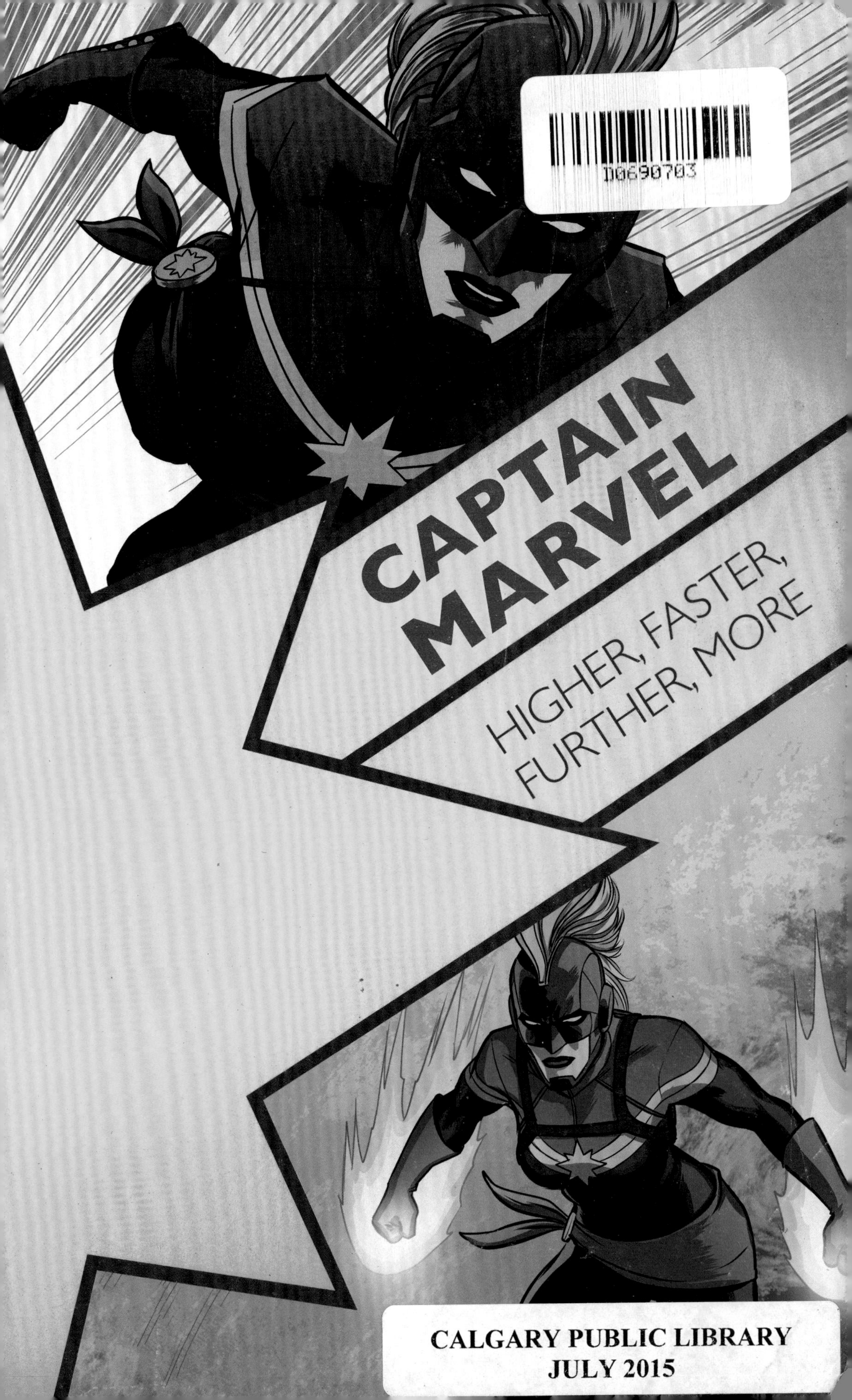
CAPTAIN MARVEL
HIGHER, FASTER, FURTHER, MORE

WRITER KELLY SUE DeCONNICK

ARTIST DAVID LOPEZ

COLOR ARTIST LEE LOUGHRIDGE

LETTERER VC'S JOE CARAMAGNA

COVER ART DAVID LOPEZ

ASSISTANT EDITOR DEVIN LEWIS

EDITOR SANA AMANAT

SENIOR EDITORS STEPHEN WACKER & NICK LOWE

COLLECTION EDITOR: JENNIFER GRÜNWALD
ASSISTANT EDITOR: SARAH BRUNSTAD
ASSOCIATE MANAGING EDITOR: ALEX STARBUCK
EDITOR, SPECIAL PROJECTS: MARK D. BEAZLEY
SENIOR EDITOR, SPECIAL PROJECTS: JEFF YOUNGQUIST
SVP PRINT, SALES & MARKETING: DAVID GABRIEL

EDITOR IN CHIEF: AXEL ALONSO
CHIEF CREATIVE OFFICER: JOE QUESADA
PUBLISHER: DAN BUCKLEY
EXECUTIVE PRODUCER: ALAN FINE

CAPTAIN MARVEL VOL. 1: HIGHER, FURTHER, FASTER, MORE. Contains material originally published in magazine form as CAPTAIN MARVEL #1-6. Third printing 2015. ISBN# 978-0-7851-9013-4. Published by MARVEL WORLDWIDE, INC., a subsidiary of MARVEL ENTERTAINMENT, LLC. OFFICE OF PUBLICATION: 135 West 50th Street, New York, NY 10020. Copyright © 2014 MARVEL No similarity between any of the names, characters, persons, and/or institutions in this magazine with those of any living or dead person or institution is intended, and any such similarity which may exist is purely coincidental. **Printed in Canada.** ALAN FINE, President, Marvel Entertainment; DAN BUCKLEY, President, TV, Publishing and Brand Management; JOE QUESADA, Chief Creative Officer; TOM BREVOORT, SVP of Publishing; DAVID BOGART, SVP of Operations & Procurement, Publishing; C.B. CEBULSKI, VP of International Development & Brand Management; DAVID GABRIEL, SVP Print, Sales & Marketing; JIM O'KEEFE, VP of Operations & Logistics; DAN CARR, Executive Director of Publishing Technology; SUSAN CRESPI, Editorial Operations Manager; ALEX MORALES, Publishing Operations Manager; STAN LEE, Chairman Emeritus. For information regarding advertising in Marvel Comics or on Marvel.com, please contact Jonathan Rheingold, VP of Custom Solutions & Ad Sales, at jrheingold@marvel.com. For Marvel subscription inquiries, please call 800-217-9158. **Manufactured between 5/20/2015 and 6/22/2015 by SOLISCO PRINTERS, SCOTT, QC, CANADA.**

10 9 8 7 6 5 4 3

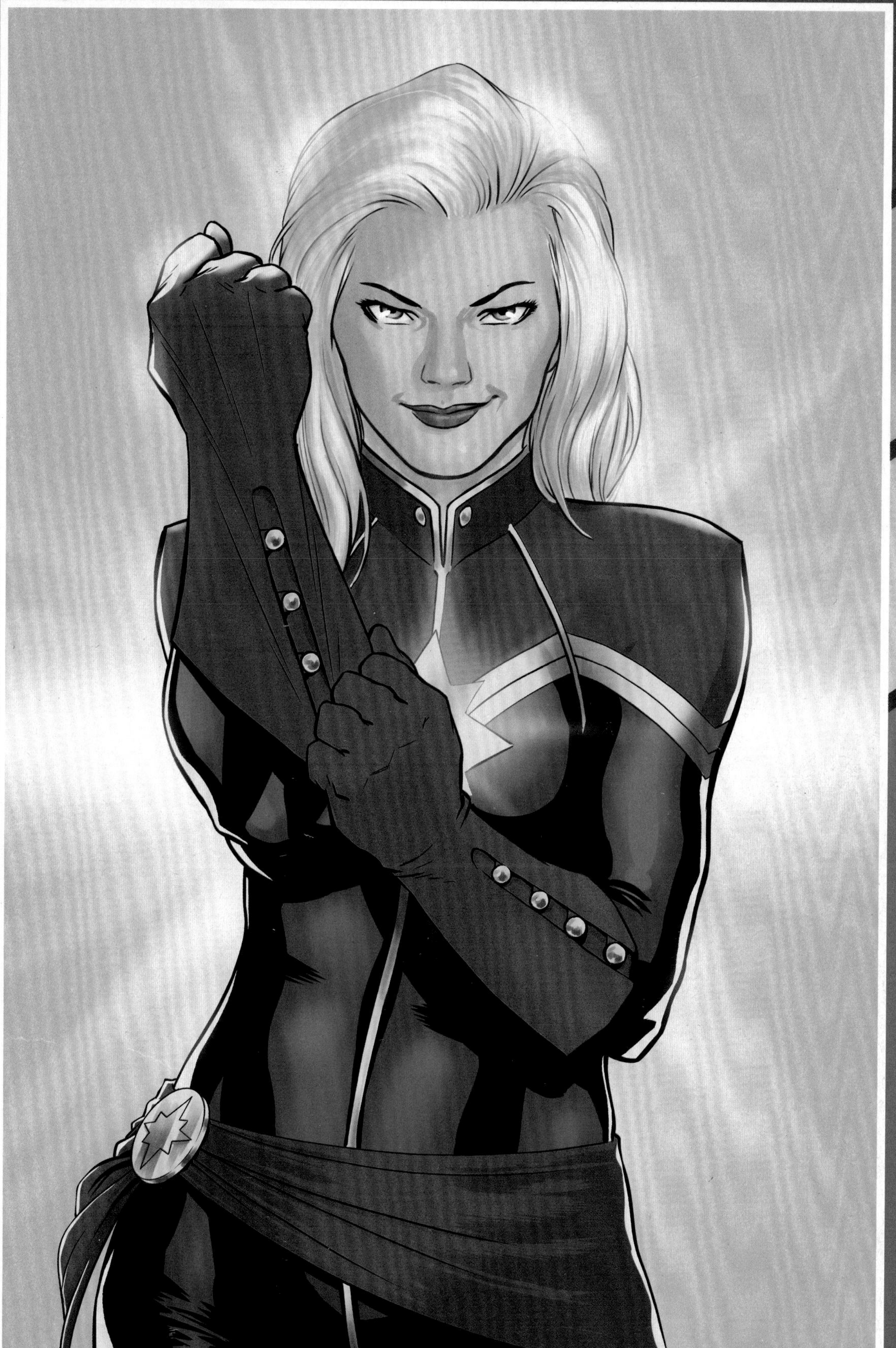

ONE

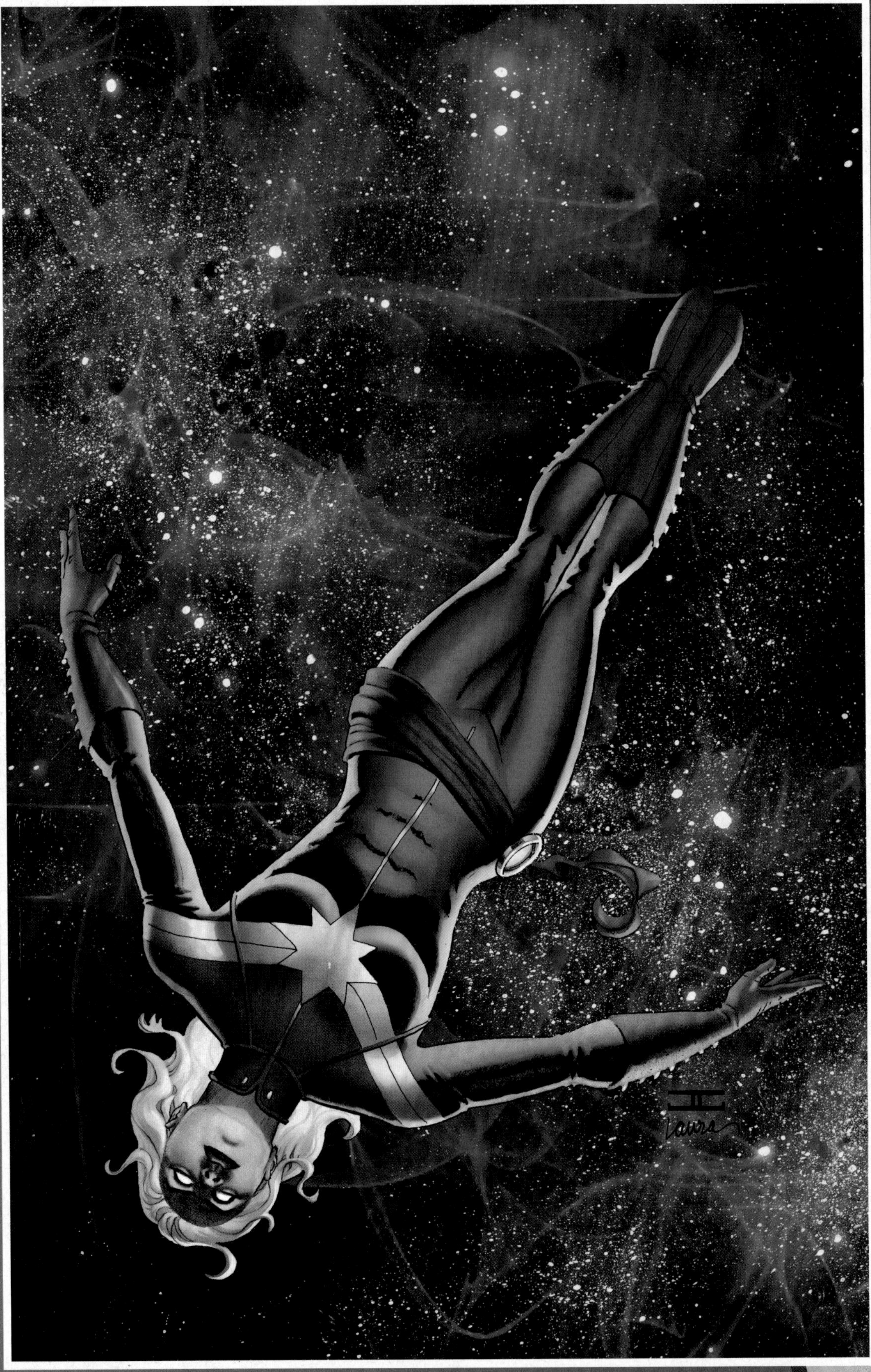

ONE VARIANT BY JOHN CASSADAY & LAURA MARTIN

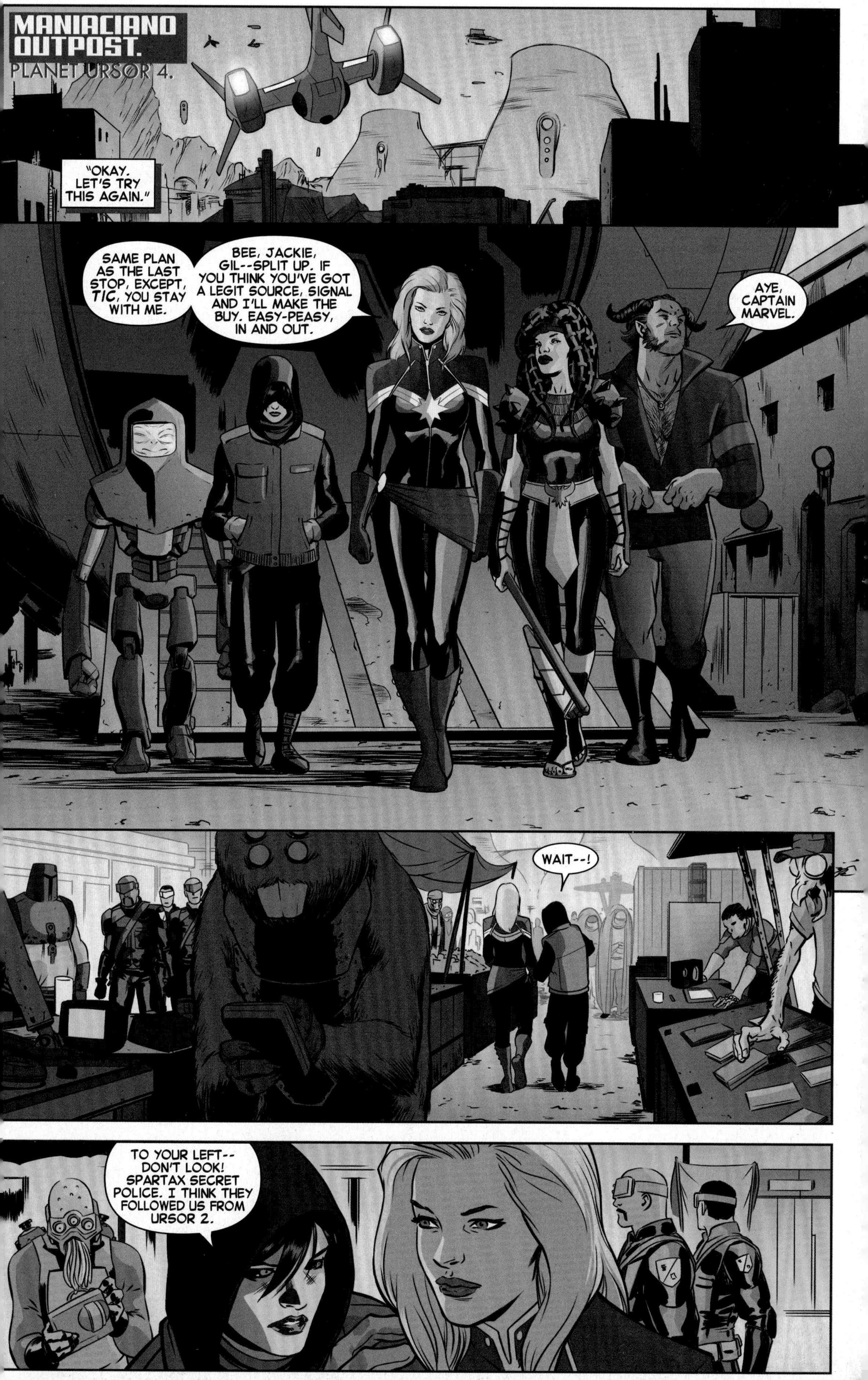
MANIACIANO OUTPOST.
PLANET URSOR 4.
"OKAY. LET'S TRY THIS AGAIN."
SAME PLAN AS THE LAST STOP, EXCEPT, TIC, YOU STAY WITH ME.
BEE, JACKIE, GIL--SPLIT UP. IF YOU THINK YOU'VE GOT A LEGIT SOURCE, SIGNAL AND I'LL MAKE THE BUY. EASY-PEASY, IN AND OUT.
AYE, CAPTAIN MARVEL.
WAIT--!
TO YOUR LEFT-- DON'T LOOK! SPARTAX SECRET POLICE. I THINK THEY FOLLOWED US FROM URSOR 2.

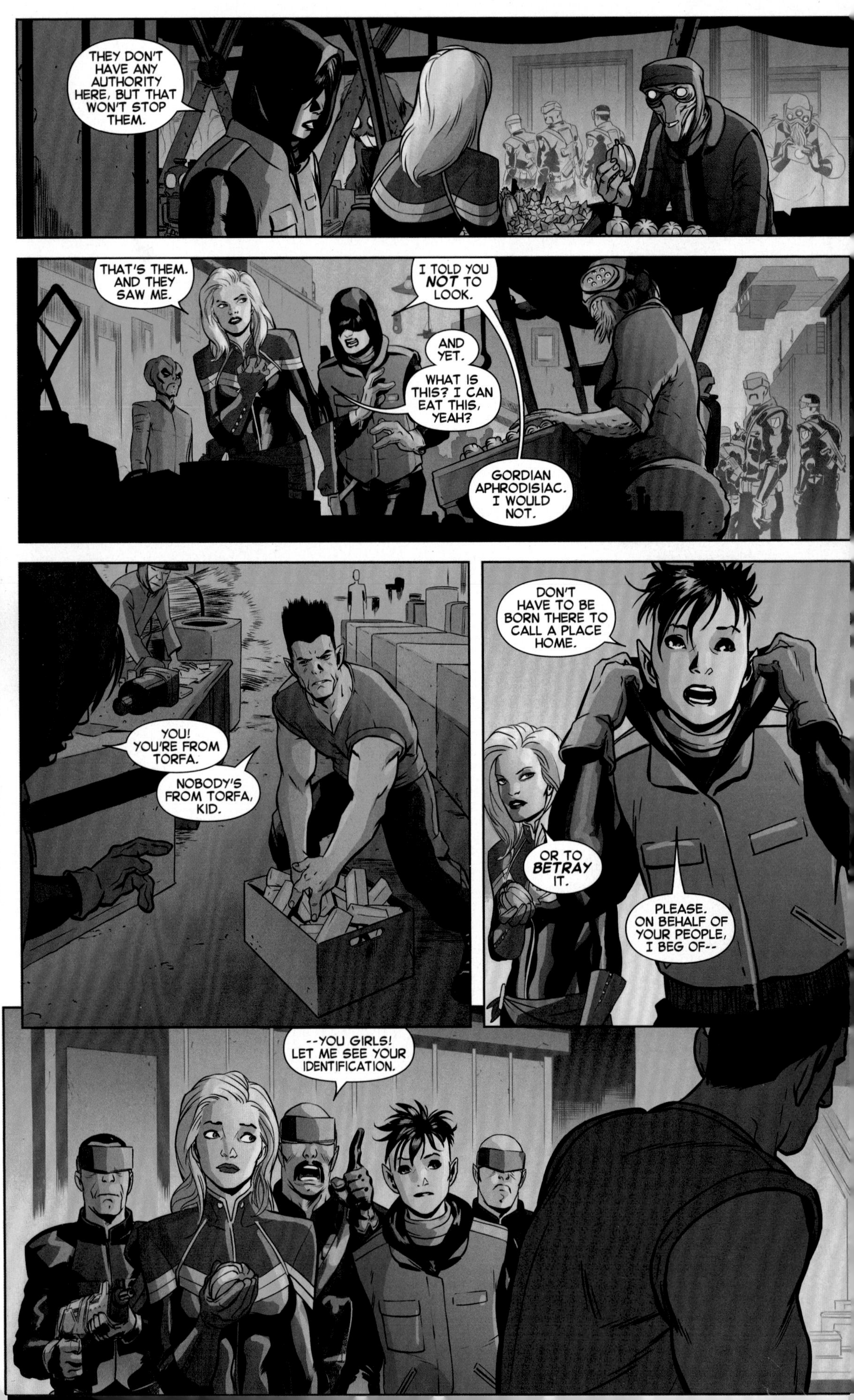
THEY DON'T HAVE ANY AUTHORITY HERE, BUT THAT WON'T STOP THEM.
THAT'S THEM. AND THEY SAW ME.
I TOLD YOU NOT TO LOOK.
AND YET.
WHAT IS THIS? I CAN EAT THIS, YEAH?
GORDIAN APHRODISIAC. I WOULD NOT.
YOU! YOU'RE FROM TORFA.
NOBODY'S FROM TORFA, KID.
DON'T HAVE TO BE BORN THERE TO CALL A PLACE HOME.
OR TO BETRAY IT.
PLEASE. ON BEHALF OF YOUR PEOPLE, I BEG OF--
--YOU GIRLS! LET ME SEE YOUR IDENTIFICATION.

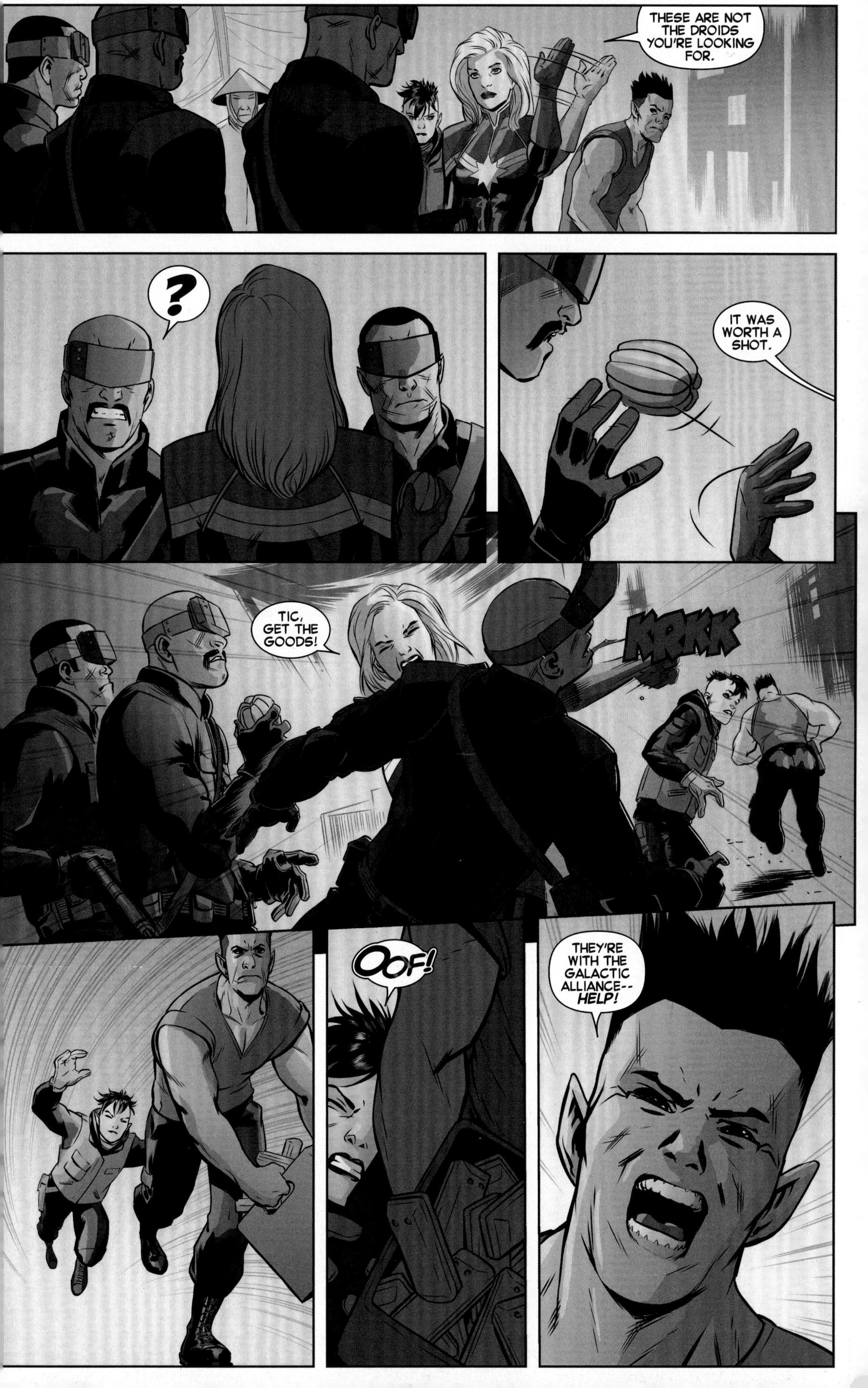
THESE ARE NOT THE DROIDS YOU'RE LOOKING FOR.
?
IT WAS WORTH A SHOT.
TIC, GET THE GOODS!
KRKK
OOF!
THEY'RE WITH THE GALACTIC ALLIANCE-- HELP!

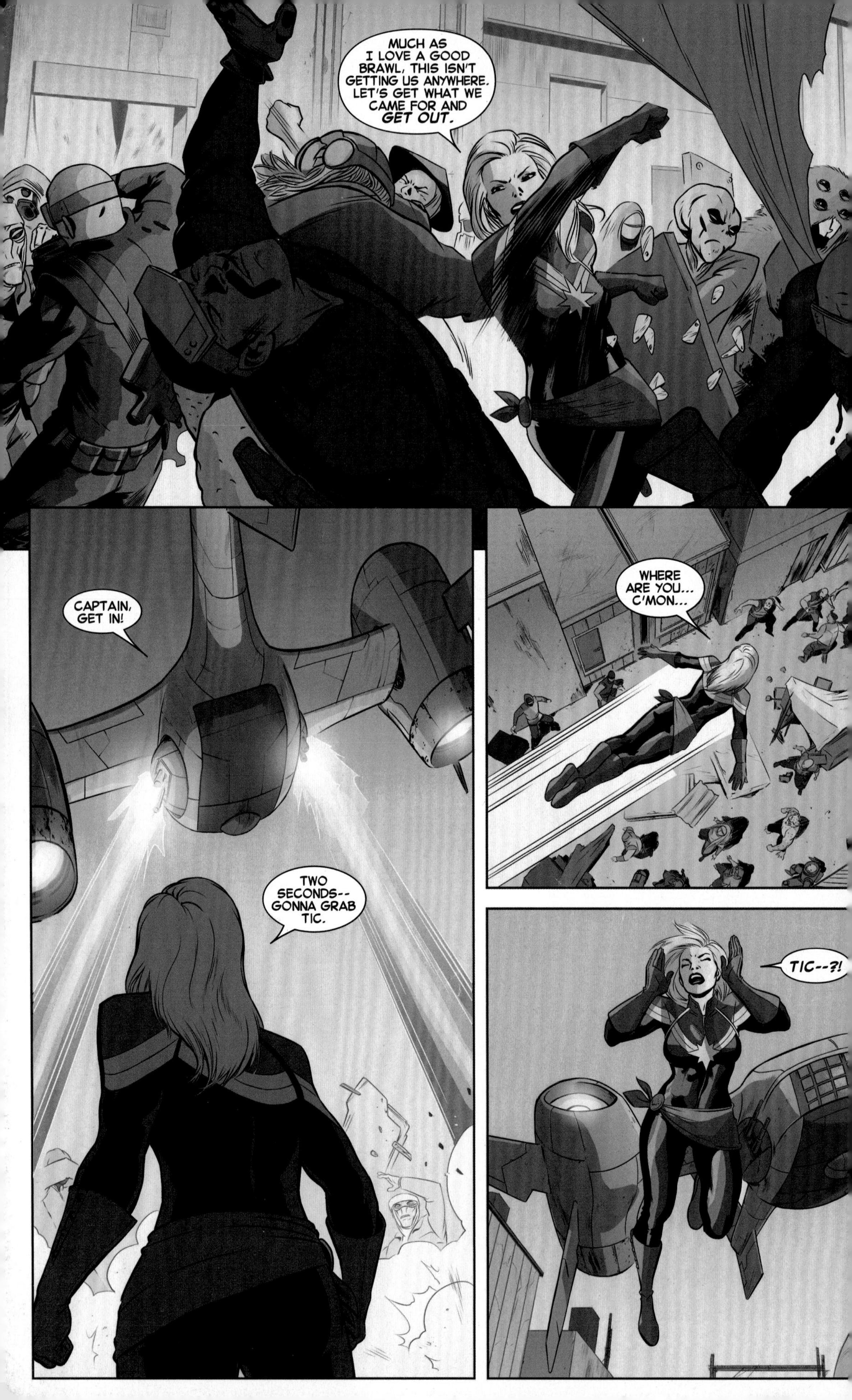
MUCH AS I LOVE A GOOD BRAWL, THIS ISN'T GETTING US ANYWHERE. LET'S GET WHAT WE CAME FOR AND GET OUT.
CAPTAIN, GET IN!
TWO SECONDS-- GONNA GRAB TIC.
WHERE ARE YOU... C'MON...
TIC--?!

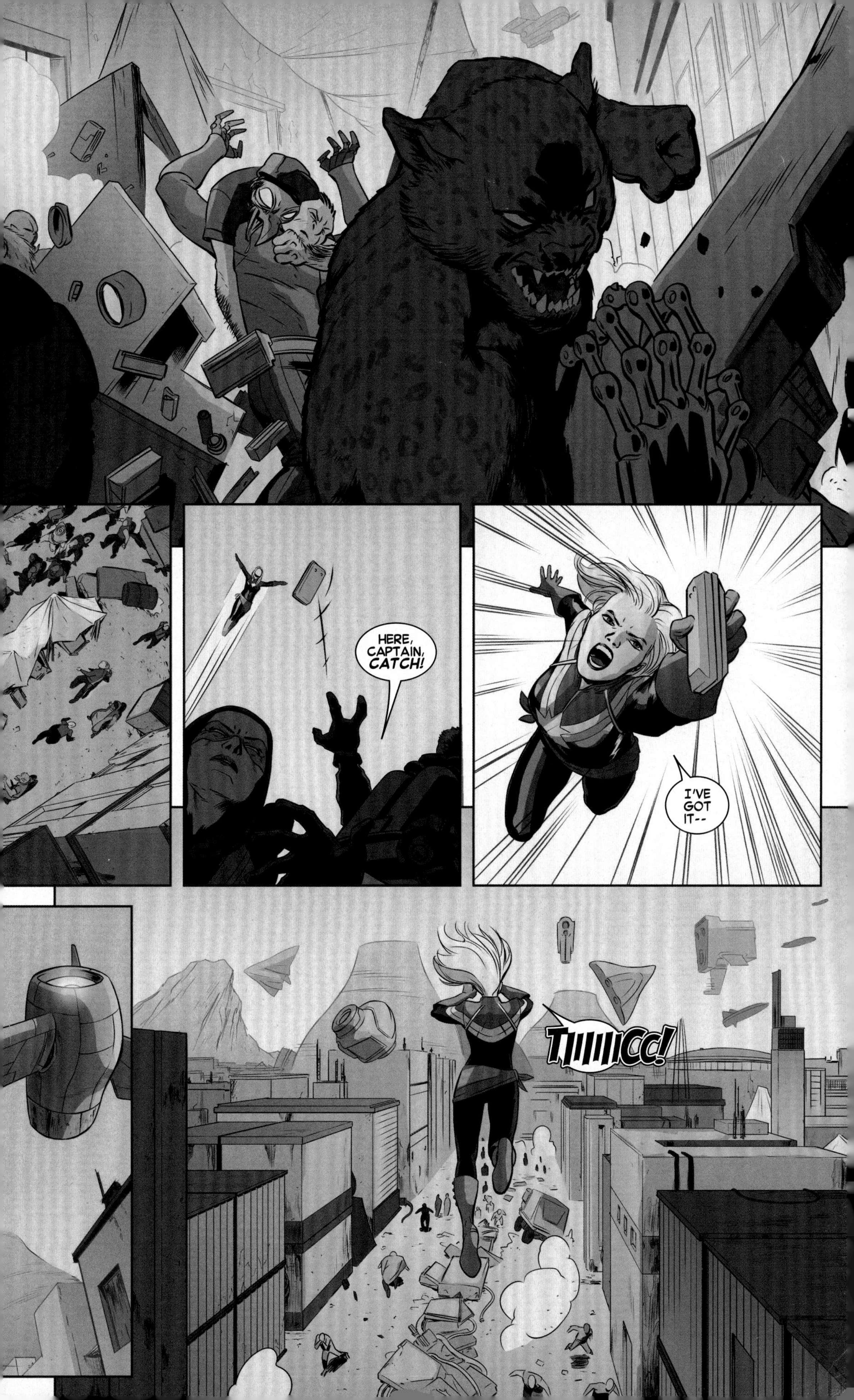
HERE, CAPTAIN, CATCH!
I'VE GOT IT--
TIIIIICC!

SIX
WEEKS
AGO.

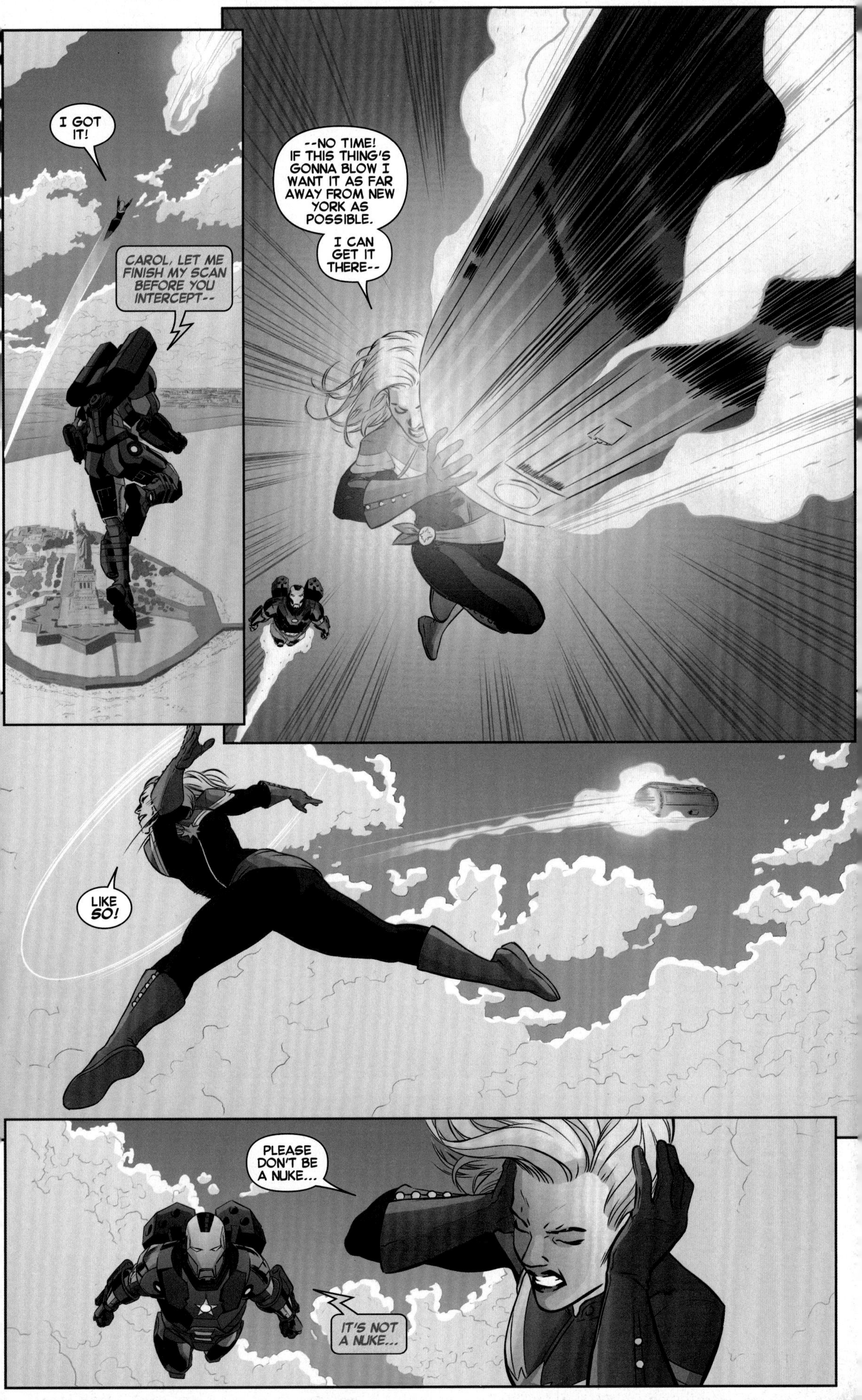
I GOT IT!
CAROL, LET ME FINISH MY SCAN BEFORE YOU INTERCEPT--
--NO TIME! IF THIS THING'S GONNA BLOW I WANT IT AS FAR AWAY FROM NEW YORK AS POSSIBLE.
I CAN GET IT THERE--
LIKE SO!
PLEASE DON'T BE A NUKE...
IT'S NOT A NUKE...

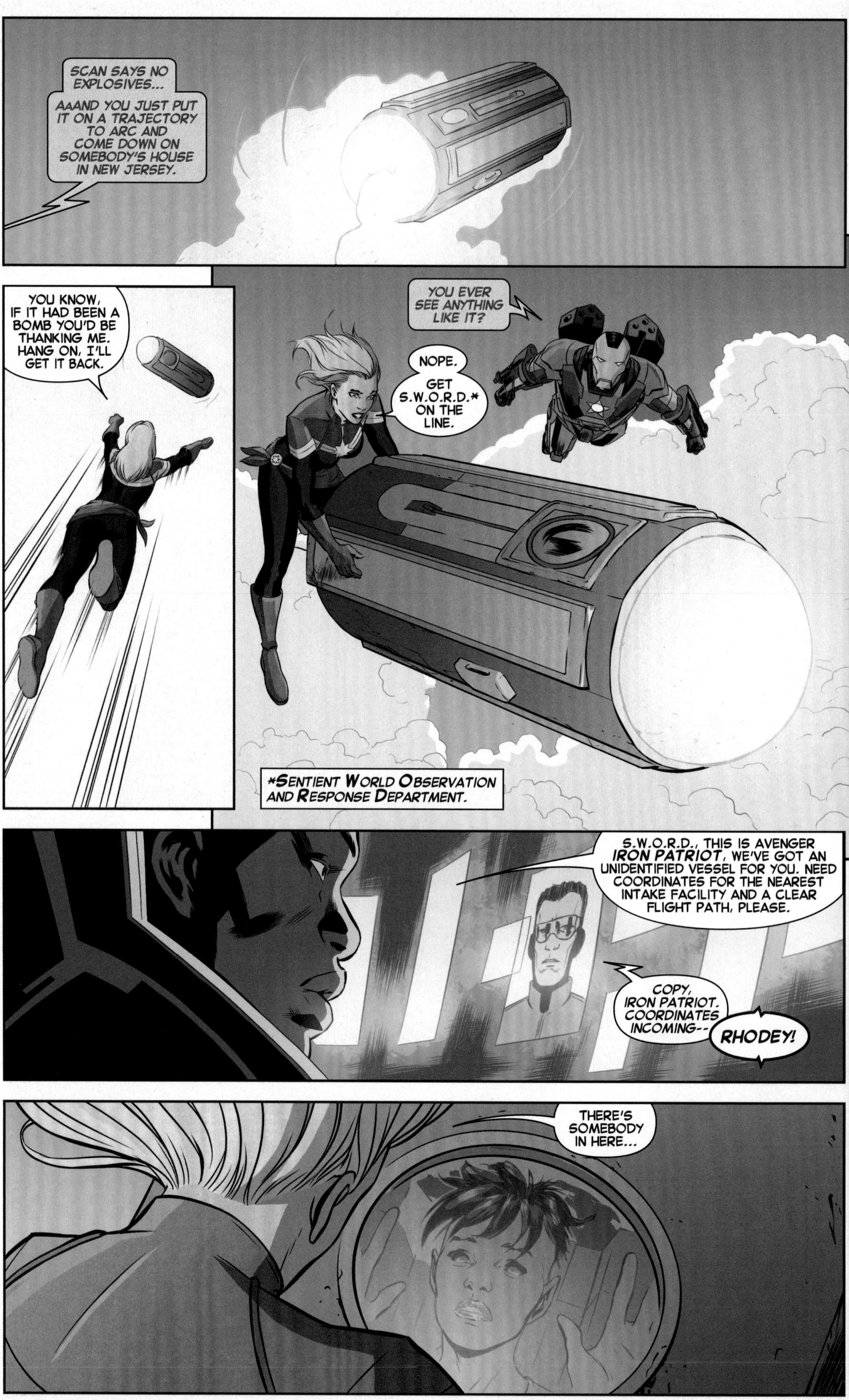
SCAN SAYS NO EXPLOSIVES...
AAAND YOU JUST PUT IT ON A TRAJECTORY TO ARC AND COME DOWN ON SOMEBODY'S HOUSE IN NEW JERSEY.
YOU KNOW, IF IT HAD BEEN A BOMB YOU'D BE THANKING ME. HANG ON, I'LL GET IT BACK.
YOU EVER SEE ANYTHING LIKE IT?
NOPE.
GET S.W.O.R.D.* ON THE LINE.
*SENTIENT WORLD OBSERVATION AND RESPONSE DEPARTMENT.
S.W.O.R.D., THIS IS AVENGER IRON PATRIOT, WE'VE GOT AN UNIDENTIFIED VESSEL FOR YOU. NEED COORDINATES FOR THE NEAREST INTAKE FACILITY AND A CLEAR FLIGHT PATH, PLEASE.
COPY, IRON PATRIOT. COORDINATES INCOMING--
RHODEY!
THERE'S SOMEBODY IN HERE...

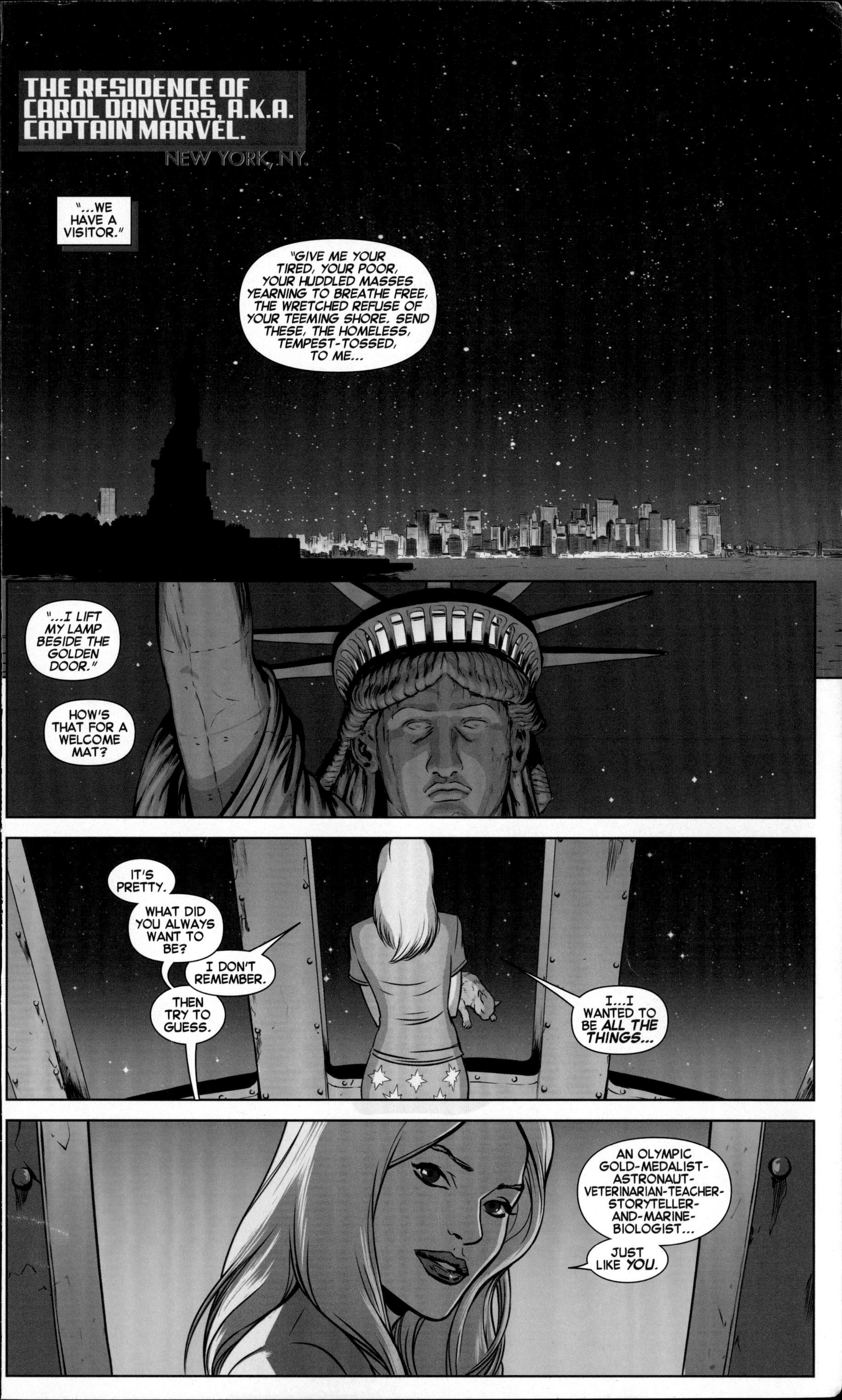
THE RESIDENCE OF CAROL DANVERS, A.K.A. CAPTAIN MARVEL.
NEW YORK, NY.
"...WE HAVE A VISITOR."
"GIVE ME YOUR TIRED, YOUR POOR, YOUR HUDDLED MASSES YEARNING TO BREATHE FREE, THE WRETCHED REFUSE OF YOUR TEEMING SHORE. SEND THESE, THE HOMELESS, TEMPEST-TOSSED, TO ME...
"...I LIFT MY LAMP BESIDE THE GOLDEN DOOR."
HOW'S THAT FOR A WELCOME MAT?
IT'S PRETTY.
WHAT DID YOU ALWAYS WANT TO BE?
I DON'T REMEMBER.
THEN TRY TO GUESS.
I...I WANTED TO BE ALL THE THINGS...
AN OLYMPIC GOLD-MEDALIST-ASTRONAUT-VETERINARIAN-TEACHER-STORYTELLER-AND-MARINE-BIOLOGIST...
JUST LIKE YOU.

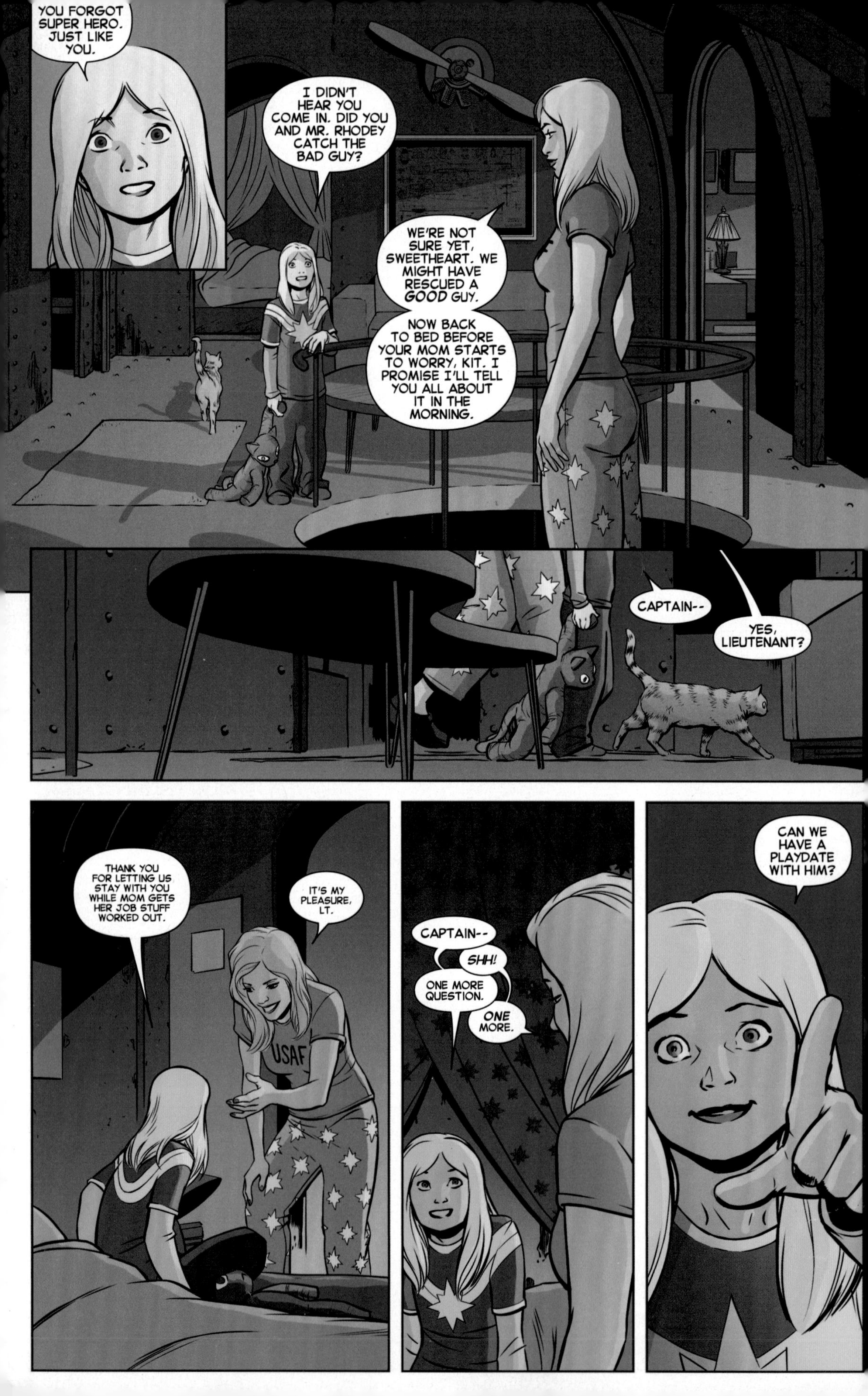
YOU FORGOT SUPER HERO. JUST LIKE YOU.
I DIDN'T HEAR YOU COME IN. DID YOU AND MR. RHODEY CATCH THE BAD GUY?
WE'RE NOT SURE YET, SWEETHEART. WE MIGHT HAVE RESCUED A *GOOD* GUY.
NOW BACK TO BED BEFORE YOUR MOM STARTS TO WORRY, KIT. I PROMISE I'LL TELL YOU ALL ABOUT IT IN THE MORNING.
CAPTAIN--
YES, LIEUTENANT?
THANK YOU FOR LETTING US STAY WITH YOU WHILE MOM GETS HER JOB STUFF WORKED OUT.
IT'S MY PLEASURE, LT.
CAPTAIN--
SHH!
ONE MORE QUESTION.
ONE MORE.
CAN WE HAVE A PLAYDATE WITH HIM?

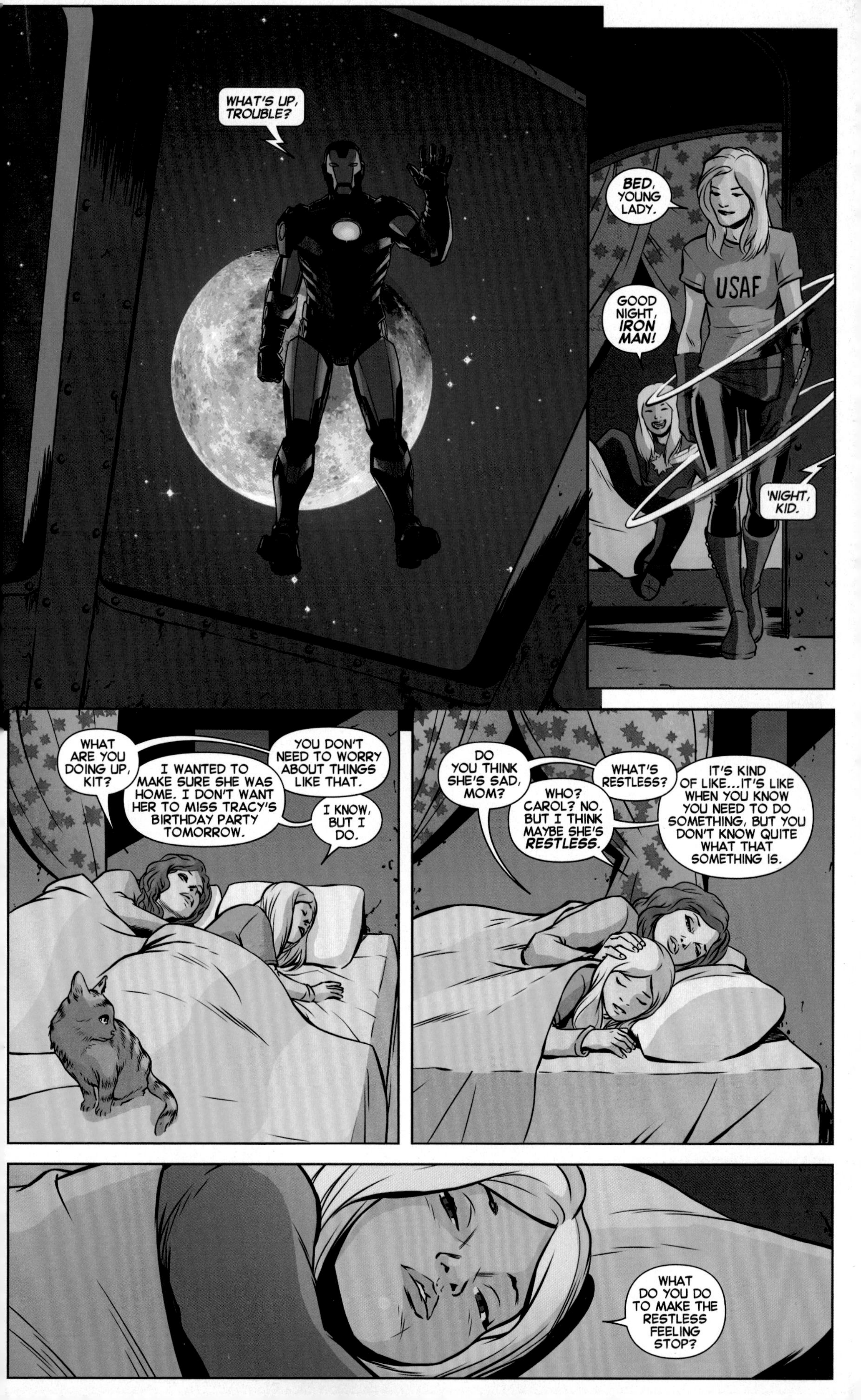
WHAT'S UP, TROUBLE?
BED, YOUNG LADY.
GOOD NIGHT, IRON MAN!
'NIGHT, KID.
WHAT ARE YOU DOING UP, KIT?
I WANTED TO MAKE SURE SHE WAS HOME. I DON'T WANT HER TO MISS TRACY'S BIRTHDAY PARTY TOMORROW.
YOU DON'T NEED TO WORRY ABOUT THINGS LIKE THAT.
I KNOW, BUT I DO.
DO YOU THINK SHE'S SAD, MOM?
WHO? CAROL? NO. BUT I THINK MAYBE SHE'S RESTLESS.
WHAT'S RESTLESS?
IT'S KIND OF LIKE...IT'S LIKE WHEN YOU KNOW YOU NEED TO DO SOMETHING, BUT YOU DON'T KNOW QUITE WHAT THAT SOMETHING IS.
WHAT DO YOU DO TO MAKE THE RESTLESS FEELING STOP?

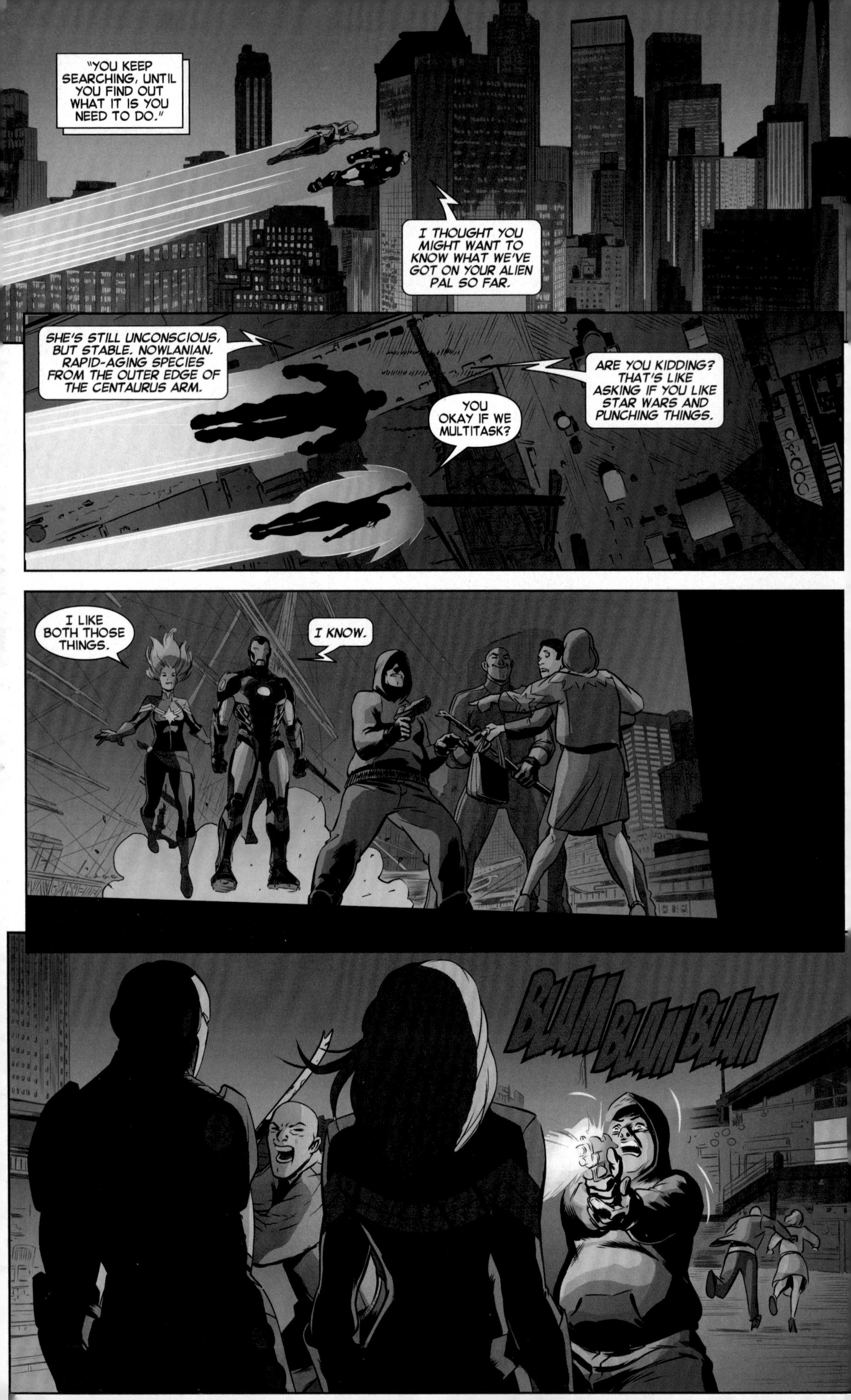
"YOU KEEP SEARCHING, UNTIL YOU FIND OUT WHAT IT IS YOU NEED TO DO."
I THOUGHT YOU MIGHT WANT TO KNOW WHAT WE'VE GOT ON YOUR ALIEN PAL SO FAR.
SHE'S STILL UNCONSCIOUS, BUT STABLE. NOWLANIAN. RAPID-AGING SPECIES FROM THE OUTER EDGE OF THE CENTAURUS ARM.
YOU OKAY IF WE MULTITASK?
ARE YOU KIDDING? THAT'S LIKE ASKING IF YOU LIKE STAR WARS AND PUNCHING THINGS.
I LIKE BOTH THOSE THINGS.
I KNOW.
BLAM BLAM BLAM

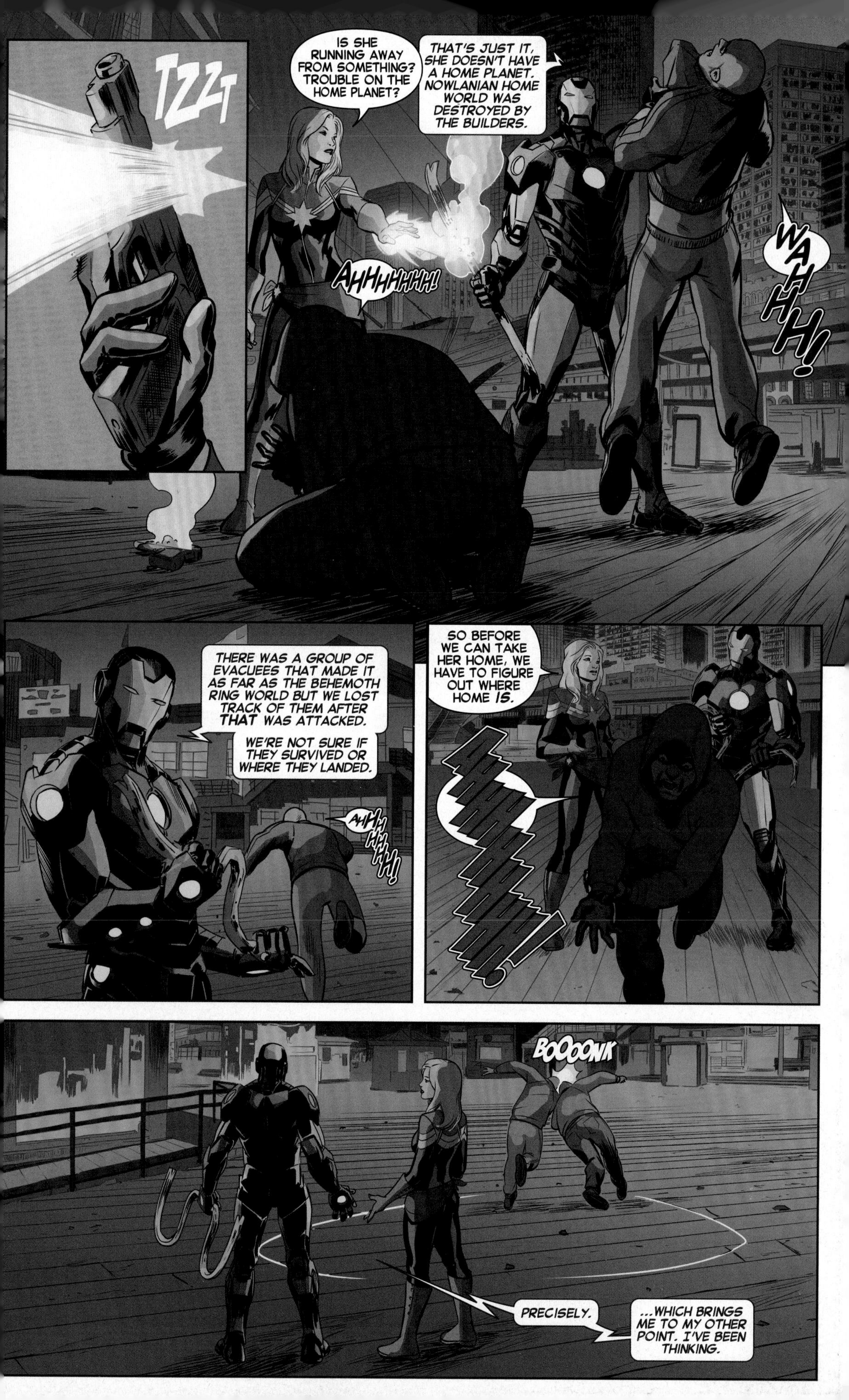
TZZT
IS SHE RUNNING AWAY FROM SOMETHING? TROUBLE ON THE HOME PLANET?
THAT'S JUST IT, SHE DOESN'T HAVE A HOME PLANET. NOWLANIAN HOME WORLD WAS DESTROYED BY THE BUILDERS.
AHHHHHHH!
WAHHHH!
THERE WAS A GROUP OF EVACUEES THAT MADE IT AS FAR AS THE BEHEMOTH RING WORLD BUT WE LOST TRACK OF THEM AFTER THAT WAS ATTACKED.
WE'RE NOT SURE IF THEY SURVIVED OR WHERE THEY LANDED.
AHHHHHH!
SO BEFORE WE CAN TAKE HER HOME, WE HAVE TO FIGURE OUT WHERE HOME IS.
BOOOONK
PRECISELY.
...WHICH BRINGS ME TO MY OTHER POINT. I'VE BEEN THINKING.

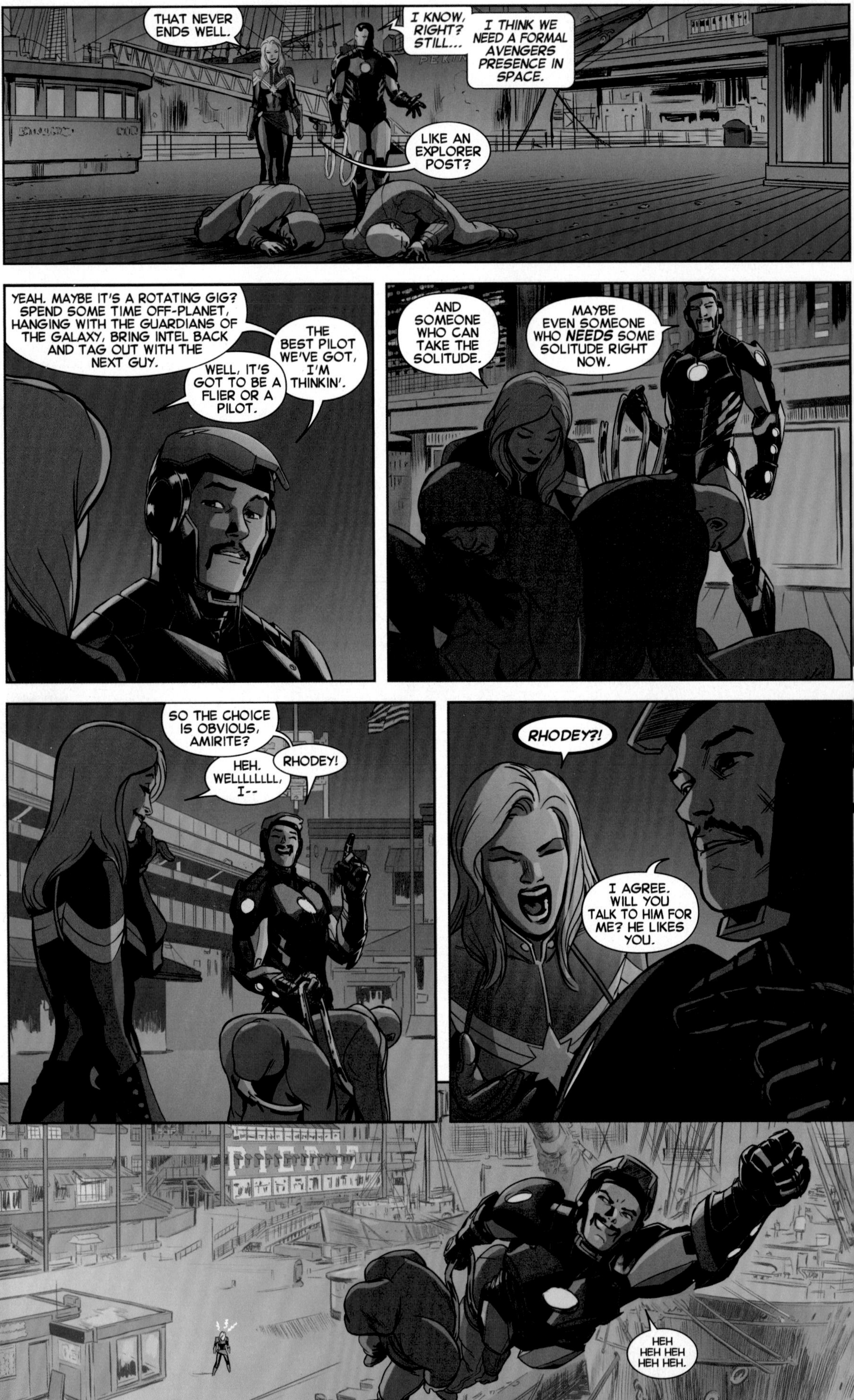
THAT NEVER ENDS WELL.
I KNOW, RIGHT? STILL...
I THINK WE NEED A FORMAL AVENGERS PRESENCE IN SPACE.
LIKE AN EXPLORER POST?
YEAH. MAYBE IT'S A ROTATING GIG? SPEND SOME TIME OFF-PLANET, HANGING WITH THE GUARDIANS OF THE GALAXY, BRING INTEL BACK AND TAG OUT WITH THE NEXT GUY.
WELL, IT'S GOT TO BE A FLIER OR A PILOT.
THE BEST PILOT WE'VE GOT, I'M THINKIN'.
AND SOMEONE WHO CAN TAKE THE SOLITUDE.
MAYBE EVEN SOMEONE WHO ***NEEDS*** SOME SOLITUDE RIGHT NOW.
SO THE CHOICE IS OBVIOUS, AMIRITE?
HEH. WELLLLLLLL, I--
RHODEY!
RHODEY?!
I AGREE. WILL YOU TALK TO HIM FOR ME? HE LIKES YOU.
PIER 17
HEH HEH HEH HEH HEH.

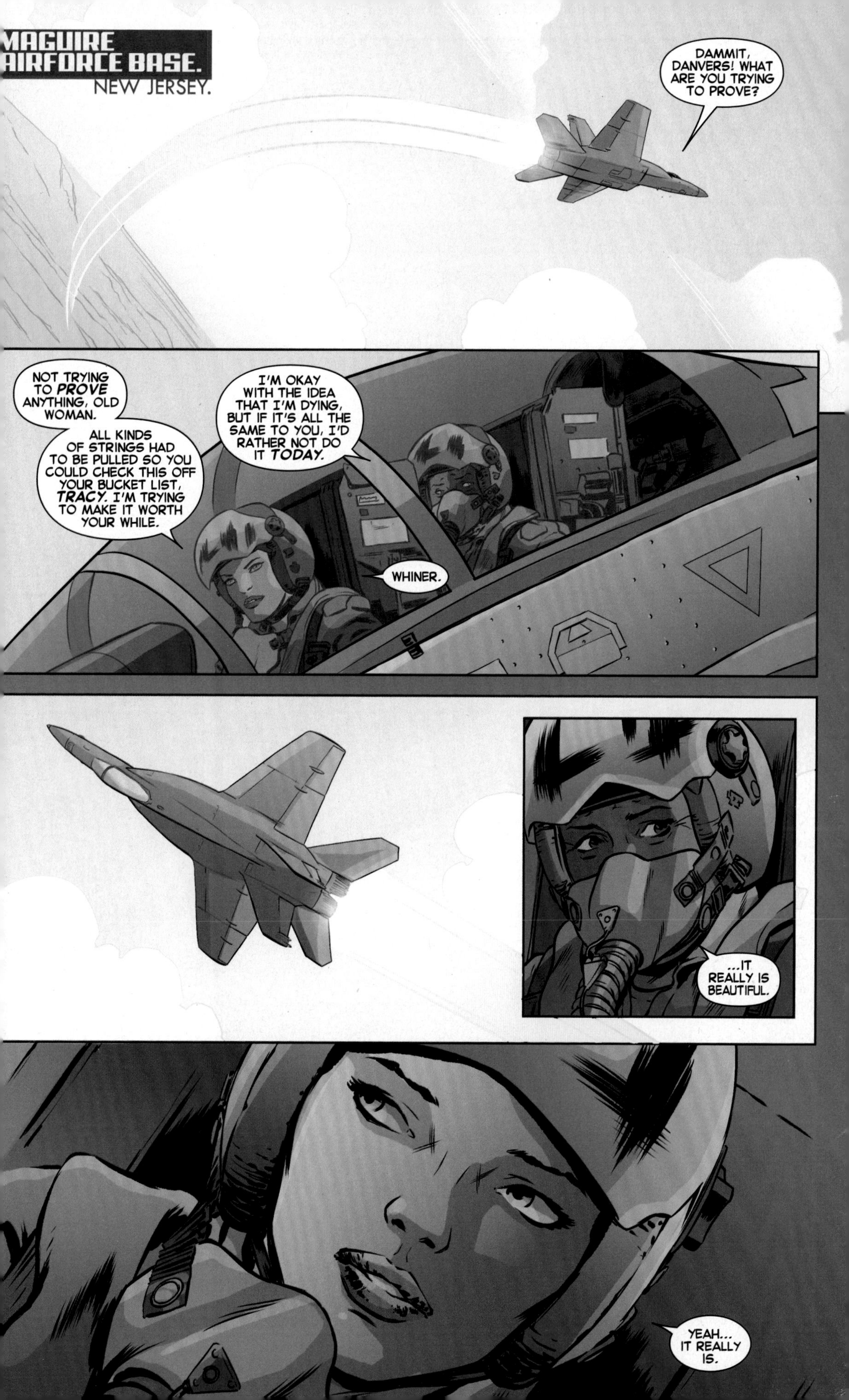
MAGUIRE AIRFORCE BASE.
NEW JERSEY.
DAMMIT, DANVERS! WHAT ARE YOU TRYING TO PROVE?
NOT TRYING TO PROVE ANYTHING, OLD WOMAN.
ALL KINDS OF STRINGS HAD TO BE PULLED SO YOU COULD CHECK THIS OFF YOUR BUCKET LIST, TRACY. I'M TRYING TO MAKE IT WORTH YOUR WHILE.
I'M OKAY WITH THE IDEA THAT I'M DYING, BUT IF IT'S ALL THE SAME TO YOU, I'D RATHER NOT DO IT TODAY.
WHINER.
...IT REALLY IS BEAUTIFUL.
YEAH... IT REALLY IS.

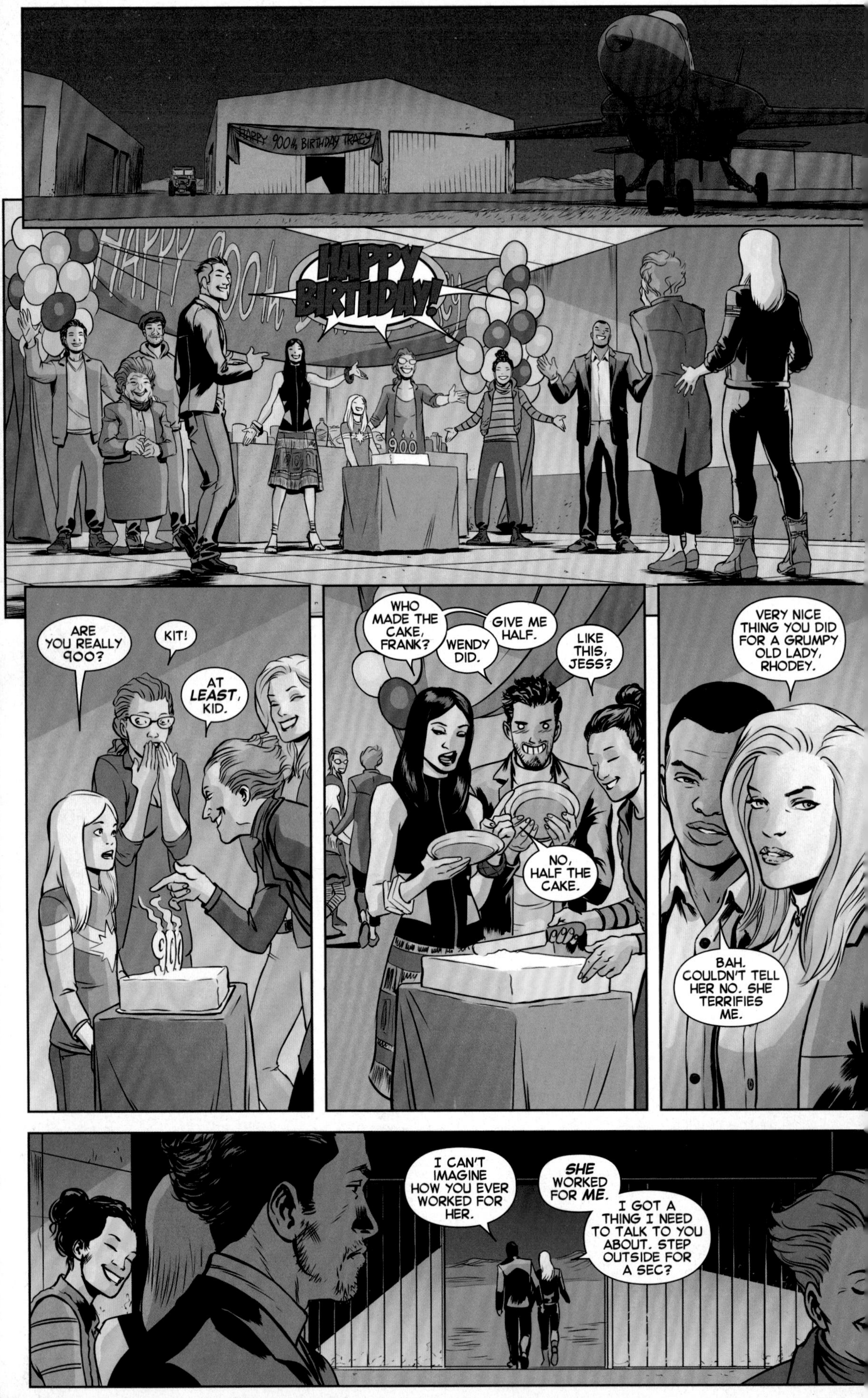
HAPPY 900th BIRTHDAY TRACY
HAPPY BIRTHDAY!
900
ARE YOU REALLY 900?
KIT!
AT LEAST, KID.
WHO MADE THE CAKE, FRANK?
WENDY DID.
GIVE ME HALF.
LIKE THIS, JESS?
NO, HALF THE CAKE.
VERY NICE THING YOU DID FOR A GRUMPY OLD LADY, RHODEY.
BAH. COULDN'T TELL HER NO. SHE TERRIFIES ME.
I CAN'T IMAGINE HOW YOU EVER WORKED FOR HER.
SHE WORKED FOR ME.
I GOT A THING I NEED TO TALK TO YOU ABOUT. STEP OUTSIDE FOR A SEC?

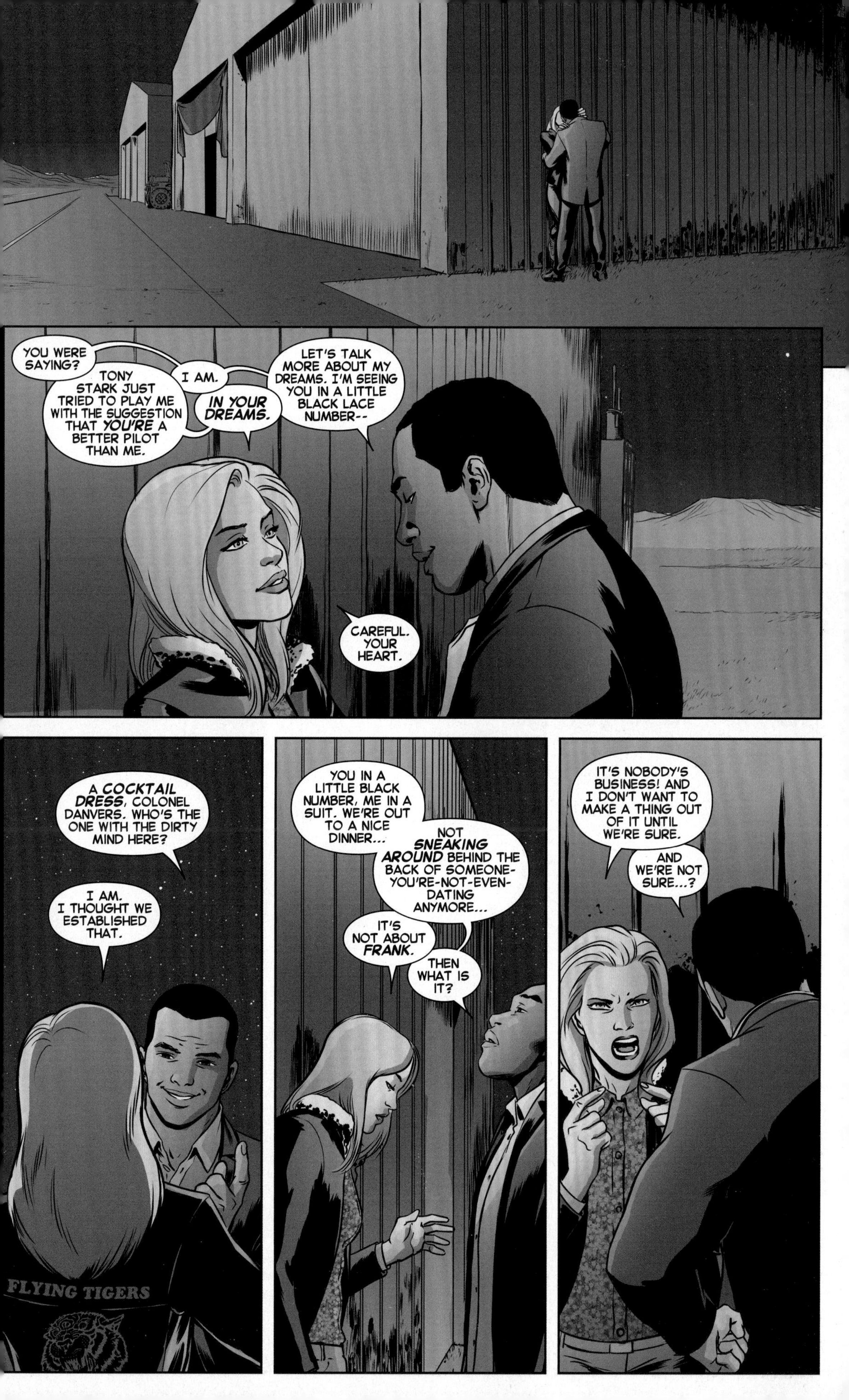
YOU WERE SAYING?
TONY STARK JUST TRIED TO PLAY ME WITH THE SUGGESTION THAT YOU'RE A BETTER PILOT THAN ME.
I AM.
IN YOUR DREAMS.
LET'S TALK MORE ABOUT MY DREAMS. I'M SEEING YOU IN A LITTLE BLACK LACE NUMBER--
CAREFUL. YOUR HEART.
A COCKTAIL DRESS, COLONEL DANVERS. WHO'S THE ONE WITH THE DIRTY MIND HERE?
I AM. I THOUGHT WE ESTABLISHED THAT.
FLYING TIGERS
YOU IN A LITTLE BLACK NUMBER, ME IN A SUIT. WE'RE OUT TO A NICE DINNER...
NOT SNEAKING AROUND BEHIND THE BACK OF SOMEONE-YOU'RE-NOT-EVEN-DATING ANYMORE...
IT'S NOT ABOUT FRANK.
THEN WHAT IS IT?
IT'S NOBODY'S BUSINESS! AND I DON'T WANT TO MAKE A THING OUT OF IT UNTIL WE'RE SURE.
AND WE'RE NOT SURE...?

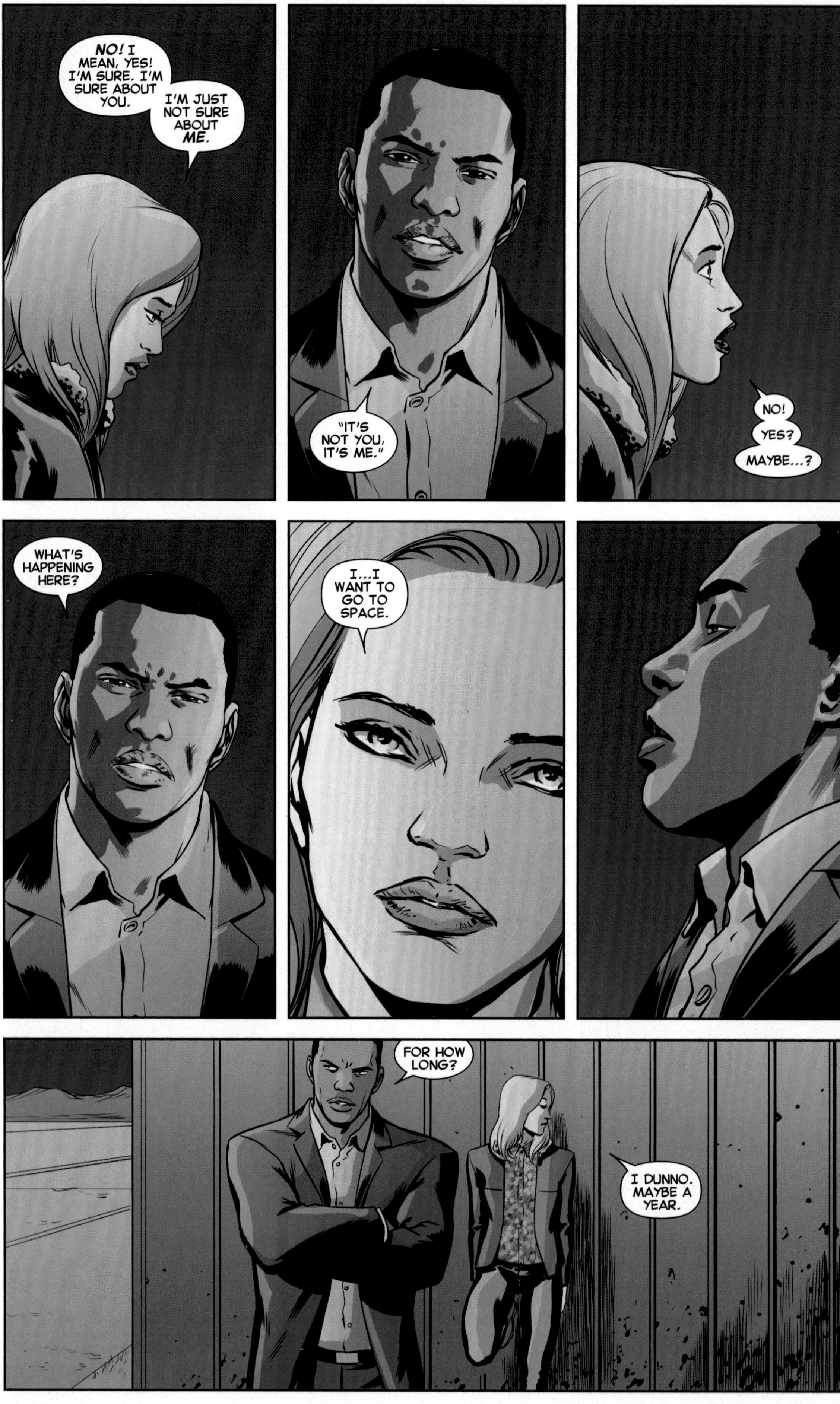
NO! I MEAN, YES! I'M SURE. I'M SURE ABOUT YOU.
I'M JUST NOT SURE ABOUT ME.
"IT'S NOT YOU, IT'S ME."
NO!
YES?
MAYBE...?
WHAT'S HAPPENING HERE?
I...I WANT TO GO TO SPACE.
FOR HOW LONG?
I DUNNO. MAYBE A YEAR.

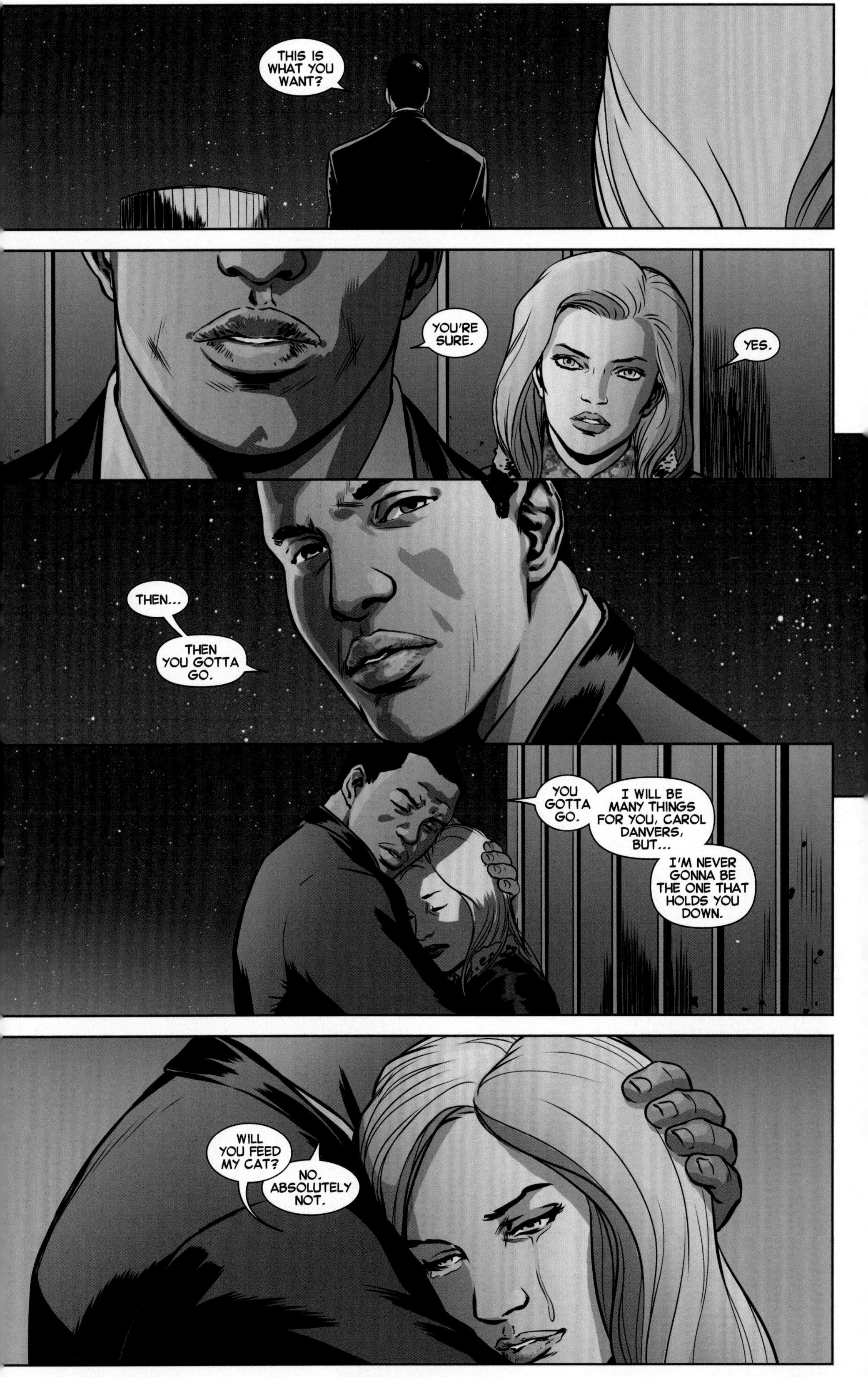
THIS IS WHAT YOU WANT?
YOU'RE SURE.
YES.
THEN...
THEN YOU GOTTA GO.
YOU GOTTA GO.
I WILL BE MANY THINGS FOR YOU, CAROL DANVERS, BUT...
I'M NEVER GONNA BE THE ONE THAT HOLDS YOU DOWN.
WILL YOU FEED MY CAT?
NO. ABSOLUTELY NOT.

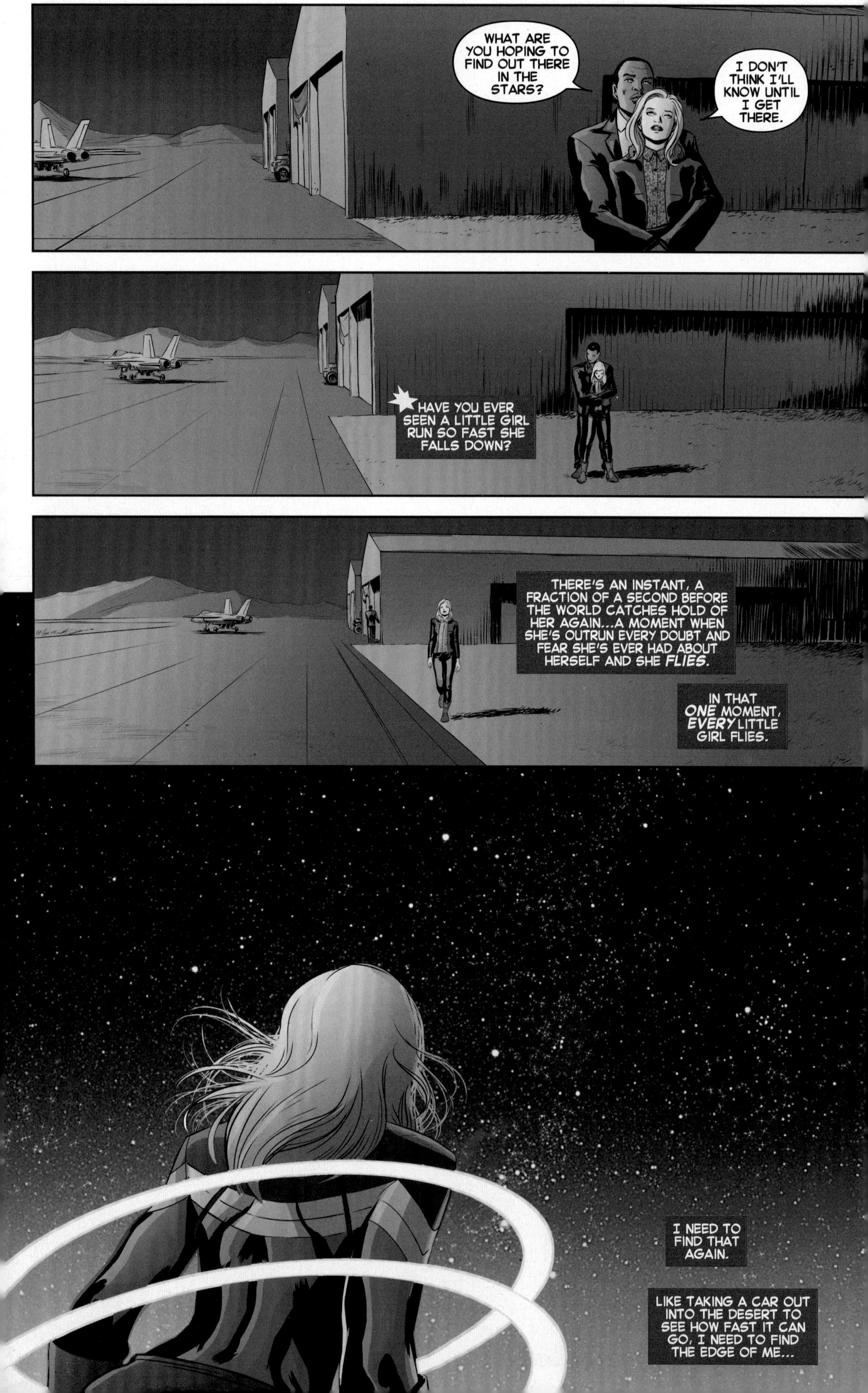

WHAT ARE YOU HOPING TO FIND OUT THERE IN THE STARS?
I DON'T THINK I'LL KNOW UNTIL I GET THERE.
HAVE YOU EVER SEEN A LITTLE GIRL RUN SO FAST SHE FALLS DOWN?
THERE'S AN INSTANT, A FRACTION OF A SECOND BEFORE THE WORLD CATCHES HOLD OF HER AGAIN...A MOMENT WHEN SHE'S OUTRUN EVERY DOUBT AND FEAR SHE'S EVER HAD ABOUT HERSELF AND SHE FLIES.
IN THAT ONE MOMENT, EVERY LITTLE GIRL FLIES.
I NEED TO FIND THAT AGAIN.
LIKE TAKING A CAR OUT INTO THE DESERT TO SEE HOW FAST IT CAN GO, I NEED TO FIND THE EDGE OF ME...

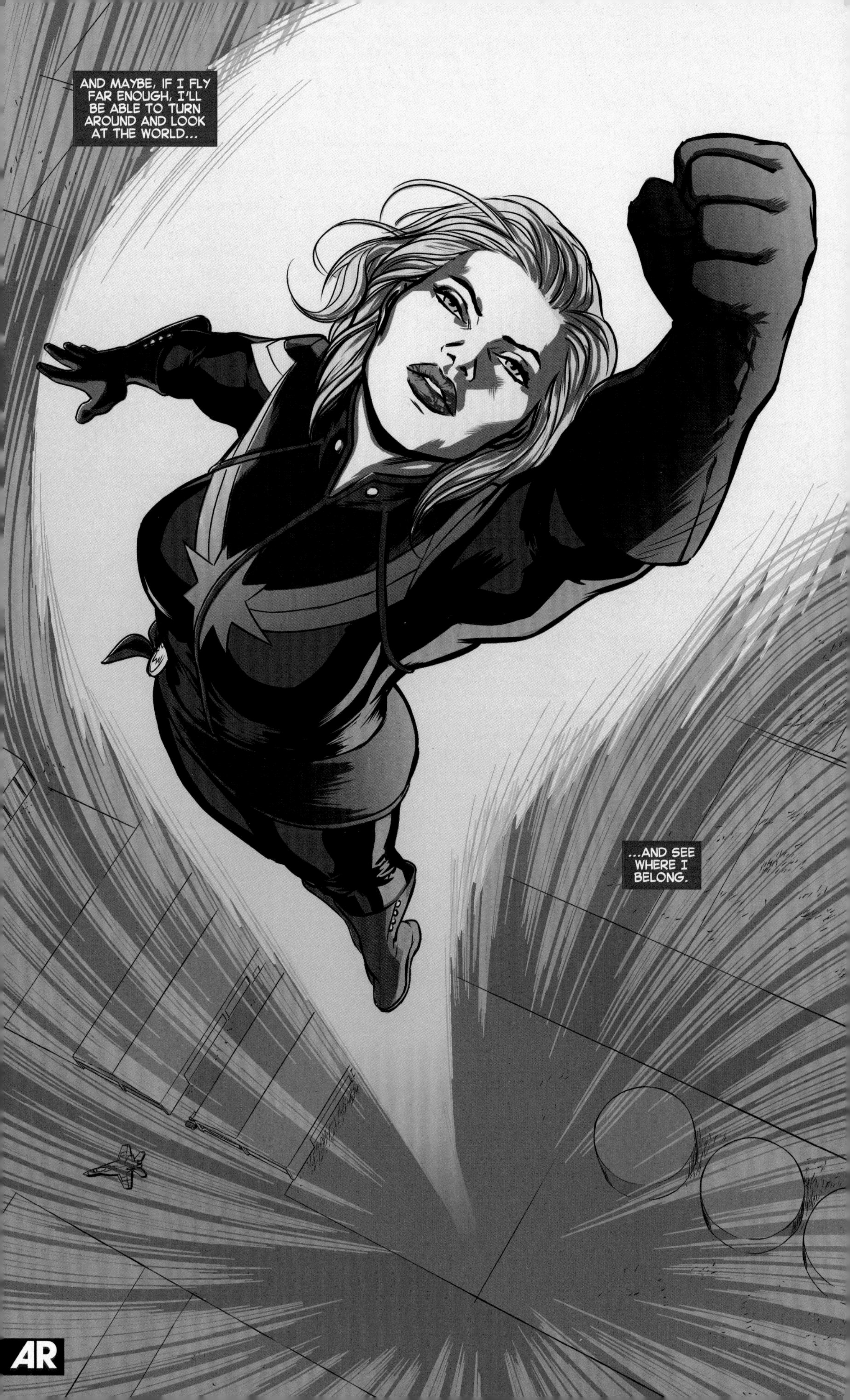
AND MAYBE, IF I FLY FAR ENOUGH, I'LL BE ABLE TO TURN AROUND AND LOOK AT THE WORLD...
...AND SEE WHERE I BELONG.

the origin of CAPTAIN MARVEL

by K*t

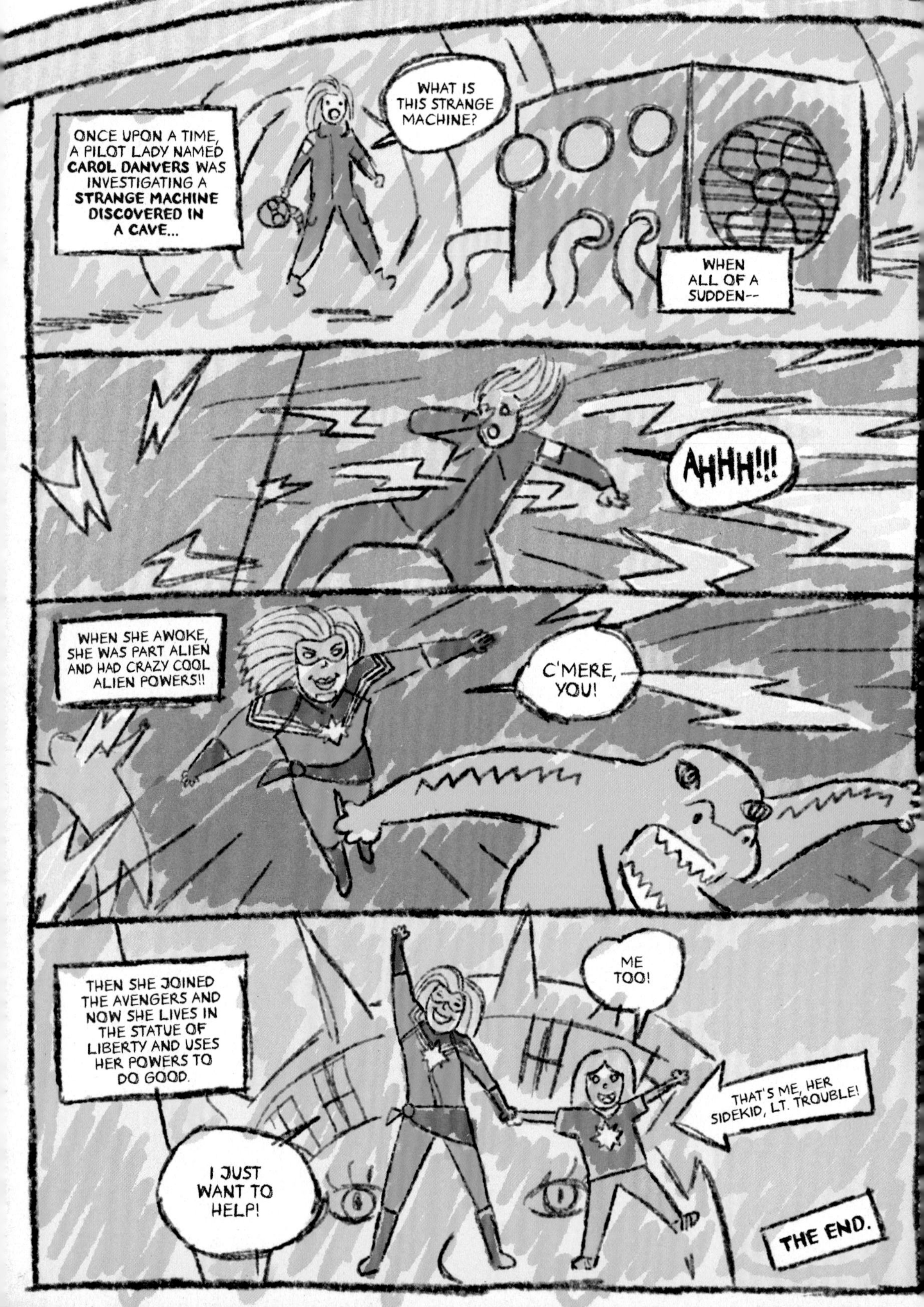
ONCE UPON A TIME, A PILOT LADY NAMED CAROL DANVERS WAS INVESTIGATING A STRANGE MACHINE DISCOVERED IN A CAVE...
WHAT IS THIS STRANGE MACHINE?
WHEN ALL OF A SUDDEN--
AHHH!!!
WHEN SHE AWOKE, SHE WAS PART ALIEN AND HAD CRAZY COOL ALIEN POWERS!!
C'MERE, YOU!
THEN SHE JOINED THE AVENGERS AND NOW SHE LIVES IN THE STATUE OF LIBERTY AND USES HER POWERS TO DO GOOD.
ME TOO!
THAT'S ME, HER SIDEKID, LT. TROUBLE!
I JUST WANT TO HELP!
THE END.

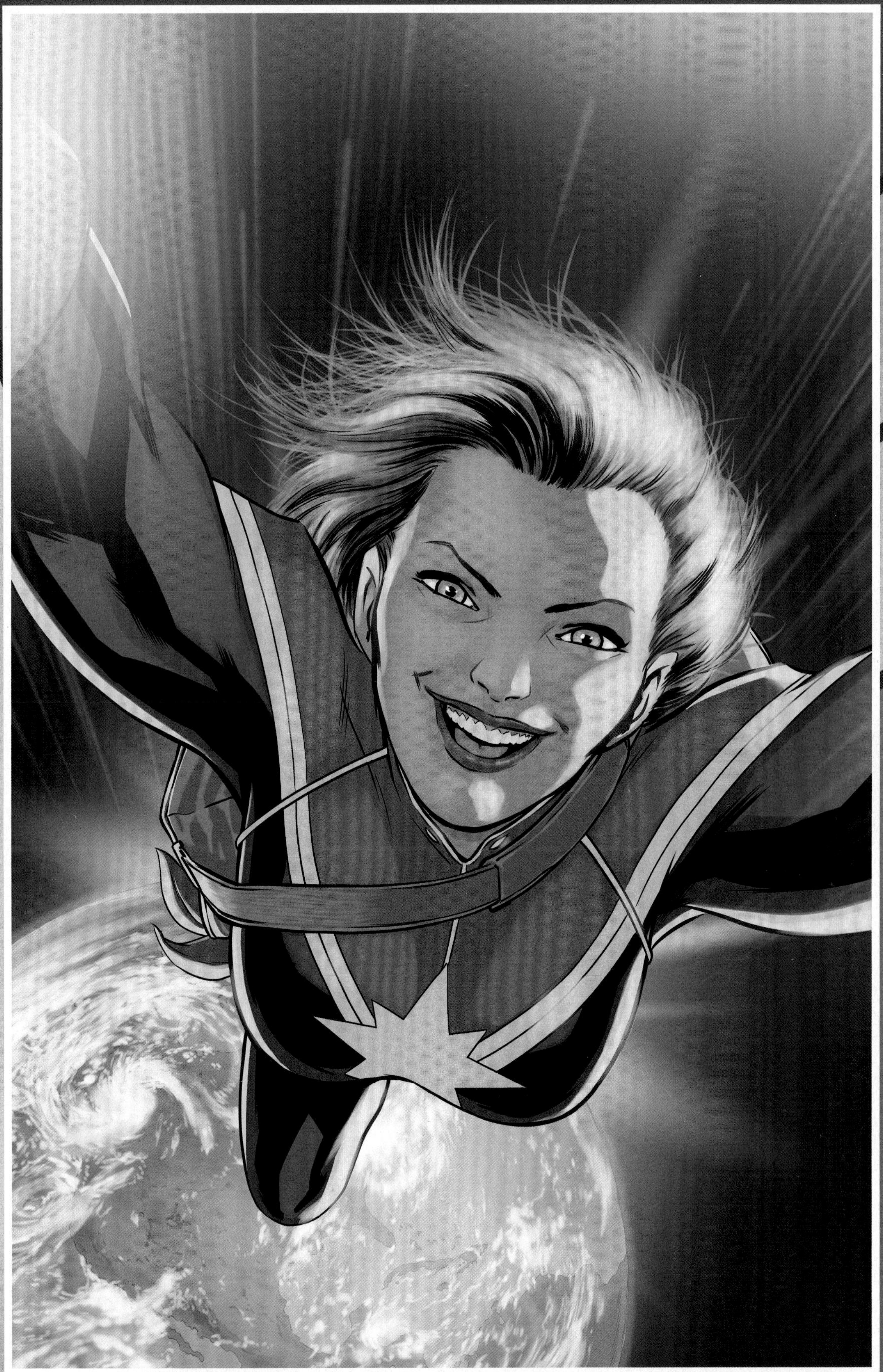

TWO

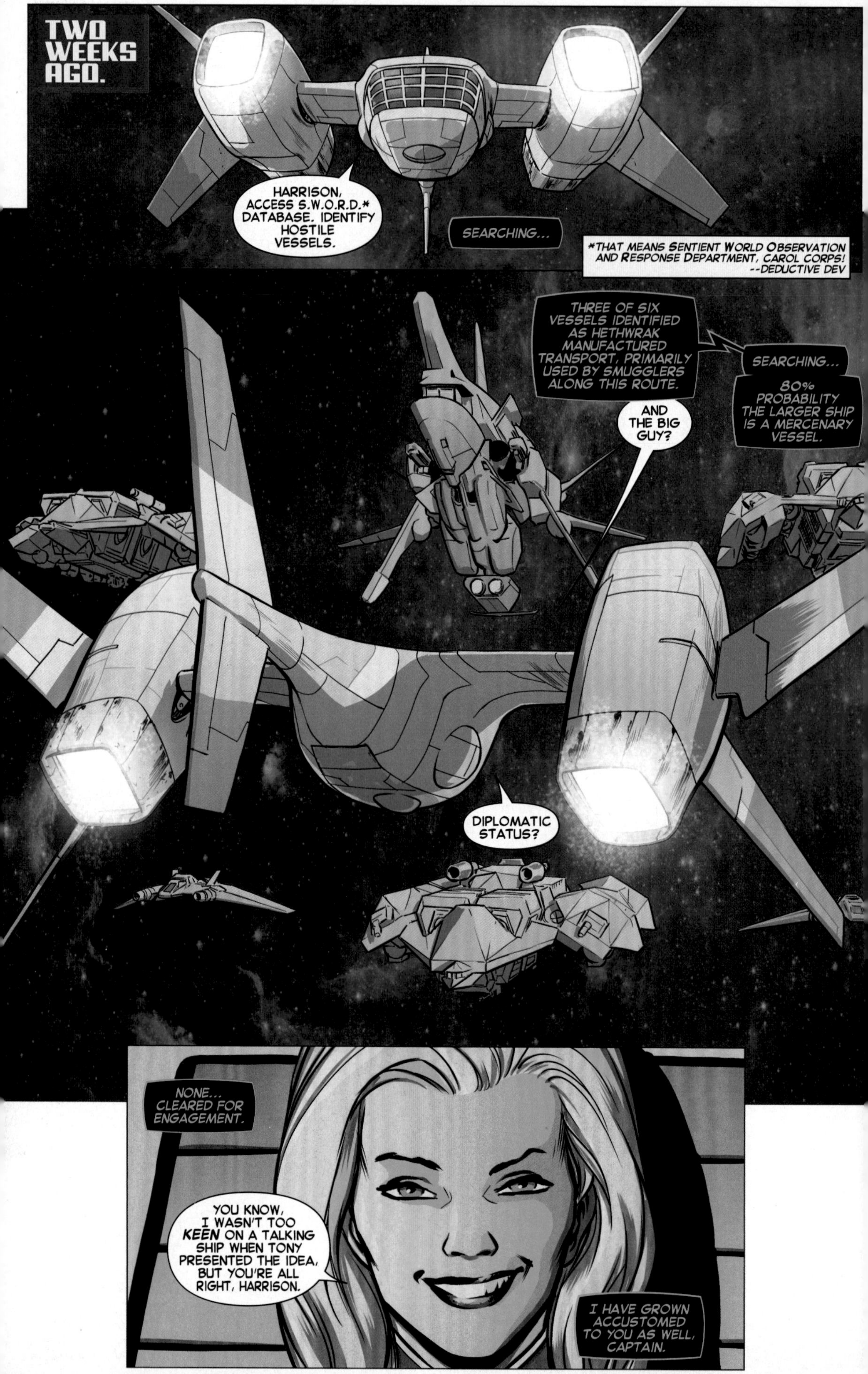
TWO WEEKS AGO.
HARRISON, ACCESS S.W.O.R.D.* DATABASE. IDENTIFY HOSTILE VESSELS.
SEARCHING...
*THAT MEANS SENTIENT WORLD OBSERVATION AND RESPONSE DEPARTMENT, CAROL CORPS! --DEDUCTIVE DEV
THREE OF SIX VESSELS IDENTIFIED AS HETHWRAK MANUFACTURED TRANSPORT, PRIMARILY USED BY SMUGGLERS ALONG THIS ROUTE.
AND THE BIG GUY?
SEARCHING...
80% PROBABILITY THE LARGER SHIP IS A MERCENARY VESSEL.
DIPLOMATIC STATUS?
NONE... CLEARED FOR ENGAGEMENT.
YOU KNOW, I WASN'T TOO KEEN ON A TALKING SHIP WHEN TONY PRESENTED THE IDEA, BUT YOU'RE ALL RIGHT, HARRISON.
I HAVE GROWN ACCUSTOMED TO YOU AS WELL, CAPTAIN.

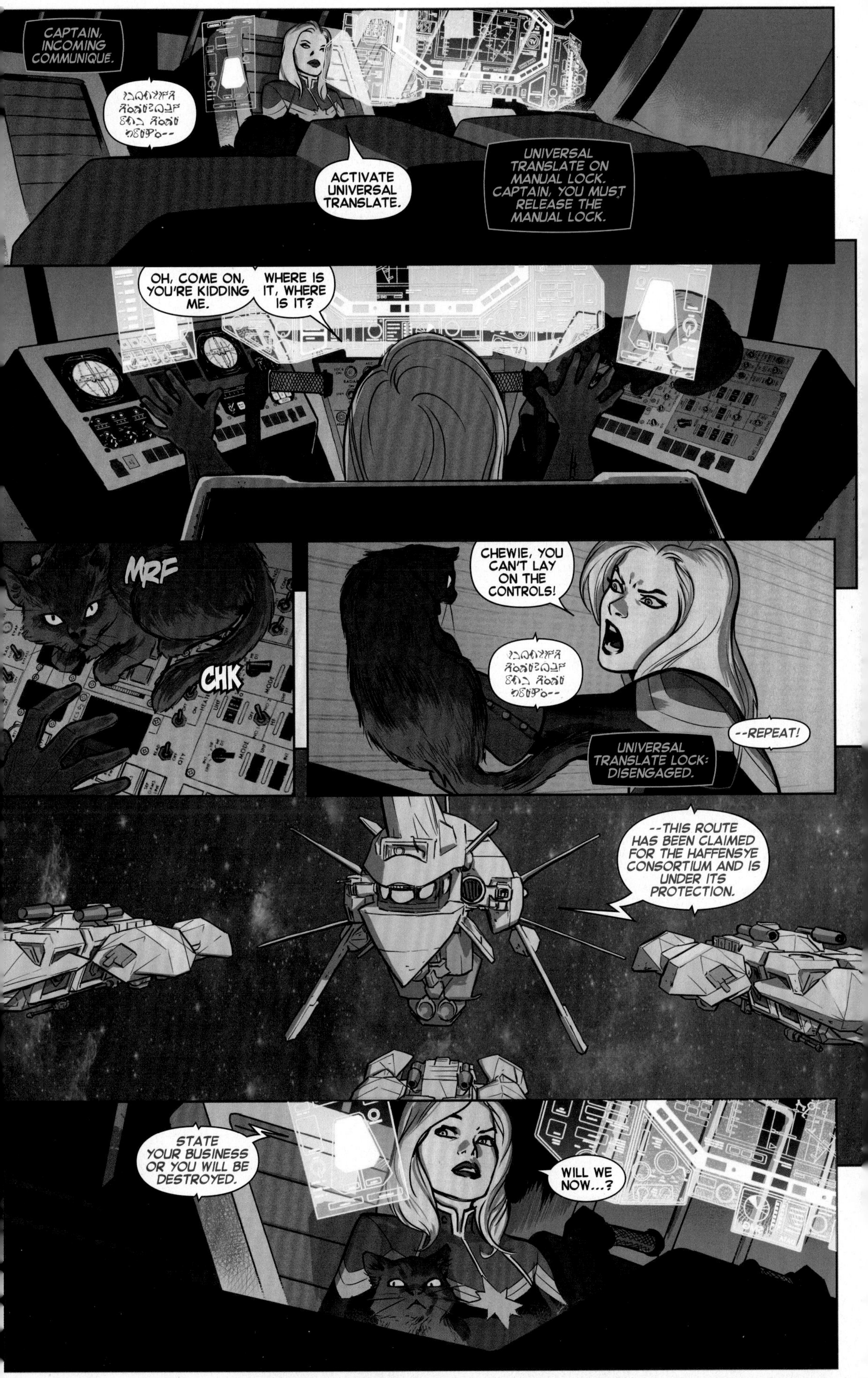
CAPTAIN, INCOMING COMMUNIQUE.
ACTIVATE UNIVERSAL TRANSLATE.
UNIVERSAL TRANSLATE ON MANUAL LOCK. CAPTAIN, YOU MUST RELEASE THE MANUAL LOCK.
OH, COME ON, YOU'RE KIDDING ME.
WHERE IS IT, WHERE IS IT?
MRF
CHK
CHEWIE, YOU CAN'T LAY ON THE CONTROLS!
UNIVERSAL TRANSLATE LOCK: DISENGAGED.
--REPEAT!
--THIS ROUTE HAS BEEN CLAIMED FOR THE HAFFENSYE CONSORTIUM AND IS UNDER ITS PROTECTION.
STATE YOUR BUSINESS OR YOU WILL BE DESTROYED.
WILL WE NOW...?

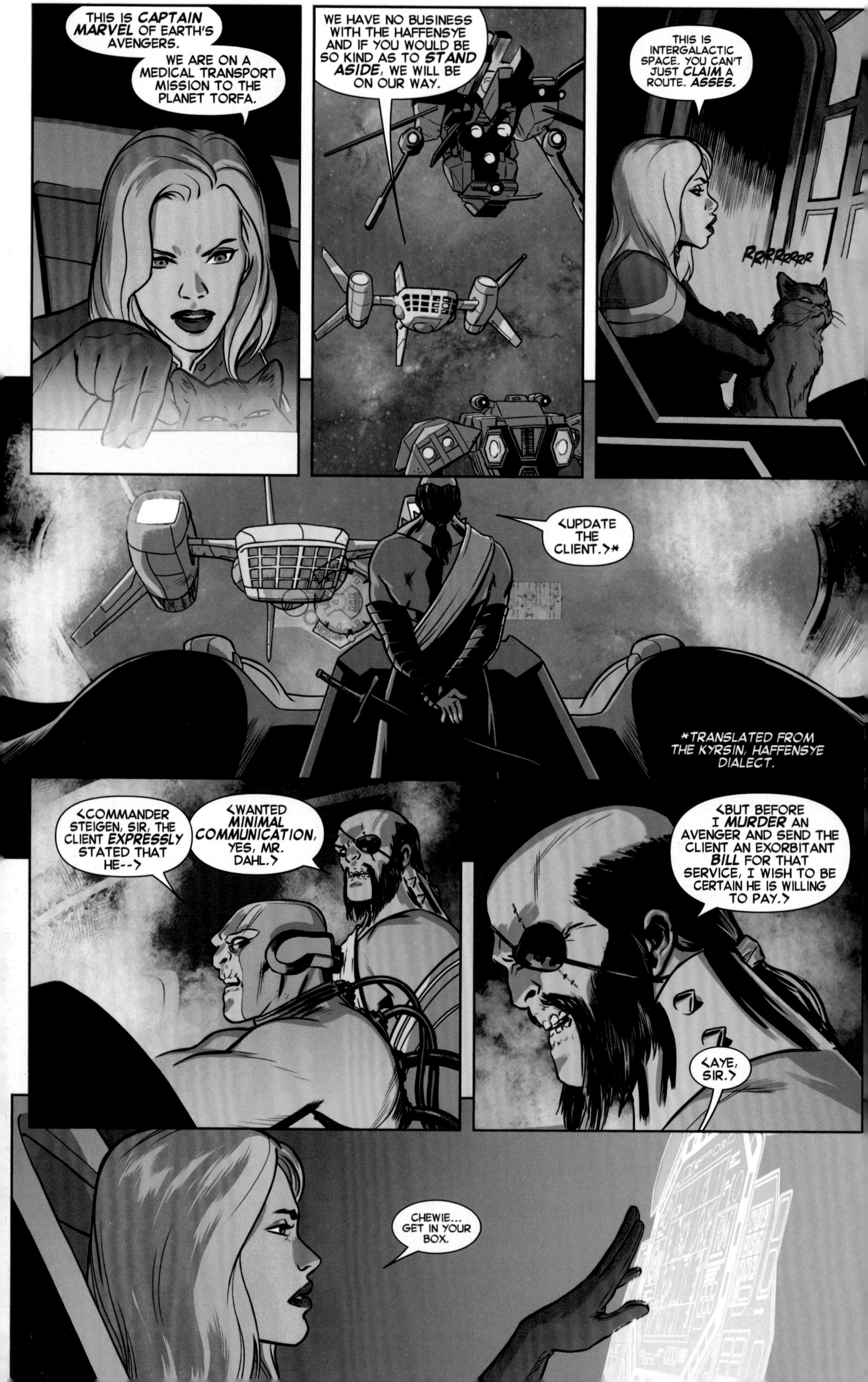
THIS IS CAPTAIN MARVEL OF EARTH'S AVENGERS.
WE ARE ON A MEDICAL TRANSPORT MISSION TO THE PLANET TORFA.
WE HAVE NO BUSINESS WITH THE HAFFENSYE AND IF YOU WOULD BE SO KIND AS TO STAND ASIDE, WE WILL BE ON OUR WAY.
THIS IS INTERGALACTIC SPACE. YOU CAN'T JUST CLAIM A ROUTE. ASSES.
RRRRRRRR
<UPDATE THE CLIENT.>*
*TRANSLATED FROM THE KYRSIN, HAFFENSYE DIALECT.
<COMMANDER STEIGEN, SIR, THE CLIENT EXPRESSLY STATED THAT HE-->
<WANTED MINIMAL COMMUNICATION, YES, MR. DAHL.>
<BUT BEFORE I MURDER AN AVENGER AND SEND THE CLIENT AN EXORBITANT BILL FOR THAT SERVICE, I WISH TO BE CERTAIN HE IS WILLING TO PAY.>
<AYE, SIR.>
CHEWIE... GET IN YOUR BOX.

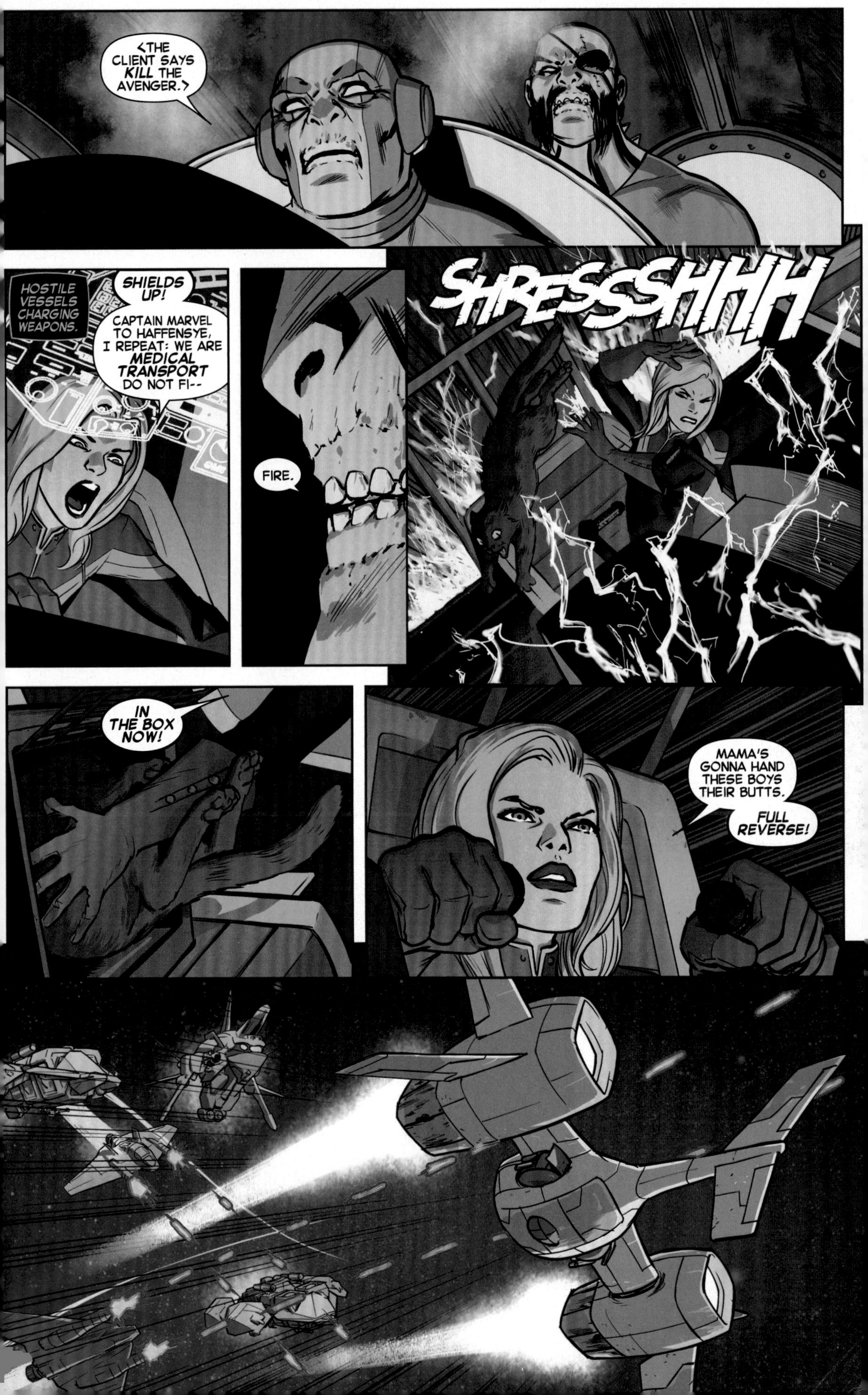
<THE CLIENT SAYS KILL THE AVENGER.>
HOSTILE VESSELS CHARGING WEAPONS.
SHIELDS UP!
CAPTAIN MARVEL TO HAFFENSYE, I REPEAT: WE ARE MEDICAL TRANSPORT DO NOT FI--
FIRE.
SHRESSSHHH
IN THE BOX NOW!
MAMA'S GONNA HAND THESE BOYS THEIR BUTTS.
FULL REVERSE!

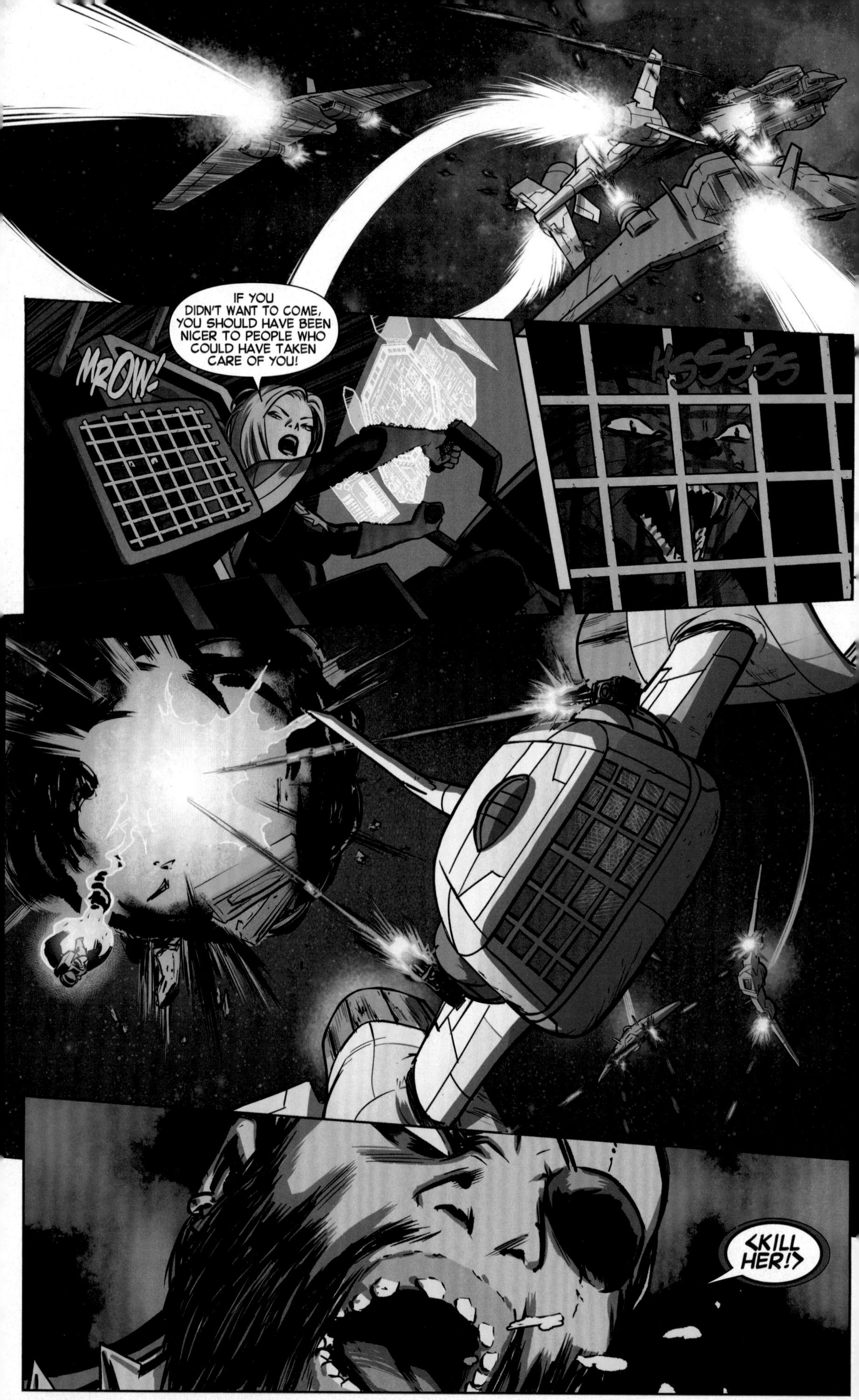
MROW!
IF YOU DIDN'T WANT TO COME, YOU SHOULD HAVE BEEN NICER TO PEOPLE WHO COULD HAVE TAKEN CARE OF YOU!
HSSSSS
<KILL HER!>

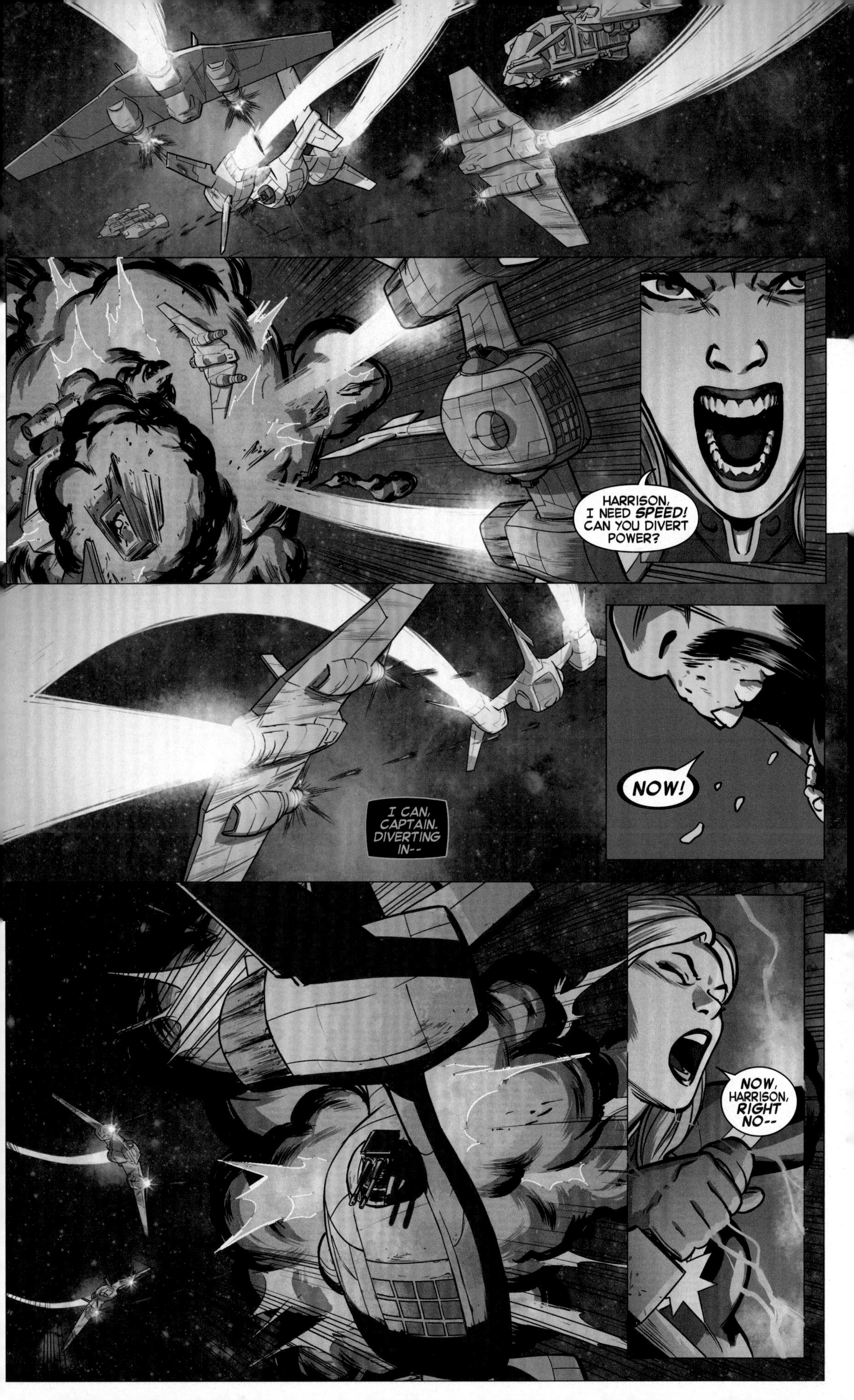
HARRISON, I NEED SPEED! CAN YOU DIVERT POWER?
NOW!
I CAN, CAPTAIN. DIVERTING IN--
NOW, HARRISON, RIGHT NO--

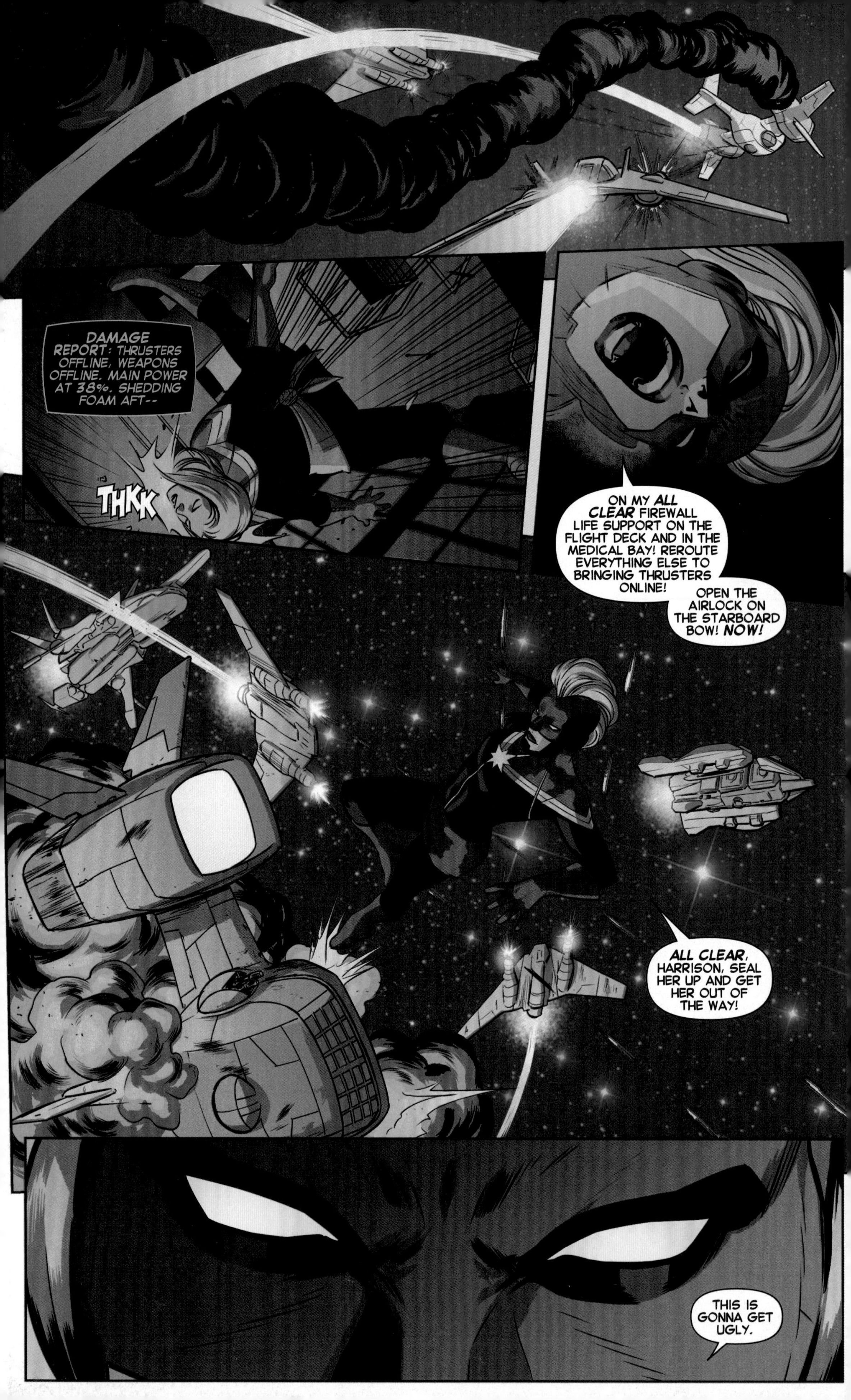
DAMAGE REPORT: THRUSTERS OFFLINE, WEAPONS OFFLINE. MAIN POWER AT 38%. SHEDDING FOAM AFT--
THKK
ON MY ALL CLEAR FIREWALL LIFE SUPPORT ON THE FLIGHT DECK AND IN THE MEDICAL BAY! REROUTE EVERYTHING ELSE TO BRINGING THRUSTERS ONLINE!
OPEN THE AIRLOCK ON THE STARBOARD BOW! NOW!
ALL CLEAR, HARRISON, SEAL HER UP AND GET HER OUT OF THE WAY!
THIS IS GONNA GET UGLY.

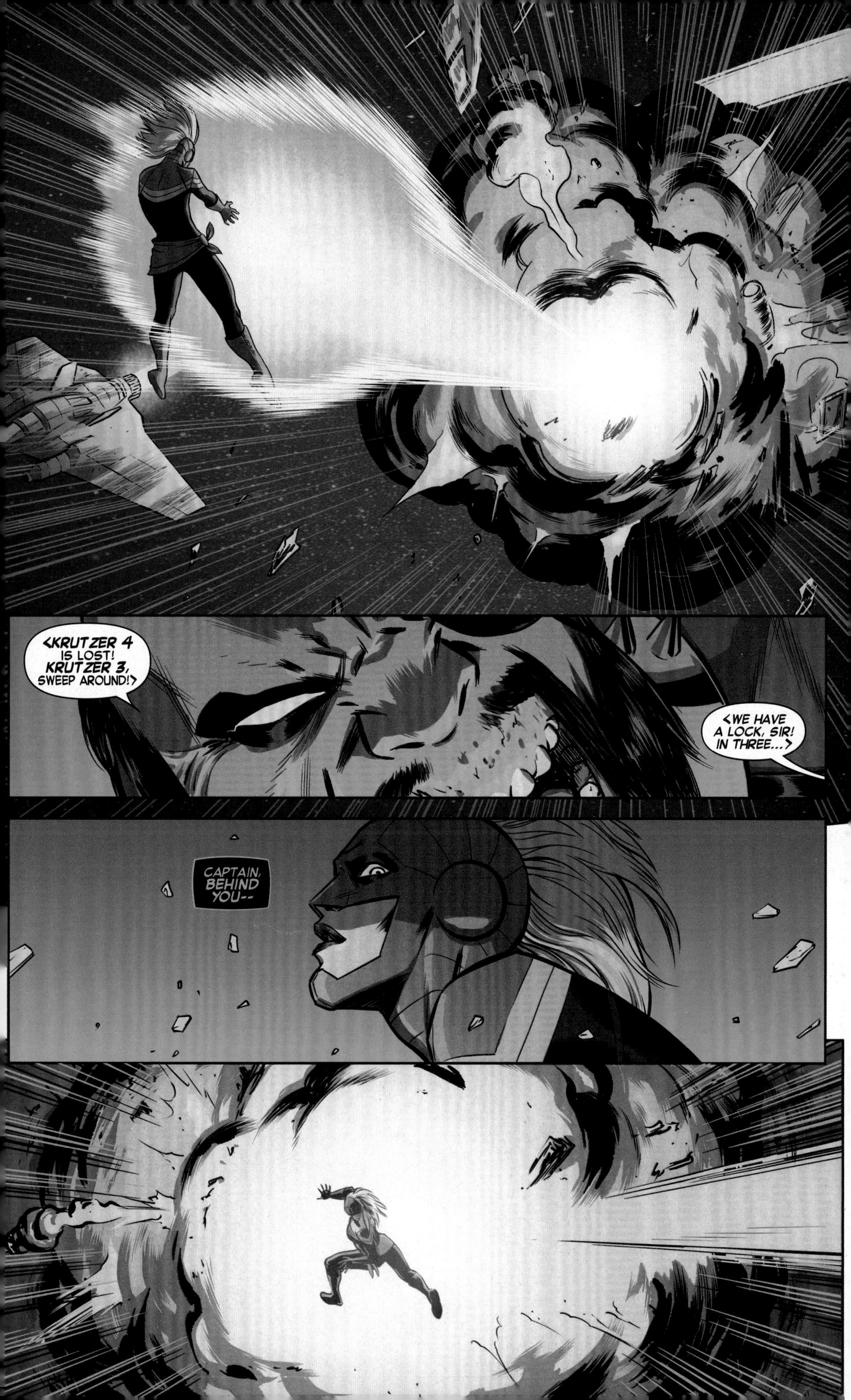
<KRUTZER 4 IS LOST! KRUTZER 3, SWEEP AROUND!>
<WE HAVE A LOCK, SIR! IN THREE...>
CAPTAIN, BEHIND YOU--

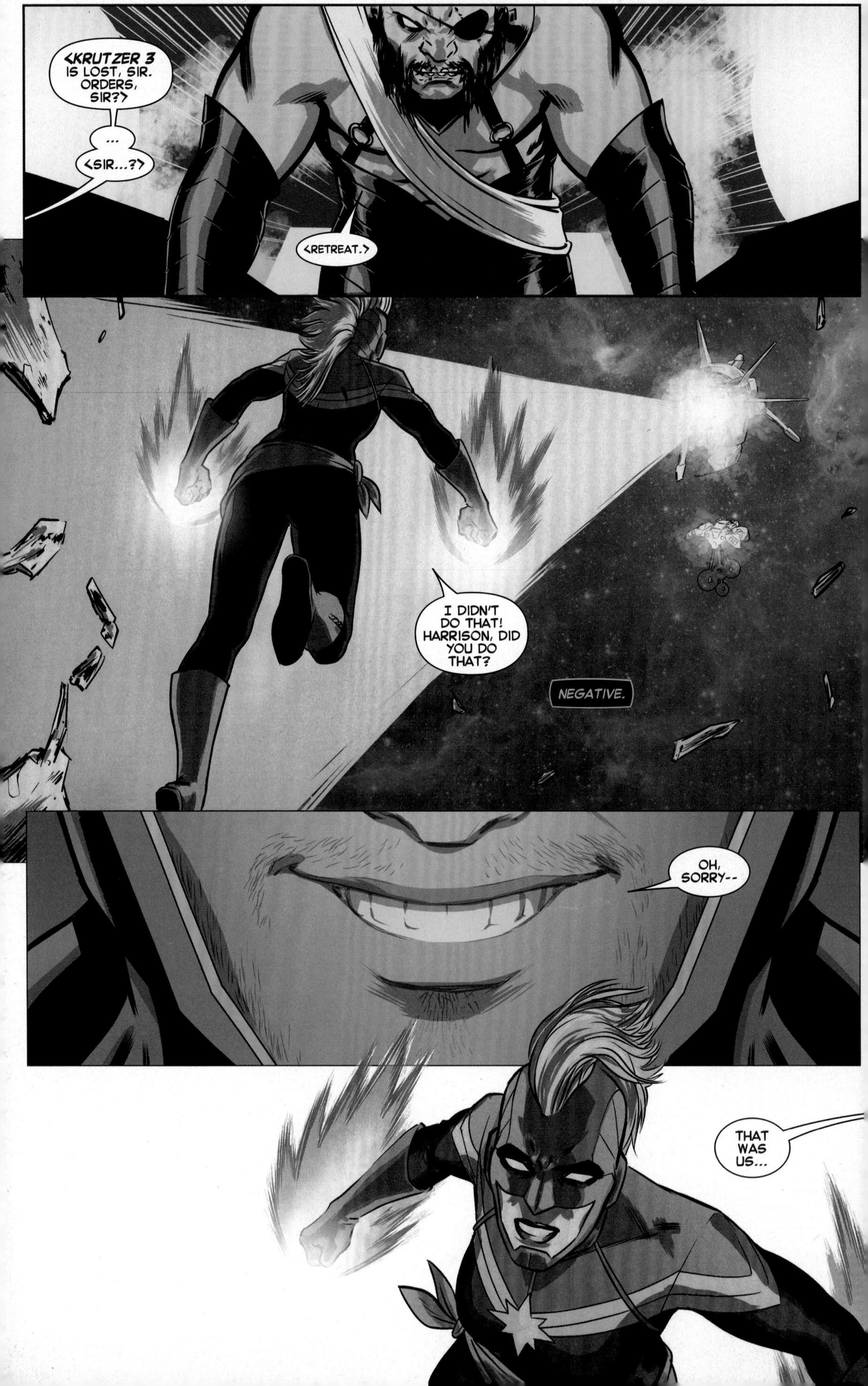
<KRUTZER 3 IS LOST, SIR. ORDERS, SIR?>
...
<SIR...?>
<RETREAT.>
I DIDN'T DO THAT! HARRISON, DID YOU DO THAT?
NEGATIVE.
OH, SORRY--
THAT WAS US...

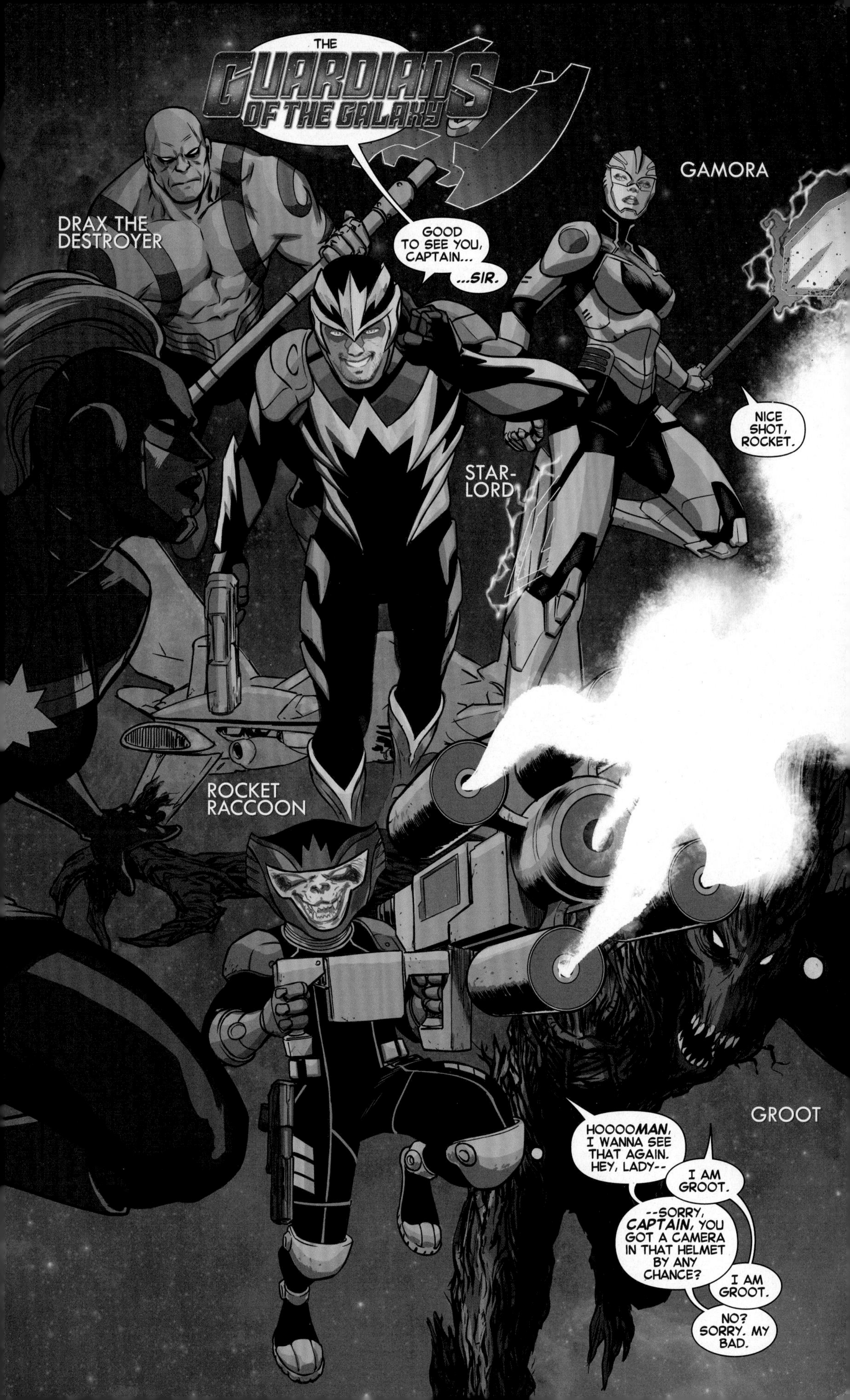
THE GUARDIANS OF THE GALAXY
DRAX THE DESTROYER
GOOD TO SEE YOU, CAPTAIN... ...SIR.
GAMORA
NICE SHOT, ROCKET.
STAR-LORD
ROCKET RACCOON
GROOT
HOOOOMAN, I WANNA SEE THAT AGAIN. HEY, LADY--
I AM GROOT.
--SORRY, CAPTAIN, YOU GOT A CAMERA IN THAT HELMET BY ANY CHANCE?
I AM GROOT.
NO? SORRY. MY BAD.

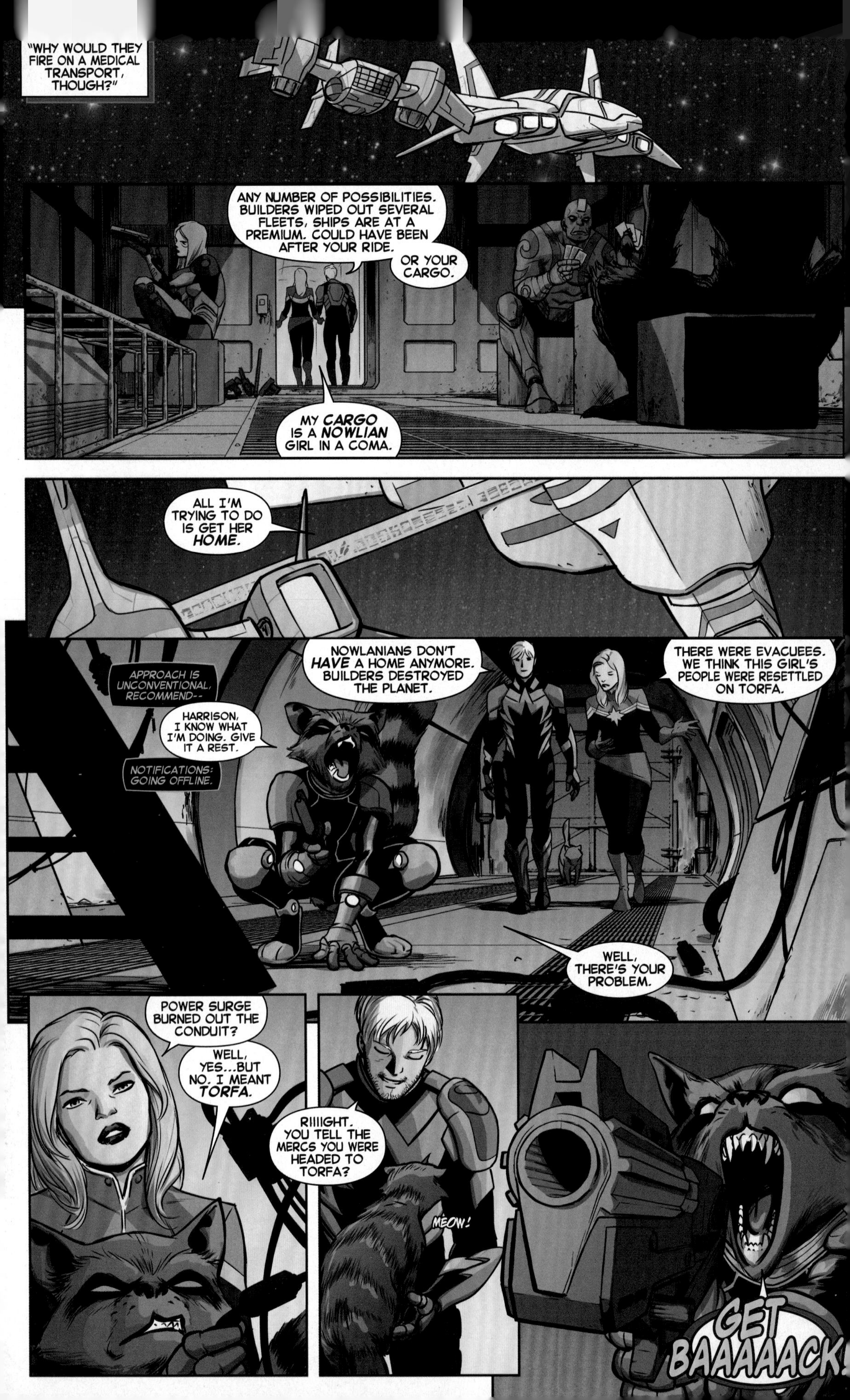
"WHY WOULD THEY FIRE ON A MEDICAL TRANSPORT, THOUGH?"
ANY NUMBER OF POSSIBILITIES. BUILDERS WIPED OUT SEVERAL FLEETS, SHIPS ARE AT A PREMIUM. COULD HAVE BEEN AFTER YOUR RIDE.
OR YOUR CARGO.
MY CARGO IS A NOWLIAN GIRL IN A COMA.
ALL I'M TRYING TO DO IS GET HER HOME.
APPROACH IS UNCONVENTIONAL, RECOMMEND--
HARRISON, I KNOW WHAT I'M DOING. GIVE IT A REST.
NOTIFICATIONS: GOING OFFLINE.
NOWLANIANS DON'T HAVE A HOME ANYMORE. BUILDERS DESTROYED THE PLANET.
THERE WERE EVACUEES. WE THINK THIS GIRL'S PEOPLE WERE RESETTLED ON TORFA.
WELL, THERE'S YOUR PROBLEM.
POWER SURGE BURNED OUT THE CONDUIT?
WELL, YES...BUT NO. I MEANT TORFA.
RIIIIGHT. YOU TELL THE MERCS YOU WERE HEADED TO TORFA?
MEOW!
GET BAAAAACK!

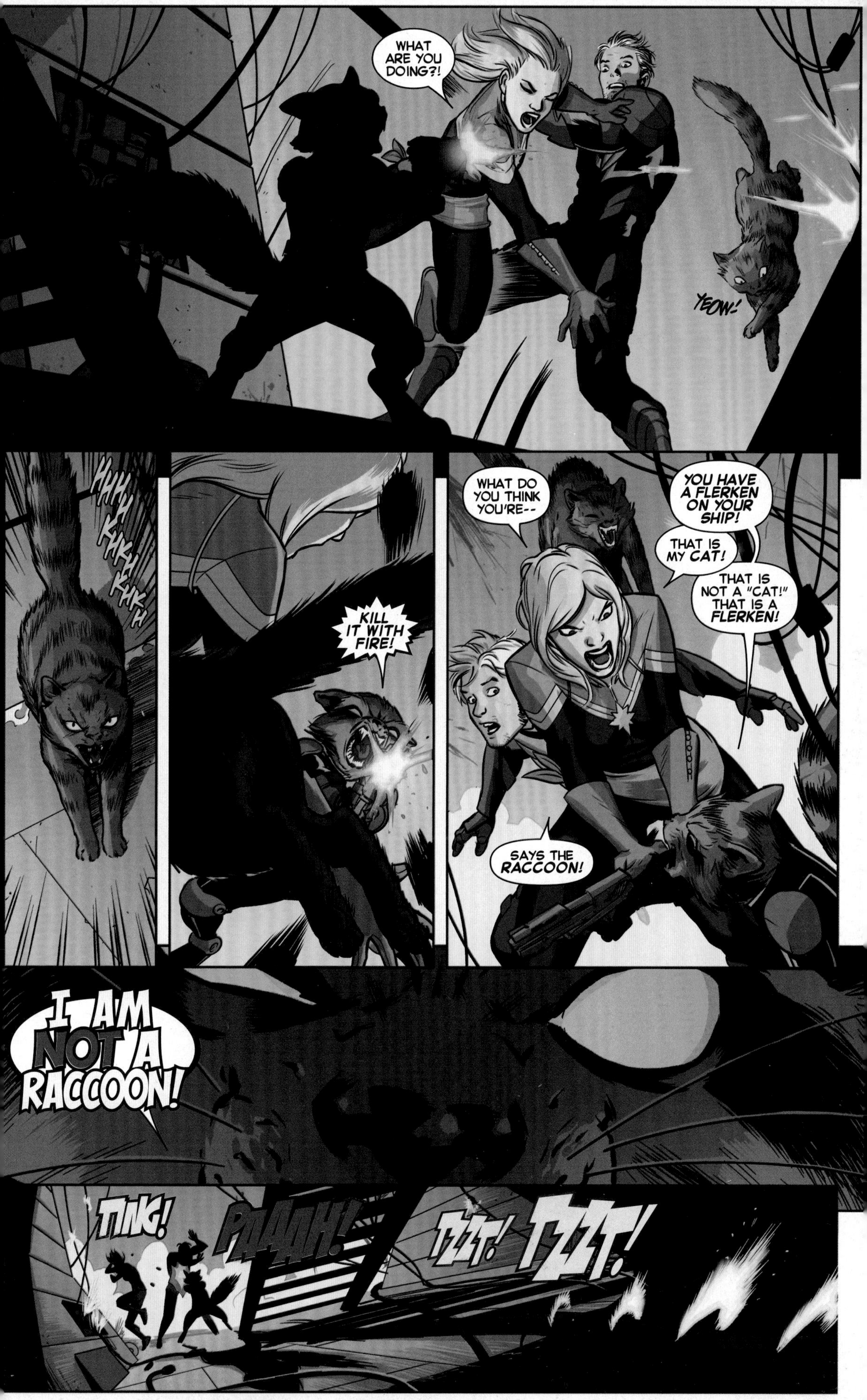
WHAT ARE YOU DOING?!
YEOW!
HHHH KHKH KHKH
KILL IT WITH FIRE!
WHAT DO YOU THINK YOU'RE--
YOU HAVE A FLERKEN ON YOUR SHIP!
THAT IS MY CAT!
THAT IS NOT A "CAT!" THAT IS A FLERKEN!
SAYS THE RACCOON!
I AM NOT A RACCOON!
TING!
PWAAH!
TZZT! TZZT!

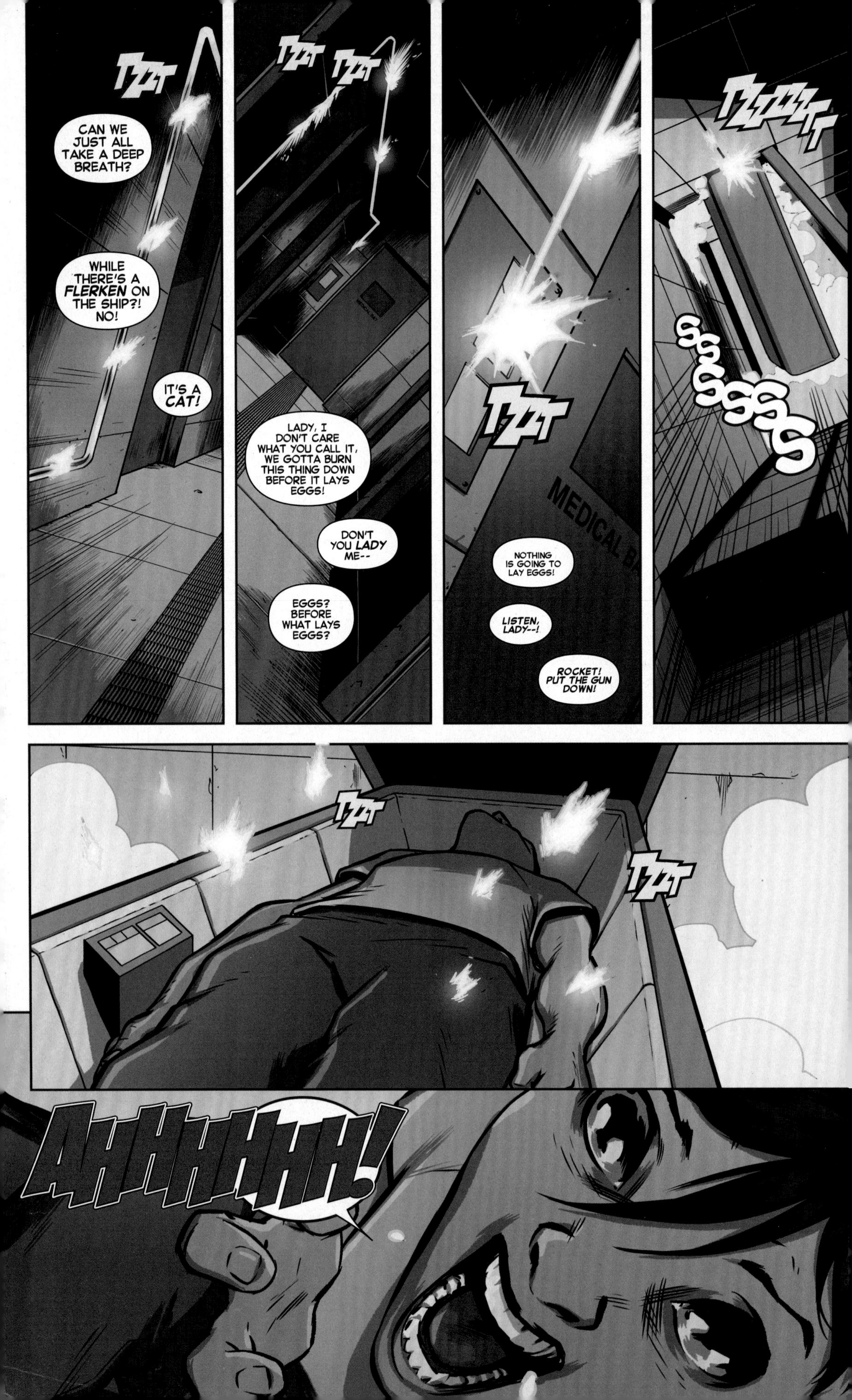
TZZT
CAN WE JUST ALL TAKE A DEEP BREATH?
WHILE THERE'S A FLERKEN ON THE SHIP?! NO!
IT'S A CAT!
TZZT TZZT
LADY, I DON'T CARE WHAT YOU CALL IT, WE GOTTA BURN THIS THING DOWN BEFORE IT LAYS EGGS!
DON'T YOU LADY ME--
EGGS? BEFORE WHAT LAYS EGGS?
TZZT
MEDICAL BA
NOTHING IS GOING TO LAY EGGS!
LISTEN, LADY--!
ROCKET! PUT THE GUN DOWN!
TZZZZZZT
SSSSSSSS
TZZT
TZZT
AHHHHHH!

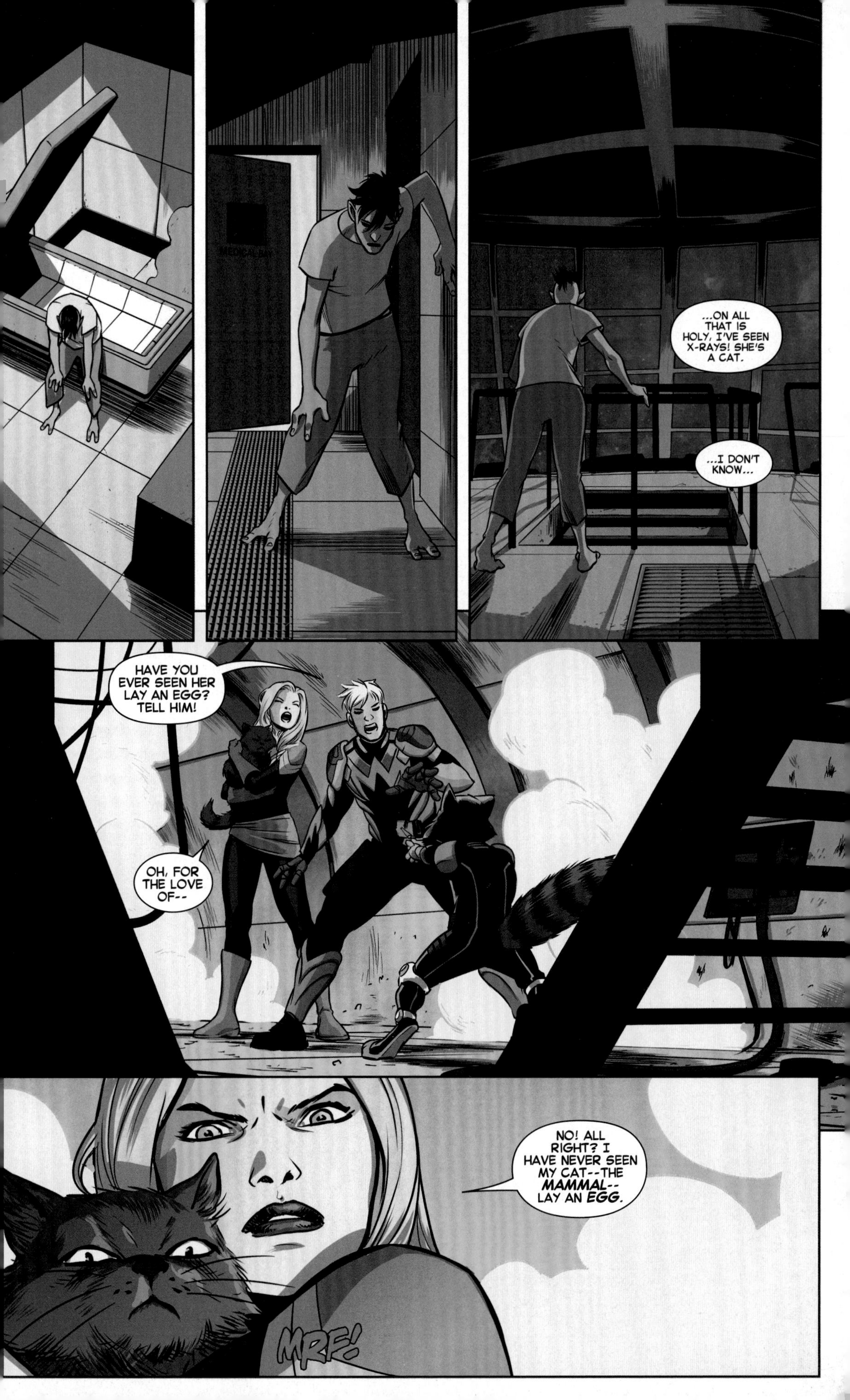
...ON ALL THAT IS HOLY, I'VE SEEN X-RAYS! SHE'S A CAT.
...I DON'T KNOW...
HAVE YOU EVER SEEN HER LAY AN EGG? TELL HIM!
OH, FOR THE LOVE OF--
NO! ALL RIGHT? I HAVE NEVER SEEN MY CAT--THE MAMMAL--LAY AN EGG.
MRF!

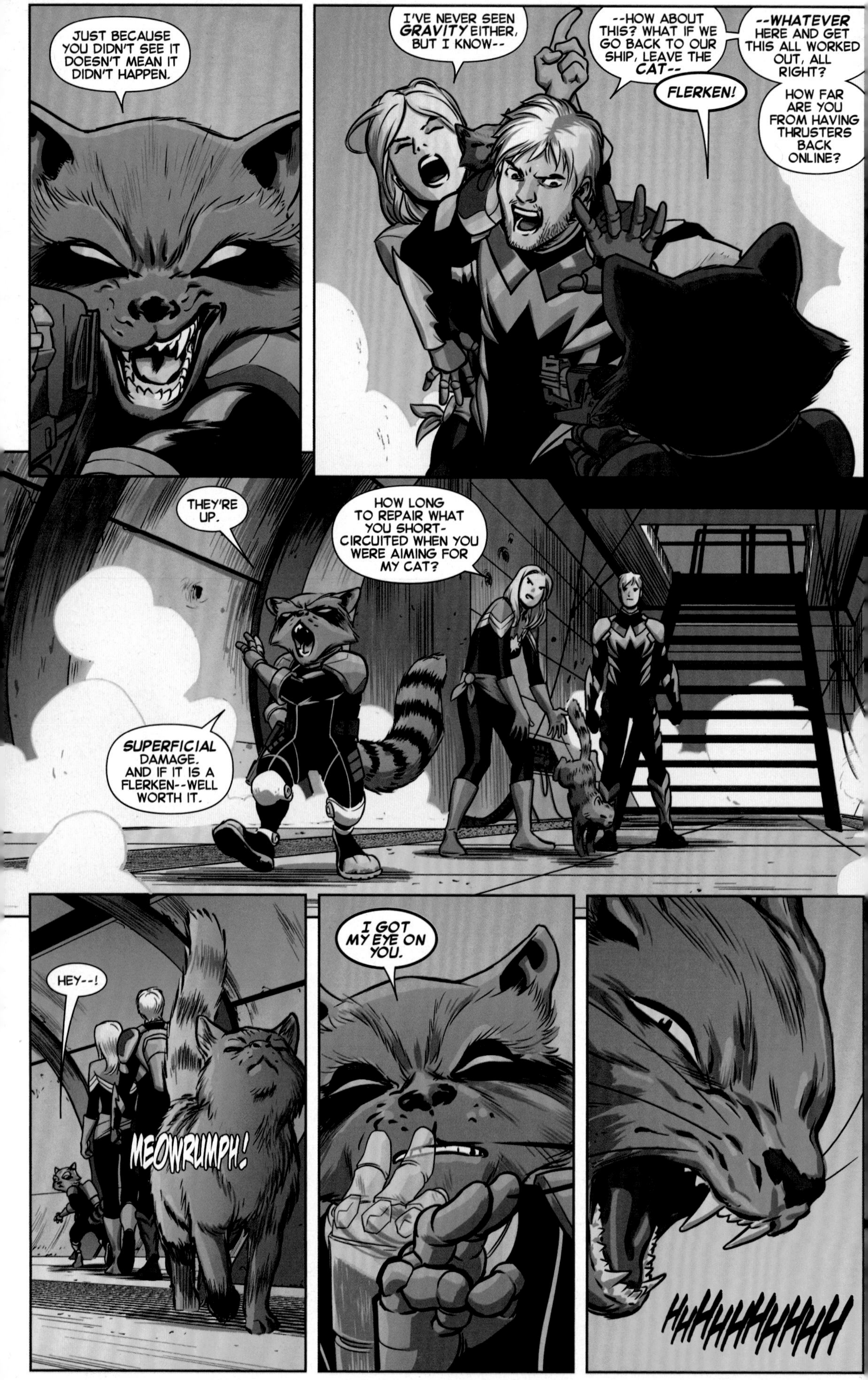

JUST BECAUSE YOU DIDN'T SEE IT DOESN'T MEAN IT DIDN'T HAPPEN.
I'VE NEVER SEEN GRAVITY EITHER, BUT I KNOW--
--HOW ABOUT THIS? WHAT IF WE GO BACK TO OUR SHIP, LEAVE THE CAT--
FLERKEN!
--WHATEVER HERE AND GET THIS ALL WORKED OUT, ALL RIGHT?
HOW FAR ARE YOU FROM HAVING THRUSTERS BACK ONLINE?
THEY'RE UP.
HOW LONG TO REPAIR WHAT YOU SHORT-CIRCUITED WHEN YOU WERE AIMING FOR MY CAT?
SUPERFICIAL DAMAGE. AND IF IT IS A FLERKEN--WELL WORTH IT.
HEY--!
MEOWRUMPH!
I GOT MY EYE ON YOU.
HHHHHHHHHH

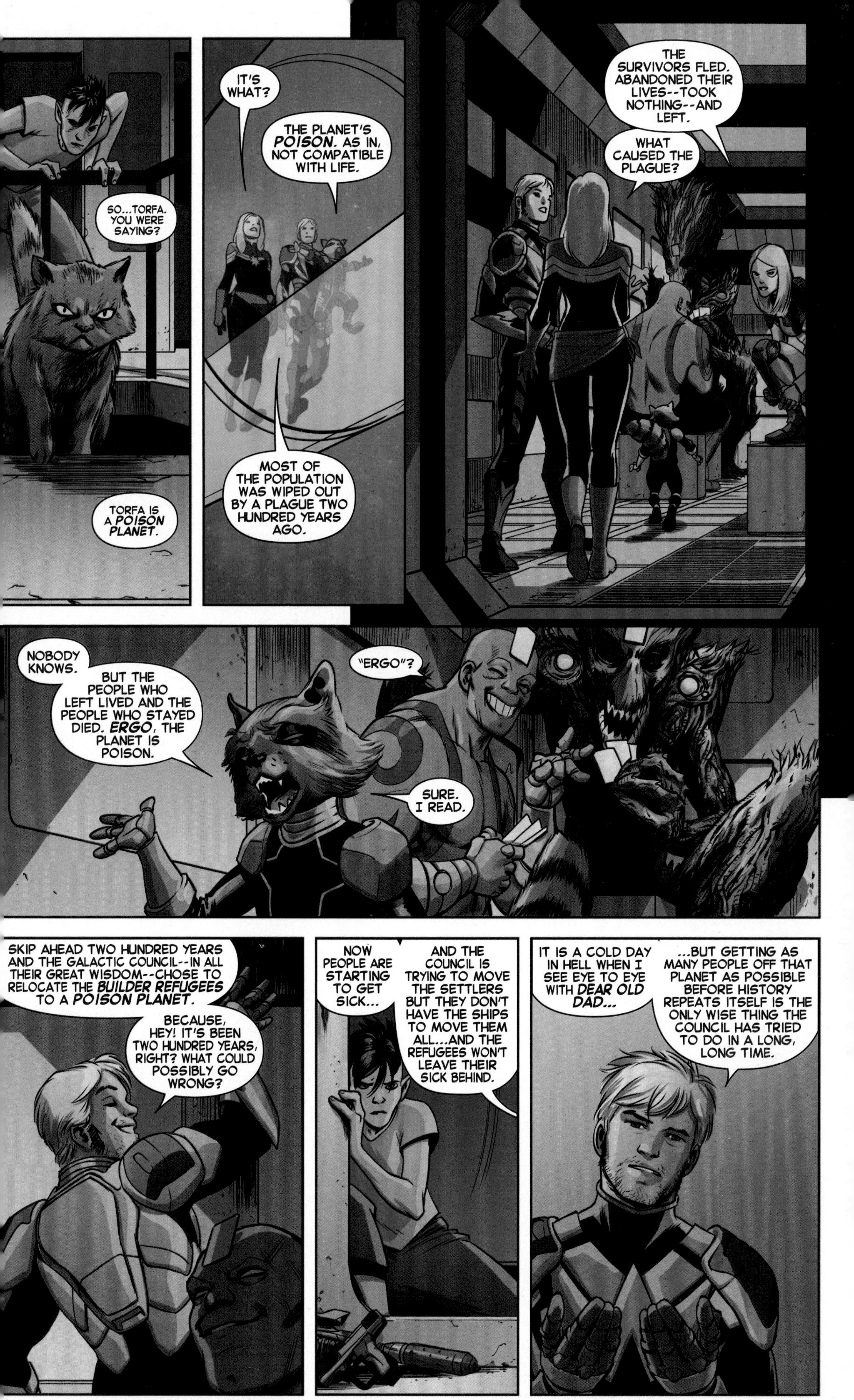
SO...TORFA. YOU WERE SAYING?
TORFA IS A POISON PLANET.
IT'S WHAT?
THE PLANET'S POISON. AS IN, NOT COMPATIBLE WITH LIFE.
MOST OF THE POPULATION WAS WIPED OUT BY A PLAGUE TWO HUNDRED YEARS AGO.
THE SURVIVORS FLED. ABANDONED THEIR LIVES--TOOK NOTHING--AND LEFT.
WHAT CAUSED THE PLAGUE?
NOBODY KNOWS.
BUT THE PEOPLE WHO LEFT LIVED AND THE PEOPLE WHO STAYED DIED. ERGO, THE PLANET IS POISON.
"ERGO"?
SURE. I READ.
SKIP AHEAD TWO HUNDRED YEARS AND THE GALACTIC COUNCIL--IN ALL THEIR GREAT WISDOM--CHOSE TO RELOCATE THE BUILDER REFUGEES TO A POISON PLANET.
BECAUSE, HEY! IT'S BEEN TWO HUNDRED YEARS, RIGHT? WHAT COULD POSSIBLY GO WRONG?
NOW PEOPLE ARE STARTING TO GET SICK...
AND THE COUNCIL IS TRYING TO MOVE THE SETTLERS BUT THEY DON'T HAVE THE SHIPS TO MOVE THEM ALL...AND THE REFUGEES WON'T LEAVE THEIR SICK BEHIND.
IT IS A COLD DAY IN HELL WHEN I SEE EYE TO EYE WITH DEAR OLD DAD...
...BUT GETTING AS MANY PEOPLE OFF THAT PLANET AS POSSIBLE BEFORE HISTORY REPEATS ITSELF IS THE ONLY WISE THING THE COUNCIL HAS TRIED TO DO IN A LONG, LONG TIME.

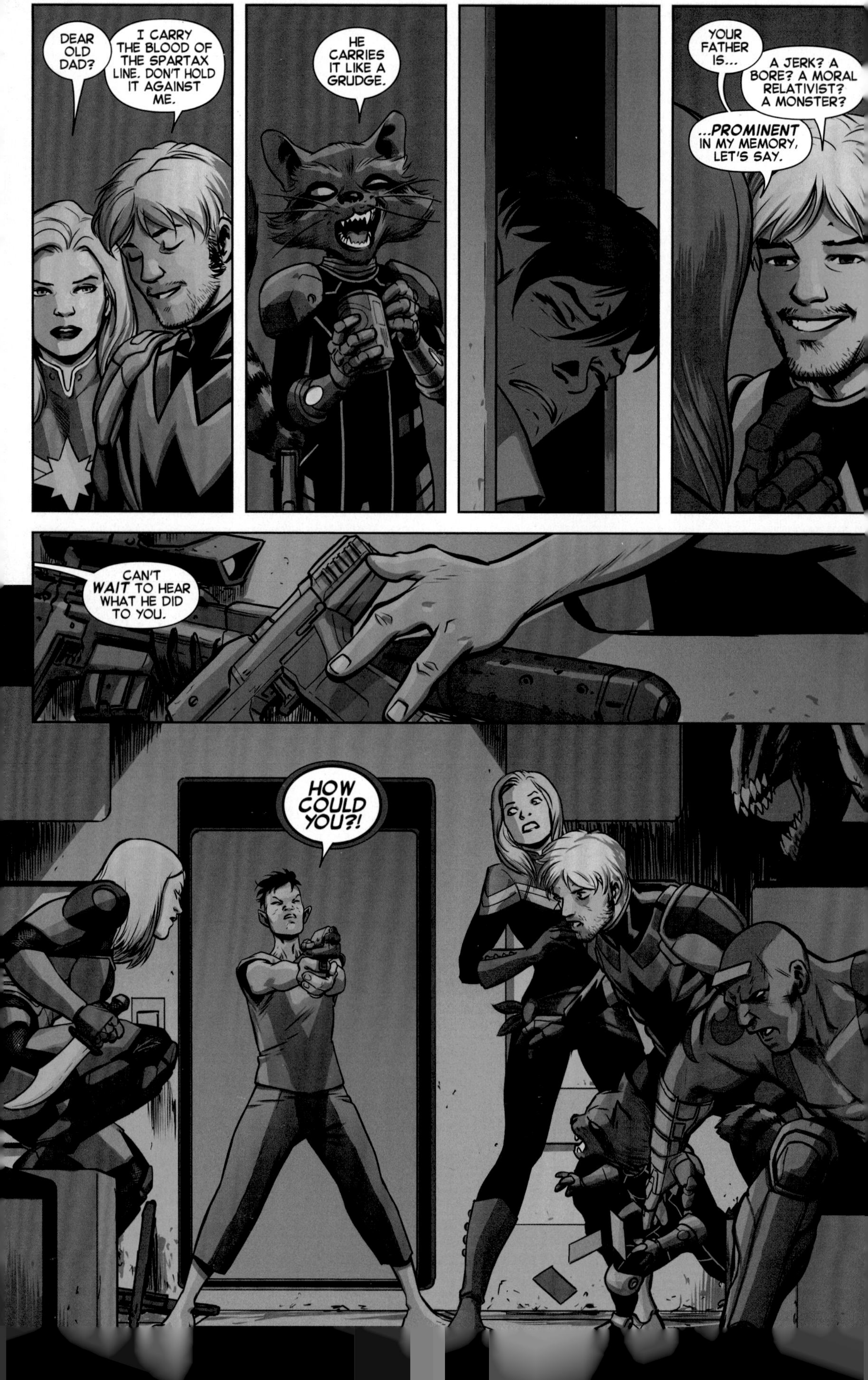
DEAR OLD DAD?
I CARRY THE BLOOD OF THE SPARTAX LINE. DON'T HOLD IT AGAINST ME.
HE CARRIES IT LIKE A GRUDGE.
YOUR FATHER IS...
A JERK? A BORE? A MORAL RELATIVIST? A MONSTER?
...PROMINENT IN MY MEMORY, LET'S SAY.
CAN'T WAIT TO HEAR WHAT HE DID TO YOU.
HOW COULD YOU?!

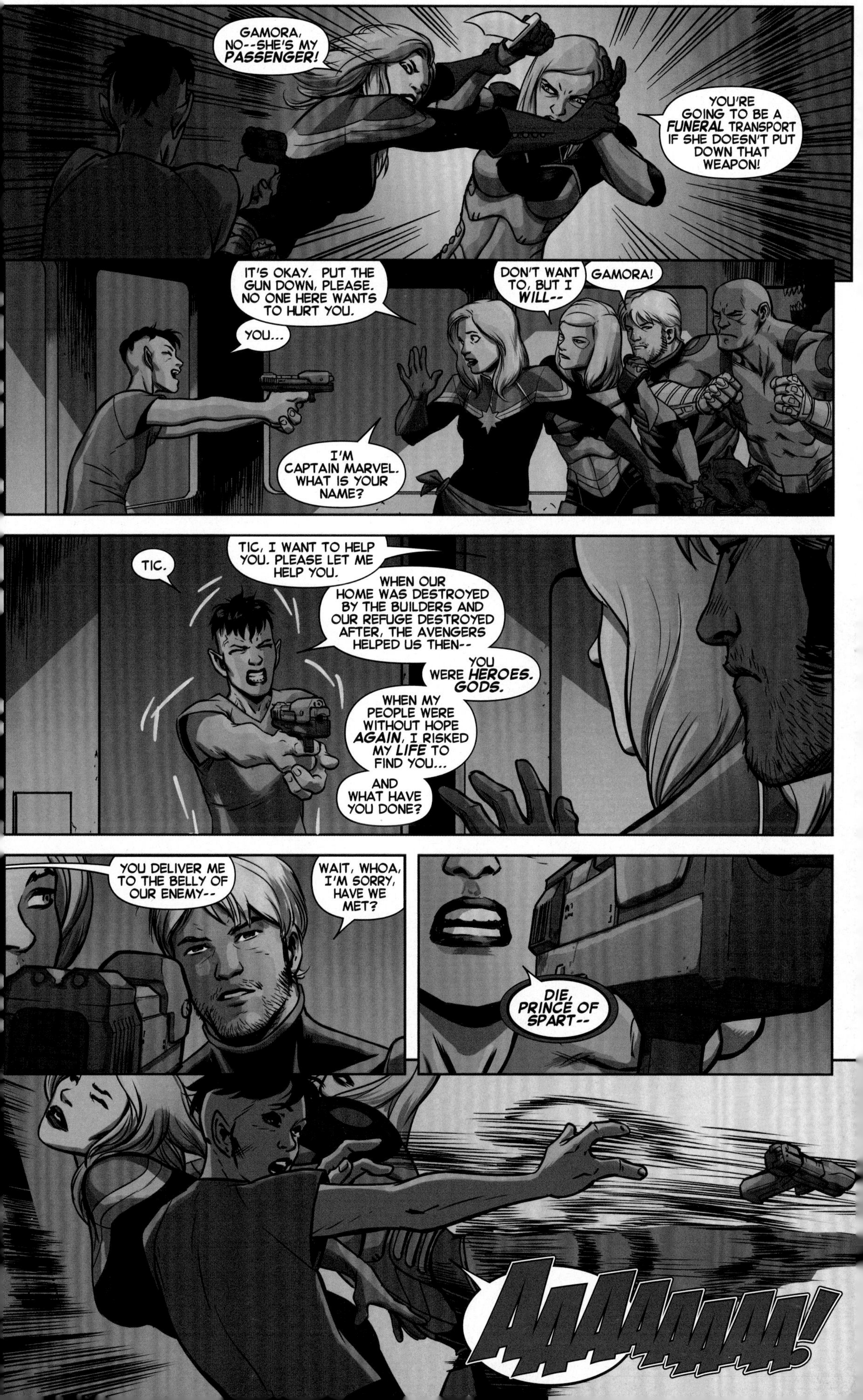
GAMORA, NO--SHE'S MY PASSENGER!
YOU'RE GOING TO BE A FUNERAL TRANSPORT IF SHE DOESN'T PUT DOWN THAT WEAPON!
IT'S OKAY. PUT THE GUN DOWN, PLEASE. NO ONE HERE WANTS TO HURT YOU.
YOU...
DON'T WANT TO, BUT I WILL--
GAMORA!
I'M CAPTAIN MARVEL. WHAT IS YOUR NAME?
TIC.
TIC, I WANT TO HELP YOU. PLEASE LET ME HELP YOU.
WHEN OUR HOME WAS DESTROYED BY THE BUILDERS AND OUR REFUGE DESTROYED AFTER, THE AVENGERS HELPED US THEN--
YOU WERE HEROES. GODS.
WHEN MY PEOPLE WERE WITHOUT HOPE AGAIN, I RISKED MY LIFE TO FIND YOU...
AND WHAT HAVE YOU DONE?
YOU DELIVER ME TO THE BELLY OF OUR ENEMY--
WAIT, WHOA, I'M SORRY, HAVE WE MET?
DIE, PRINCE OF SPART--
AAAAAAAA!

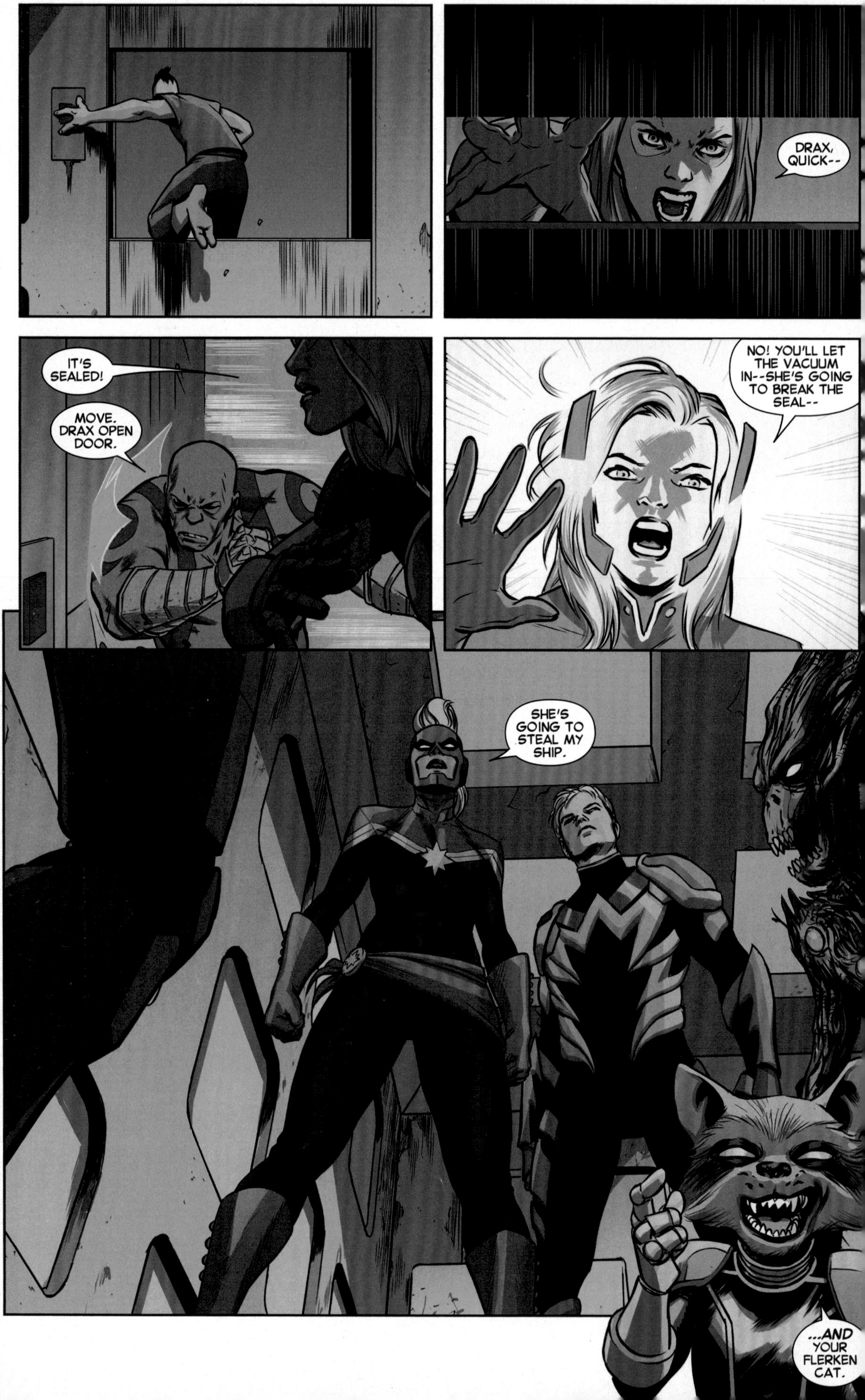
DRAX, QUICK--
IT'S SEALED!
MOVE. DRAX OPEN DOOR.
NO! YOU'LL LET THE VACUUM IN--SHE'S GOING TO BREAK THE SEAL--
SHE'S GOING TO STEAL MY SHIP.
...AND YOUR FLERKEN CAT.

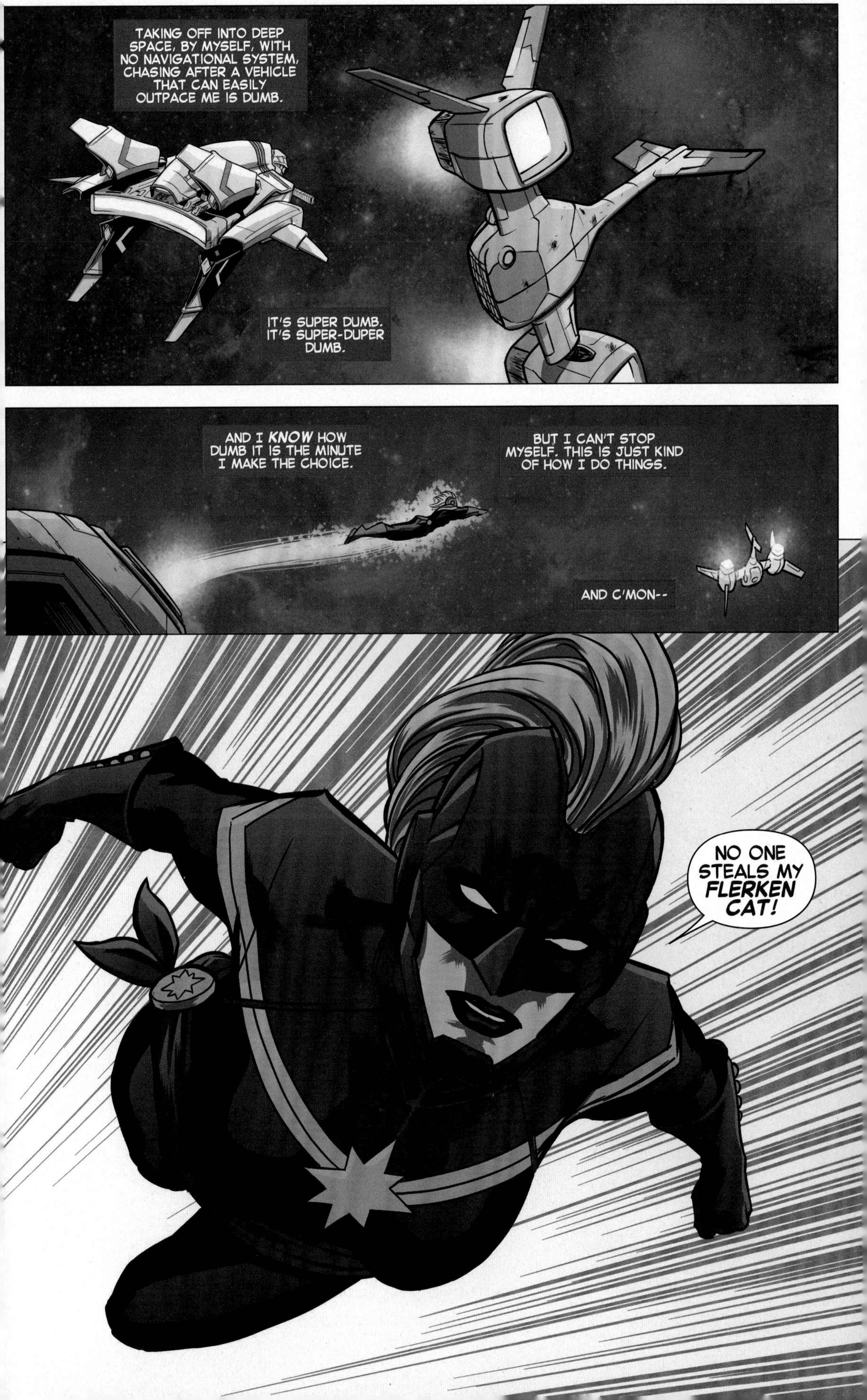
TAKING OFF INTO DEEP SPACE, BY MYSELF, WITH NO NAVIGATIONAL SYSTEM, CHASING AFTER A VEHICLE THAT CAN EASILY OUTPACE ME IS DUMB.
IT'S SUPER DUMB. IT'S SUPER-DUPER DUMB.
AND I KNOW HOW DUMB IT IS THE MINUTE I MAKE THE CHOICE.
BUT I CAN'T STOP MYSELF. THIS IS JUST KIND OF HOW I DO THINGS.
AND C'MON--
NO ONE STEALS MY FLERKEN CAT!

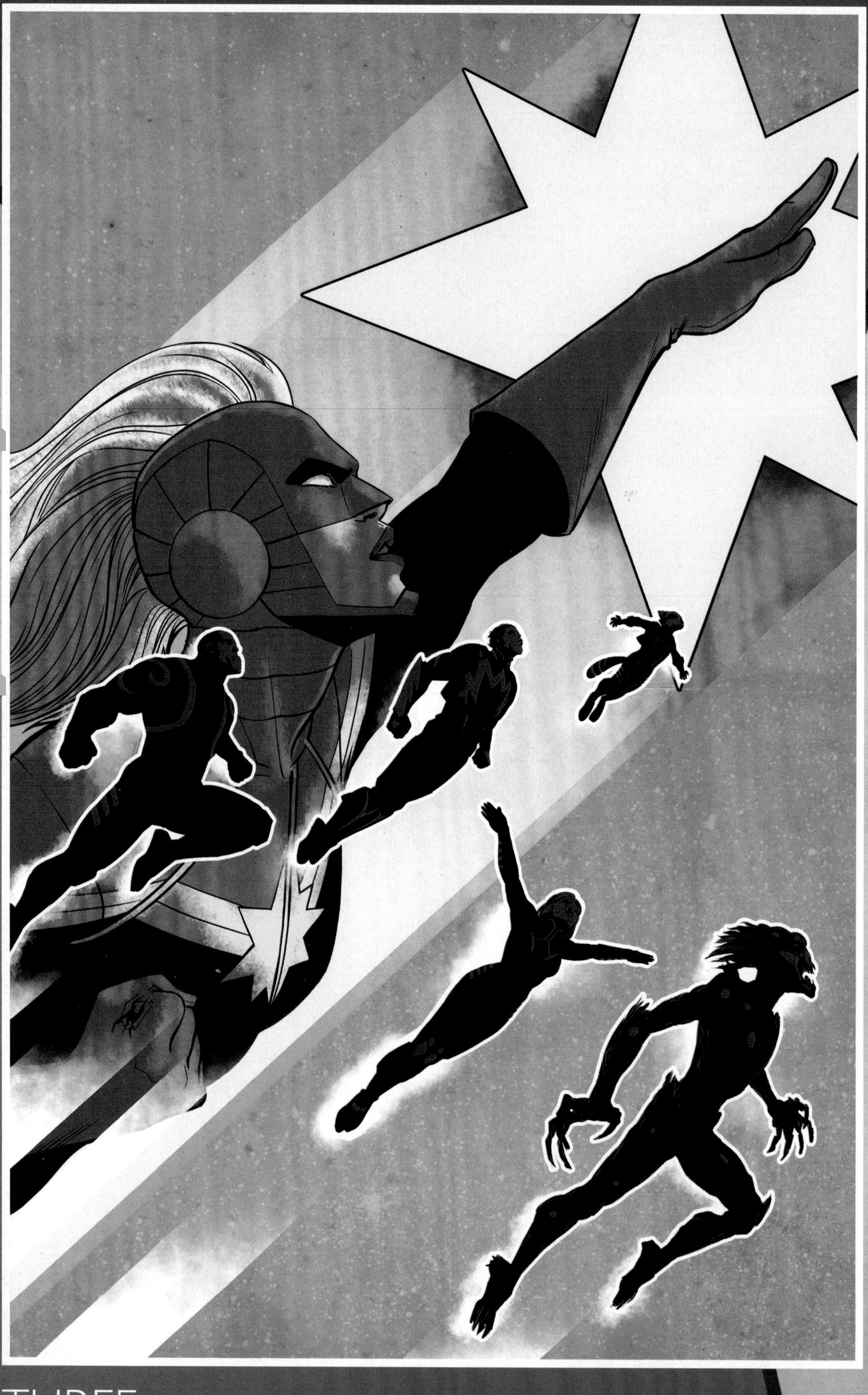

THREE

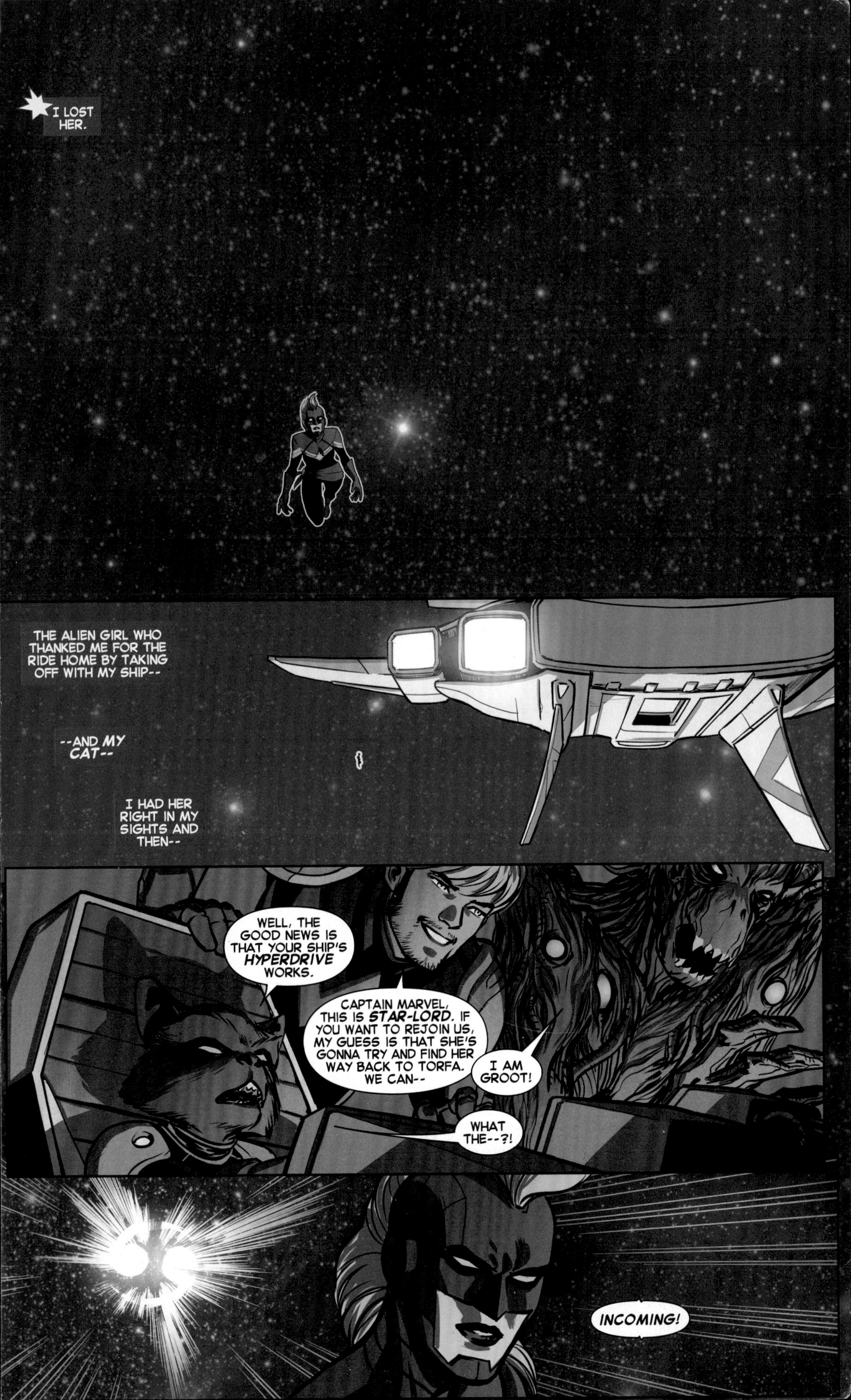

I LOST HER.
THE ALIEN GIRL WHO THANKED ME FOR THE RIDE HOME BY TAKING OFF WITH MY SHIP--
--AND MY CAT--
I HAD HER RIGHT IN MY SIGHTS AND THEN--
WELL, THE GOOD NEWS IS THAT YOUR SHIP'S HYPERDRIVE WORKS.
CAPTAIN MARVEL, THIS IS STAR-LORD. IF YOU WANT TO REJOIN US, MY GUESS IS THAT SHE'S GONNA TRY AND FIND HER WAY BACK TO TORFA. WE CAN--
I AM GROOT!
WHAT THE--?!
INCOMING!

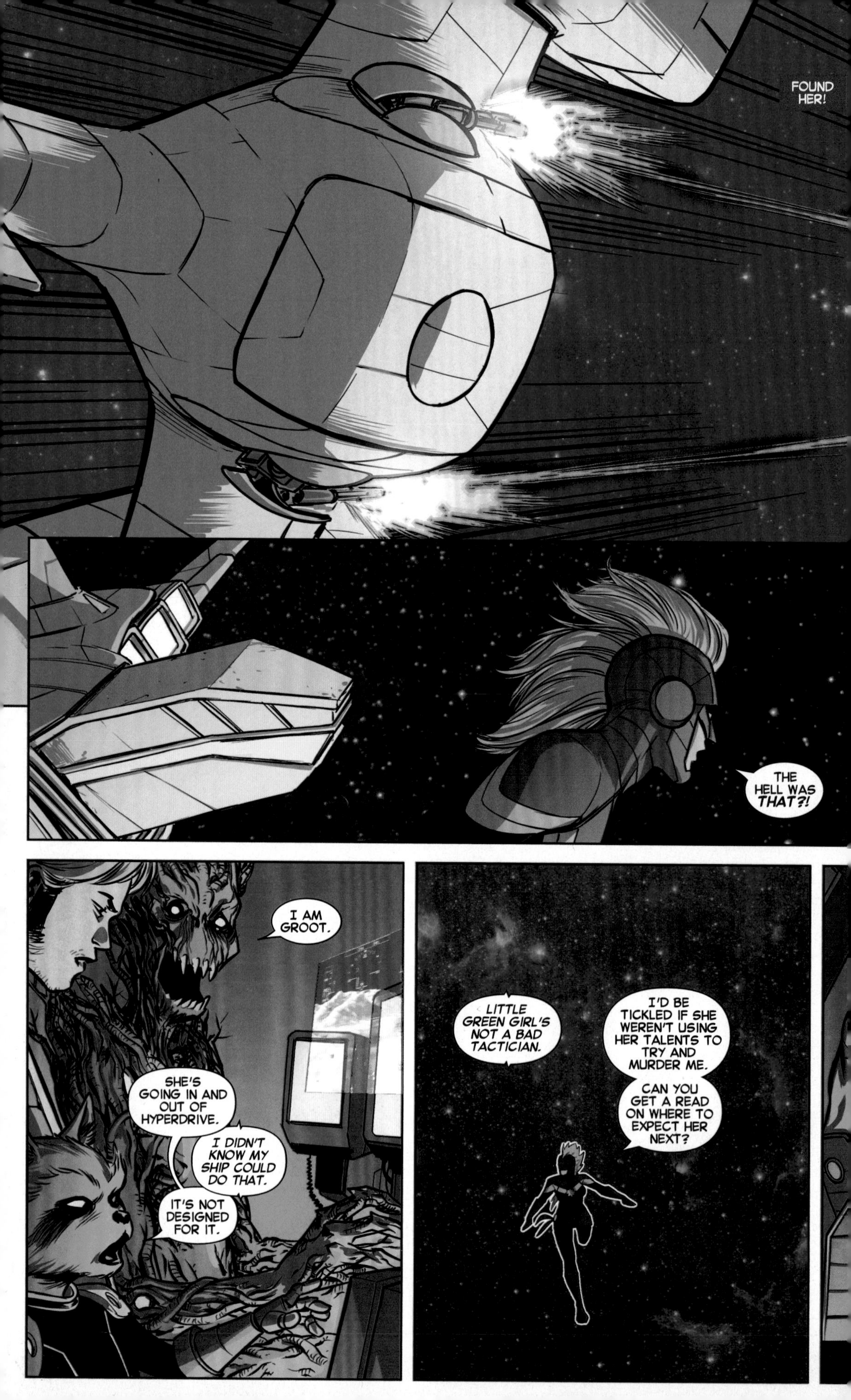
FOUND HER!
THE HELL WAS THAT?!
I AM GROOT.
SHE'S GOING IN AND OUT OF HYPERDRIVE.
I DIDN'T KNOW MY SHIP COULD DO THAT.
IT'S NOT DESIGNED FOR IT.
LITTLE GREEN GIRL'S NOT A BAD TACTICIAN.
I'D BE TICKLED IF SHE WEREN'T USING HER TALENTS TO TRY AND MURDER ME.
CAN YOU GET A READ ON WHERE TO EXPECT HER NEXT?

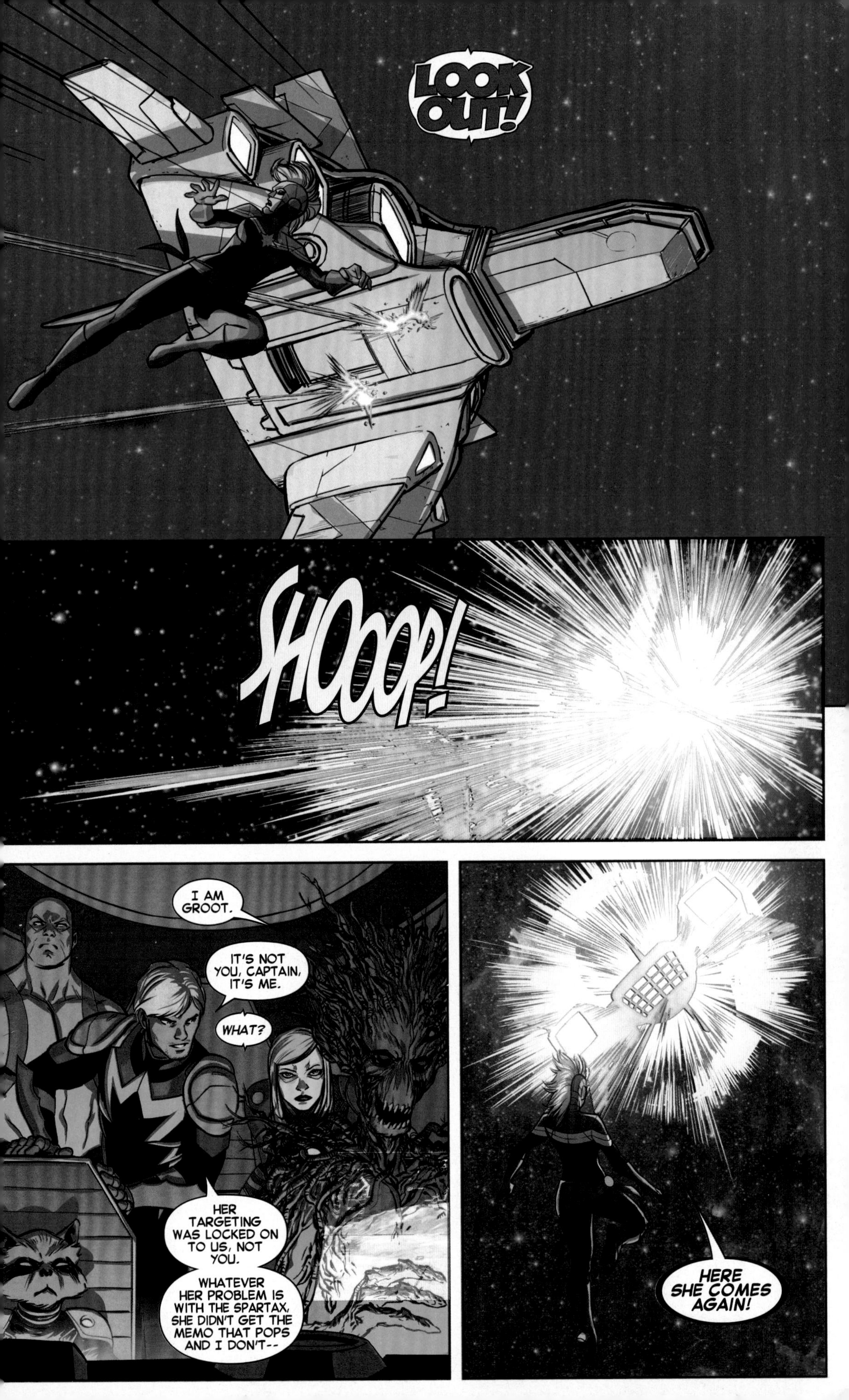
LOOK OUT!
SHOOOP!
I AM GROOT.
IT'S NOT YOU, CAPTAIN, IT'S ME.
WHAT?
HER TARGETING WAS LOCKED ON TO US, NOT YOU.
WHATEVER HER PROBLEM IS WITH THE SPARTAX, SHE DIDN'T GET THE MEMO THAT POPS AND I DON'T--
HERE SHE COMES AGAIN!

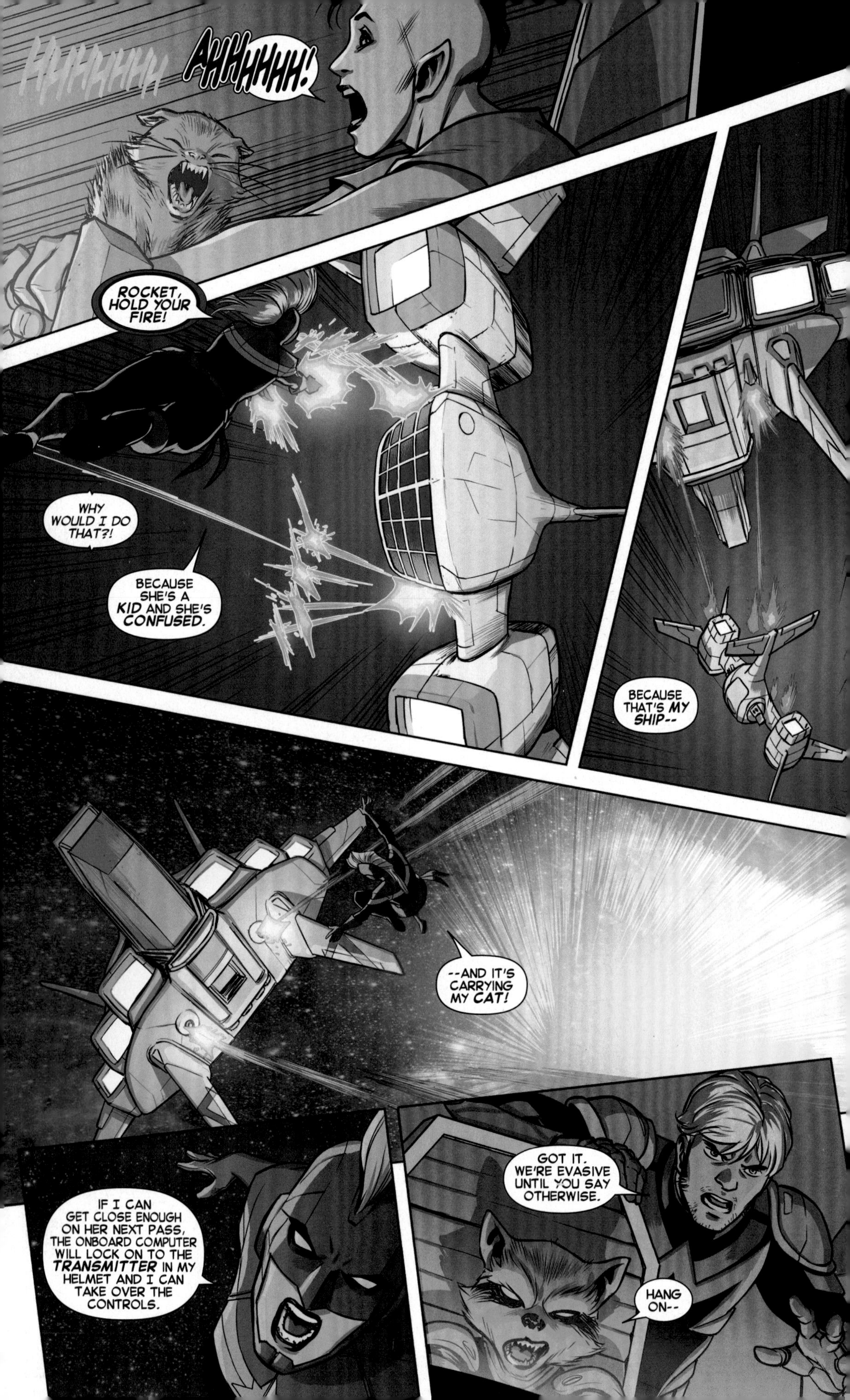
HHHHHHH
AHHHHHH!
ROCKET, HOLD YOUR FIRE!
WHY WOULD I DO THAT?!
BECAUSE SHE'S A KID AND SHE'S CONFUSED.
BECAUSE THAT'S MY SHIP--
--AND IT'S CARRYING MY CAT!
IF I CAN GET CLOSE ENOUGH ON HER NEXT PASS, THE ONBOARD COMPUTER WILL LOCK ON TO THE TRANSMITTER IN MY HELMET AND I CAN TAKE OVER THE CONTROLS.
GOT IT. WE'RE EVASIVE UNTIL YOU SAY OTHERWISE.
HANG ON--

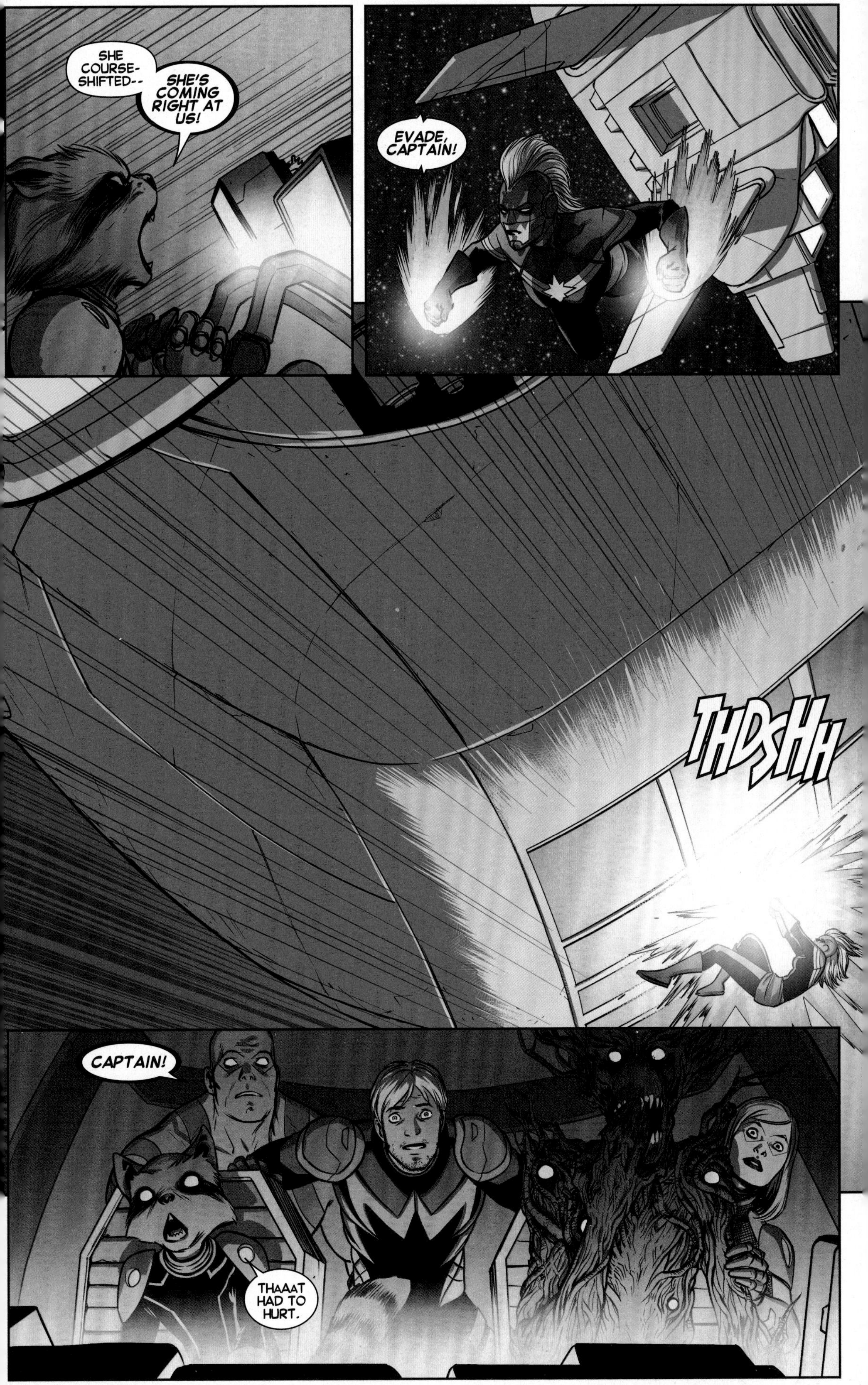
SHE COURSE-SHIFTED--
SHE'S COMING RIGHT AT US!
EVADE, CAPTAIN!
THDSHH
CAPTAIN!
THAAAT HAD TO HURT.

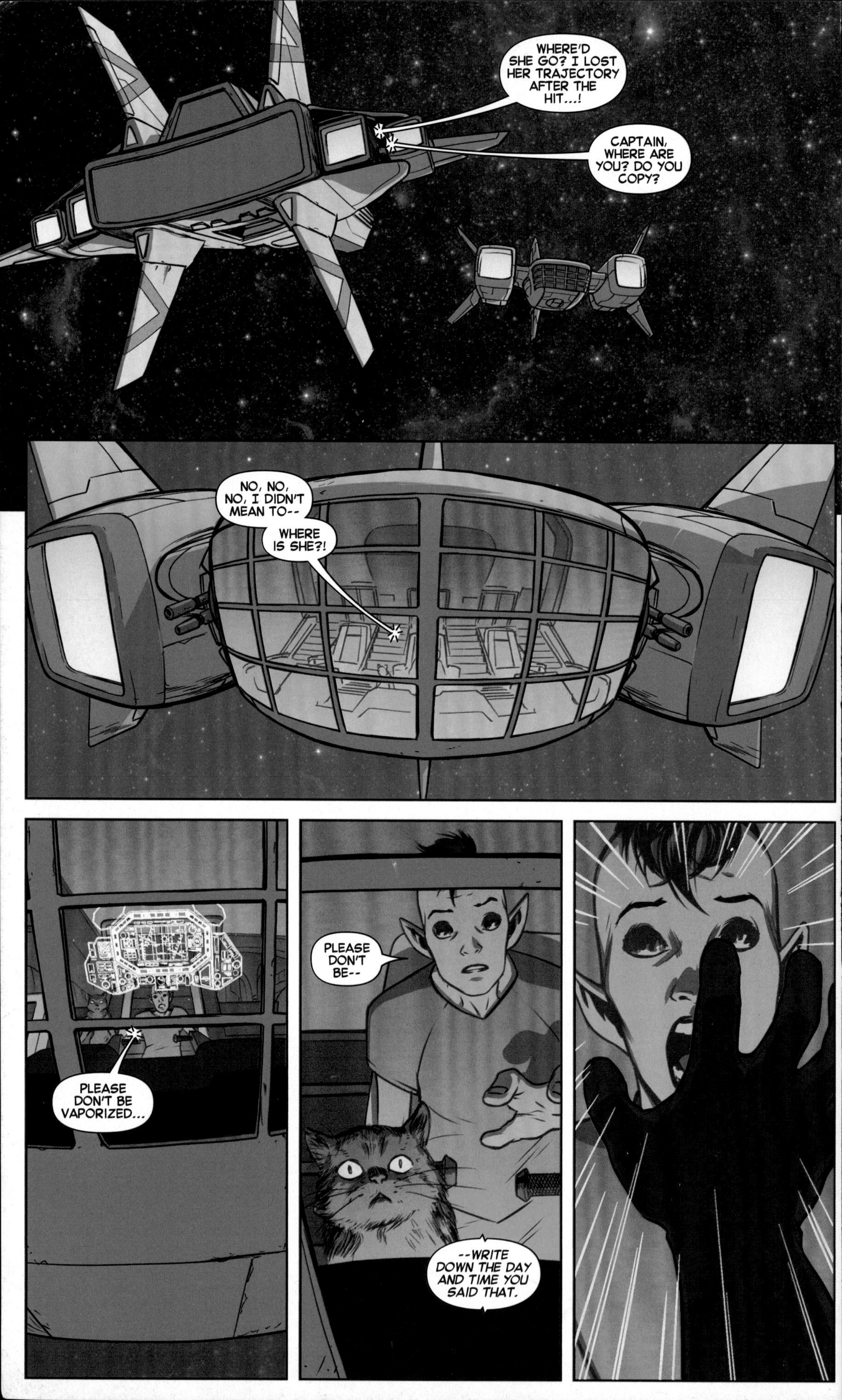
WHERE'D SHE GO? I LOST HER TRAJECTORY AFTER THE HIT...!
CAPTAIN, WHERE ARE YOU? DO YOU COPY?
NO, NO, NO, I DIDN'T MEAN TO--
WHERE IS SHE?!
PLEASE DON'T BE VAPORIZED...
PLEASE DON'T BE--
--WRITE DOWN THE DAY AND TIME YOU SAID THAT.

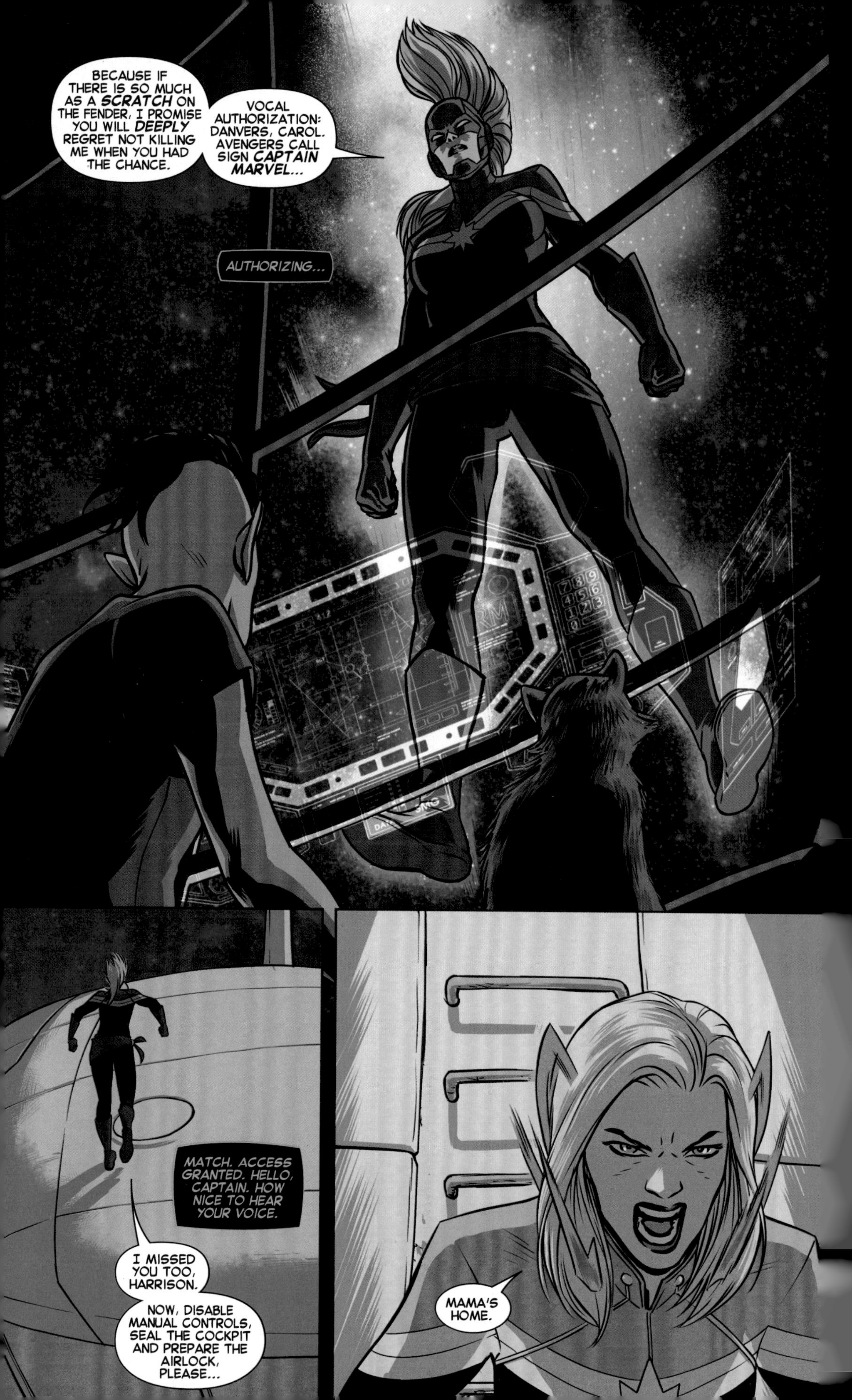

BECAUSE IF THERE IS SO MUCH AS A SCRATCH ON THE FENDER, I PROMISE YOU WILL DEEPLY REGRET NOT KILLING ME WHEN YOU HAD THE CHANCE.
VOCAL AUTHORIZATION: DANVERS, CAROL. AVENGERS CALL SIGN CAPTAIN MARVEL...
AUTHORIZING...
MATCH. ACCESS GRANTED. HELLO, CAPTAIN. HOW NICE TO HEAR YOUR VOICE.
I MISSED YOU TOO, HARRISON.
NOW, DISABLE MANUAL CONTROLS, SEAL THE COCKPIT AND PREPARE THE AIRLOCK, PLEASE...
MAMA'S HOME.

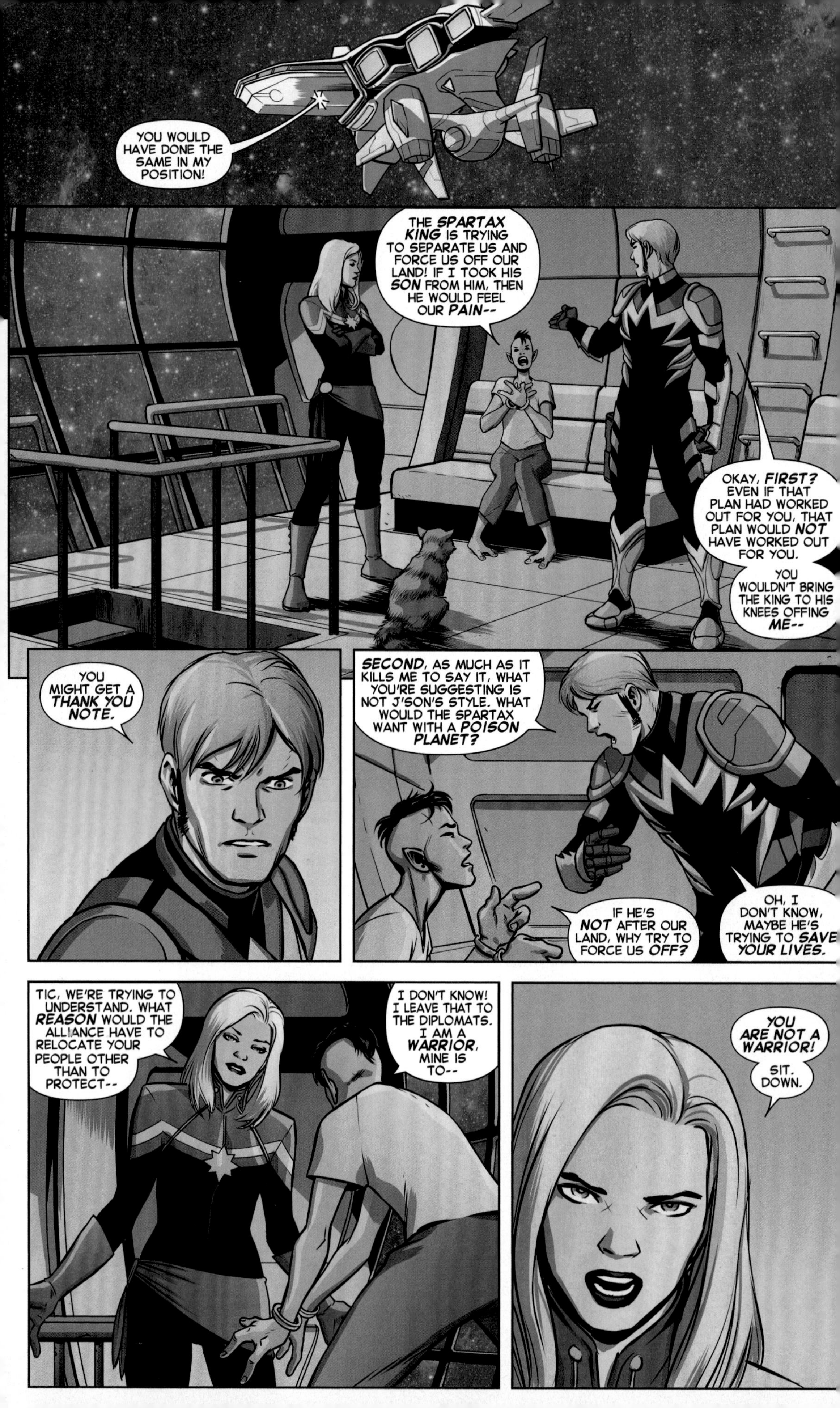
YOU WOULD HAVE DONE THE SAME IN MY POSITION!
THE SPARTAX KING IS TRYING TO SEPARATE US AND FORCE US OFF OUR LAND! IF I TOOK HIS SON FROM HIM, THEN HE WOULD FEEL OUR PAIN--
OKAY, FIRST? EVEN IF THAT PLAN HAD WORKED OUT FOR YOU, THAT PLAN WOULD NOT HAVE WORKED OUT FOR YOU.
YOU WOULDN'T BRING THE KING TO HIS KNEES OFFING ME--
YOU MIGHT GET A THANK YOU NOTE.
SECOND, AS MUCH AS IT KILLS ME TO SAY IT, WHAT YOU'RE SUGGESTING IS NOT J'SON'S STYLE. WHAT WOULD THE SPARTAX WANT WITH A POISON PLANET?
IF HE'S NOT AFTER OUR LAND, WHY TRY TO FORCE US OFF?
OH, I DON'T KNOW, MAYBE HE'S TRYING TO SAVE YOUR LIVES.
TIC, WE'RE TRYING TO UNDERSTAND. WHAT REASON WOULD THE ALLIANCE HAVE TO RELOCATE YOUR PEOPLE OTHER THAN TO PROTECT--
I DON'T KNOW! I LEAVE THAT TO THE DIPLOMATS. I AM A WARRIOR, MINE IS TO--
YOU ARE NOT A WARRIOR!
SIT. DOWN.

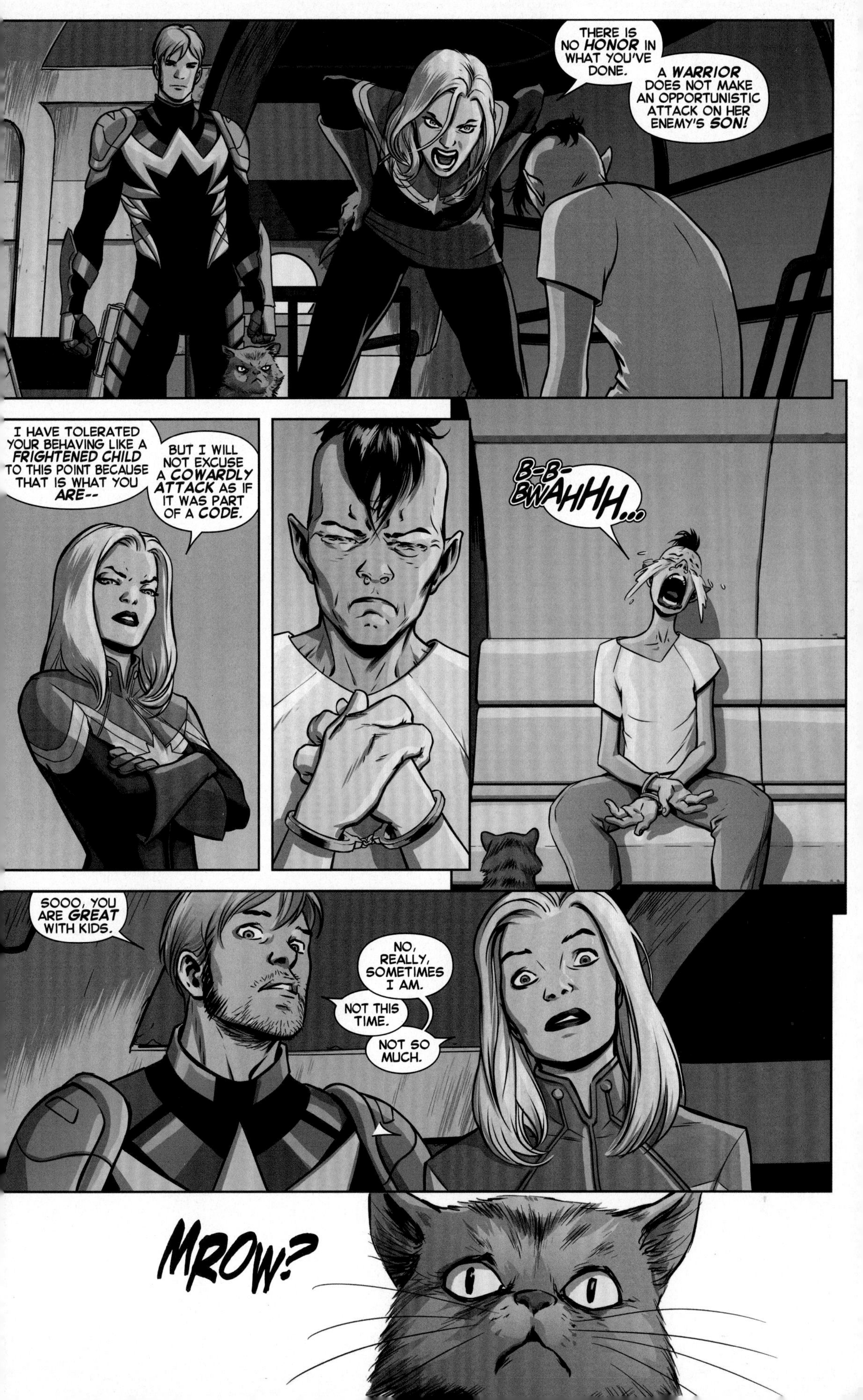
THERE IS NO HONOR IN WHAT YOU'VE DONE.
A WARRIOR DOES NOT MAKE AN OPPORTUNISTIC ATTACK ON HER ENEMY'S SON!
I HAVE TOLERATED YOUR BEHAVING LIKE A FRIGHTENED CHILD TO THIS POINT BECAUSE THAT IS WHAT YOU ARE--
BUT I WILL NOT EXCUSE A COWARDLY ATTACK AS IF IT WAS PART OF A CODE.
B-B-BWAHHH...
SOOO, YOU ARE GREAT WITH KIDS.
NO, REALLY, SOMETIMES I AM.
NOT THIS TIME.
NOT SO MUCH.
MROW?

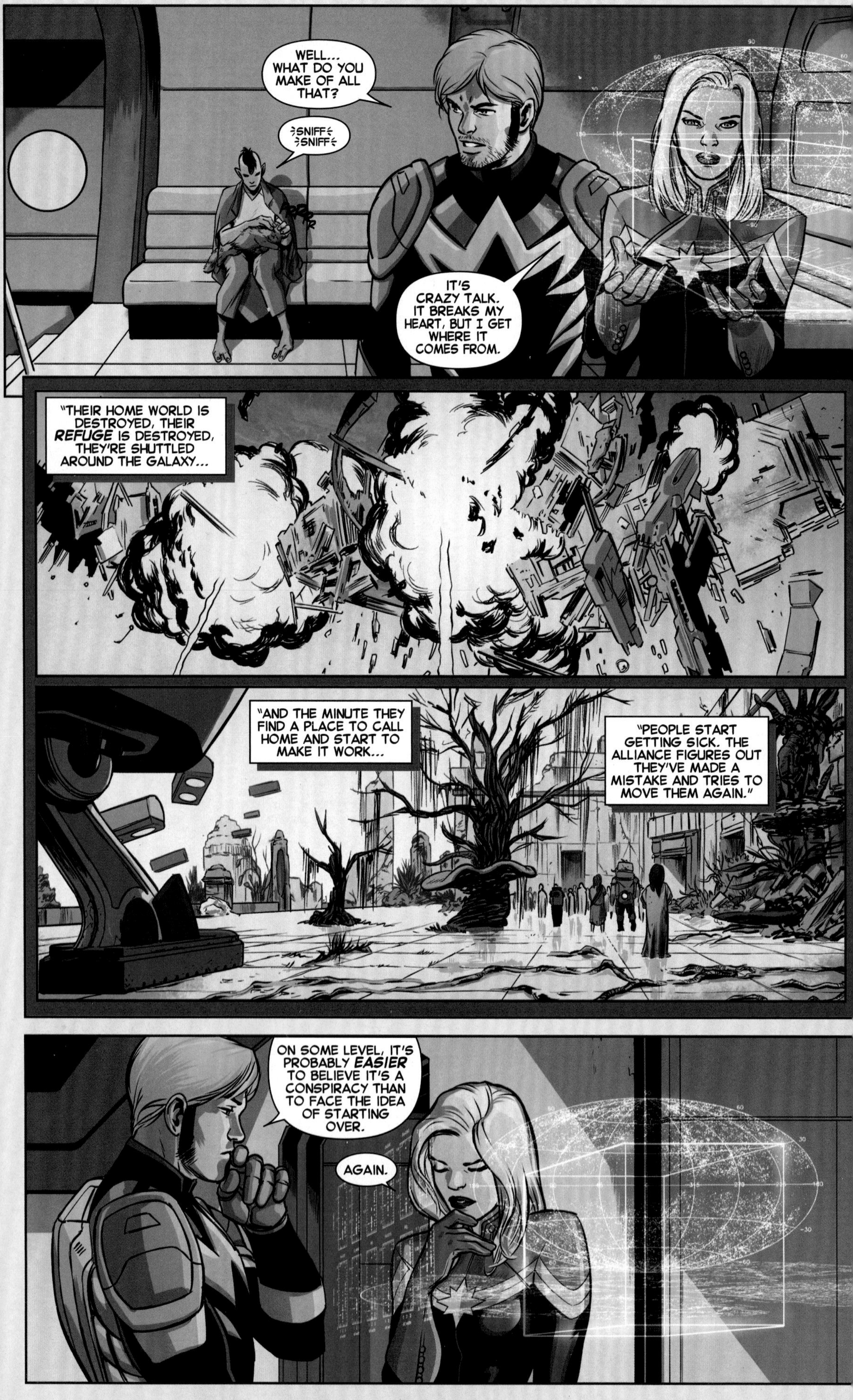
WELL... WHAT DO YOU MAKE OF ALL THAT?
SNIFF SNIFF
IT'S CRAZY TALK. IT BREAKS MY HEART, BUT I GET WHERE IT COMES FROM.
"THEIR HOME WORLD IS DESTROYED, THEIR REFUGE IS DESTROYED, THEY'RE SHUTTLED AROUND THE GALAXY...
"AND THE MINUTE THEY FIND A PLACE TO CALL HOME AND START TO MAKE IT WORK...
"PEOPLE START GETTING SICK. THE ALLIANCE FIGURES OUT THEY'VE MADE A MISTAKE AND TRIES TO MOVE THEM AGAIN."
ON SOME LEVEL, IT'S PROBABLY EASIER TO BELIEVE IT'S A CONSPIRACY THAN TO FACE THE IDEA OF STARTING OVER.
AGAIN.

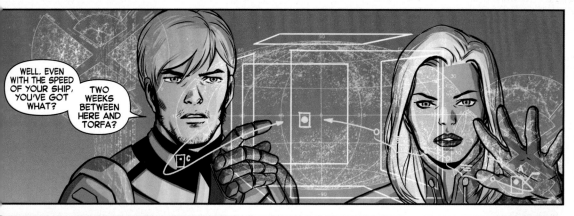

WELL. EVEN WITH THE SPEED OF YOUR SHIP, YOU'VE GOT WHAT?

TWO WEEKS BETWEEN HERE AND TORFA?

WEEK AND A HALF.

YOU OUGHT TO BE ABLE TO GAIN HER TRUST IN THAT TIME. MAYBE YOU CAN TALK SOME SENSE INTO HER.

IF *NOT*, I'M SURE I CAN MAKE SOME HEADWAY WITH THE SETTLERS' LEADERSHIP ONCE WE ARRIVE.

I'D OFFER TO HELP BUT...

NO, IF THEY THINK THE SPARTAX ARE UP TO SOMETHING, YOUR BEING THERE WOULD DO MORE HARM THAN GOOD.

FOR THE BEST, ANYWAY. I'M NOT MUCH OF A DIPLOMAT. HOW ABOUT YOU?

I'VE GOT SOME MOVES.

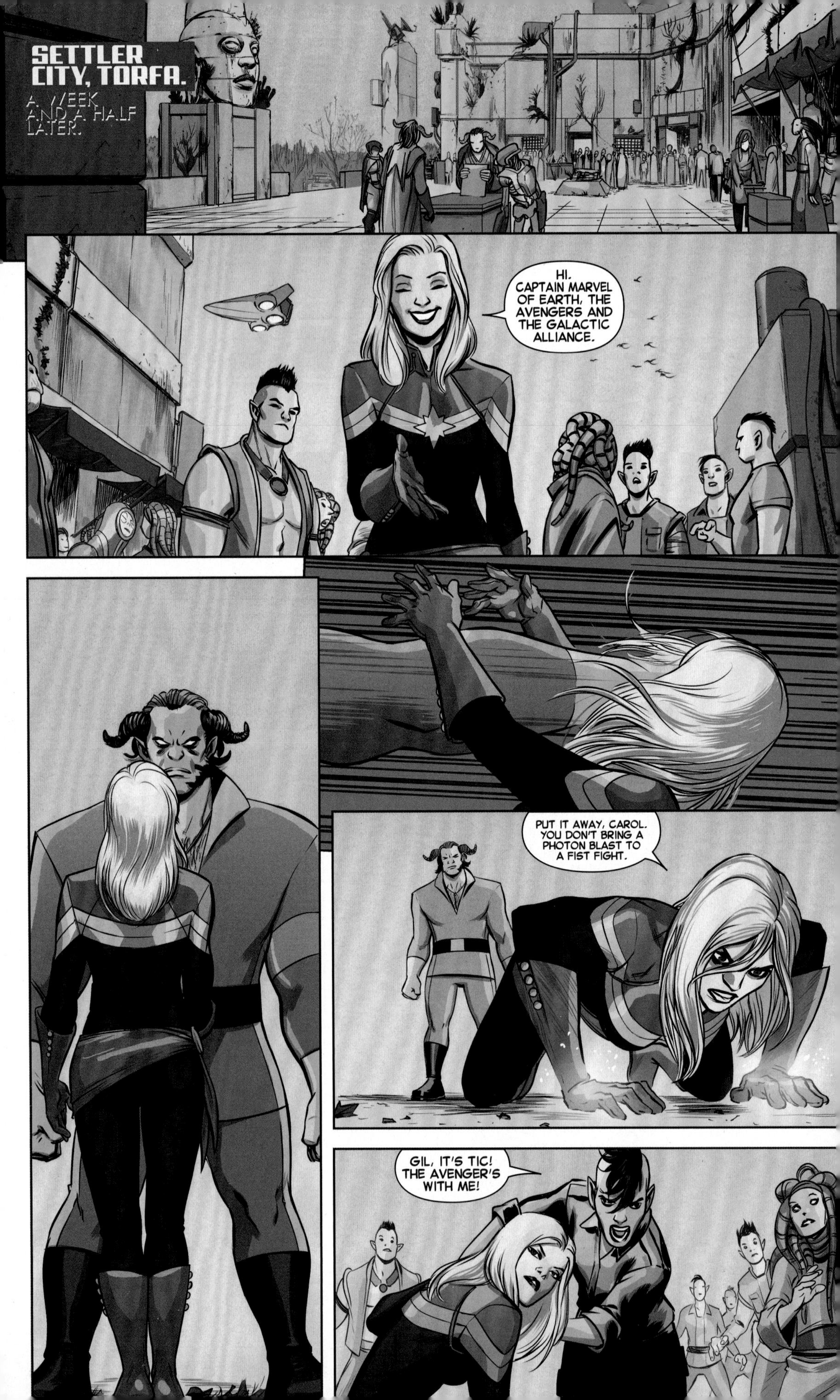
SETTLER CITY, TORFA.
A WEEK AND A HALF LATER.
HI. CAPTAIN MARVEL OF EARTH, THE AVENGERS AND THE GALACTIC ALLIANCE.
PUT IT AWAY, CAROL. YOU DON'T BRING A PHOTON BLAST TO A FIST FIGHT.
GIL, IT'S TIC! THE AVENGER'S WITH ME!

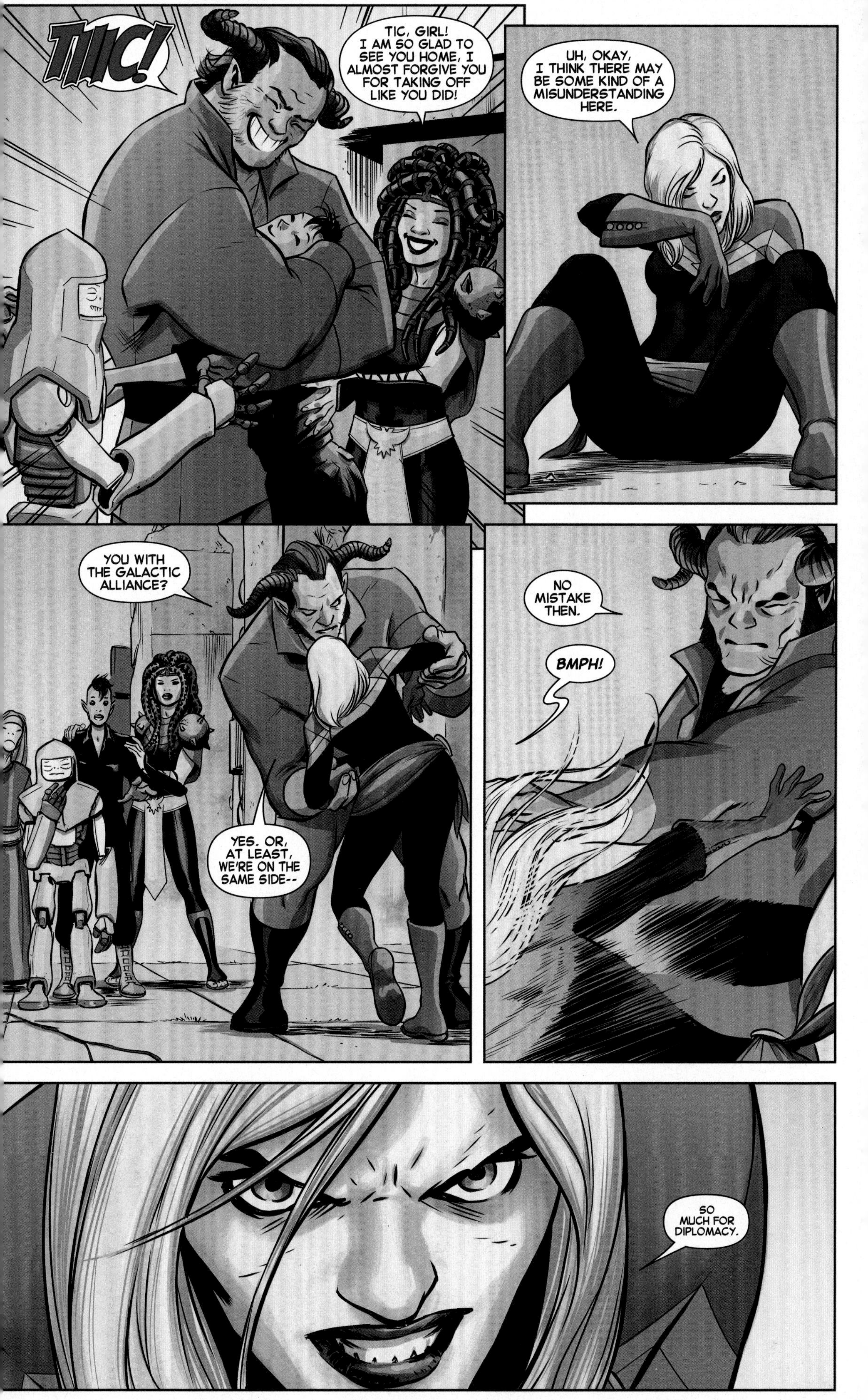
TIIC!
TIC, GIRL! I AM SO GLAD TO SEE YOU HOME, I ALMOST FORGIVE YOU FOR TAKING OFF LIKE YOU DID!
UH, OKAY, I THINK THERE MAY BE SOME KIND OF A MISUNDERSTANDING HERE.
YOU WITH THE GALACTIC ALLIANCE?
YES. OR, AT LEAST, WE'RE ON THE SAME SIDE--
NO MISTAKE THEN.
BMPH!
SO MUCH FOR DIPLOMACY.

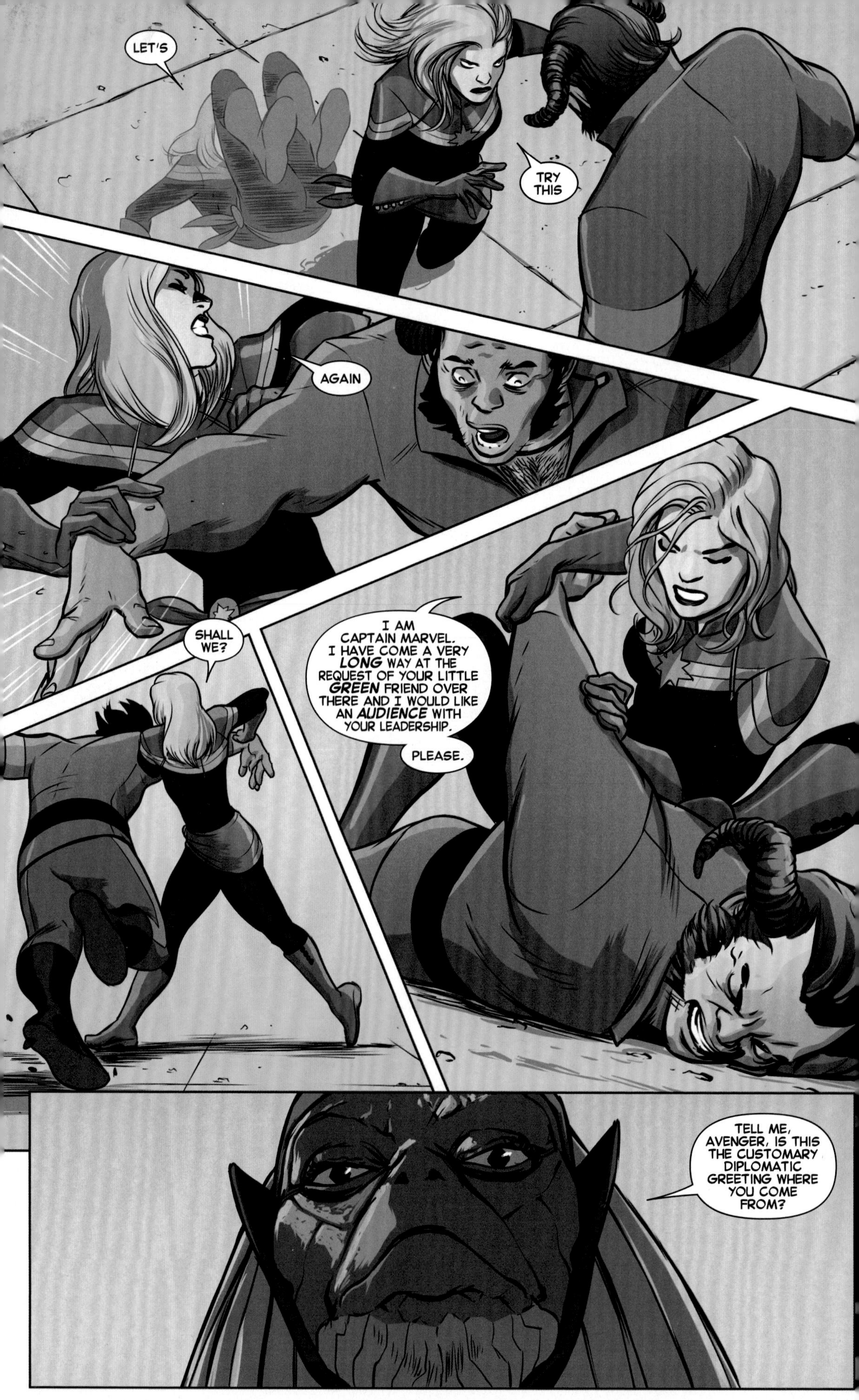
LET'S
TRY THIS
AGAIN
SHALL WE?
I AM CAPTAIN MARVEL. I HAVE COME A VERY LONG WAY AT THE REQUEST OF YOUR LITTLE GREEN FRIEND OVER THERE AND I WOULD LIKE AN AUDIENCE WITH YOUR LEADERSHIP.
PLEASE.
TELL ME, AVENGER, IS THIS THE CUSTOMARY DIPLOMATIC GREETING WHERE YOU COME FROM?

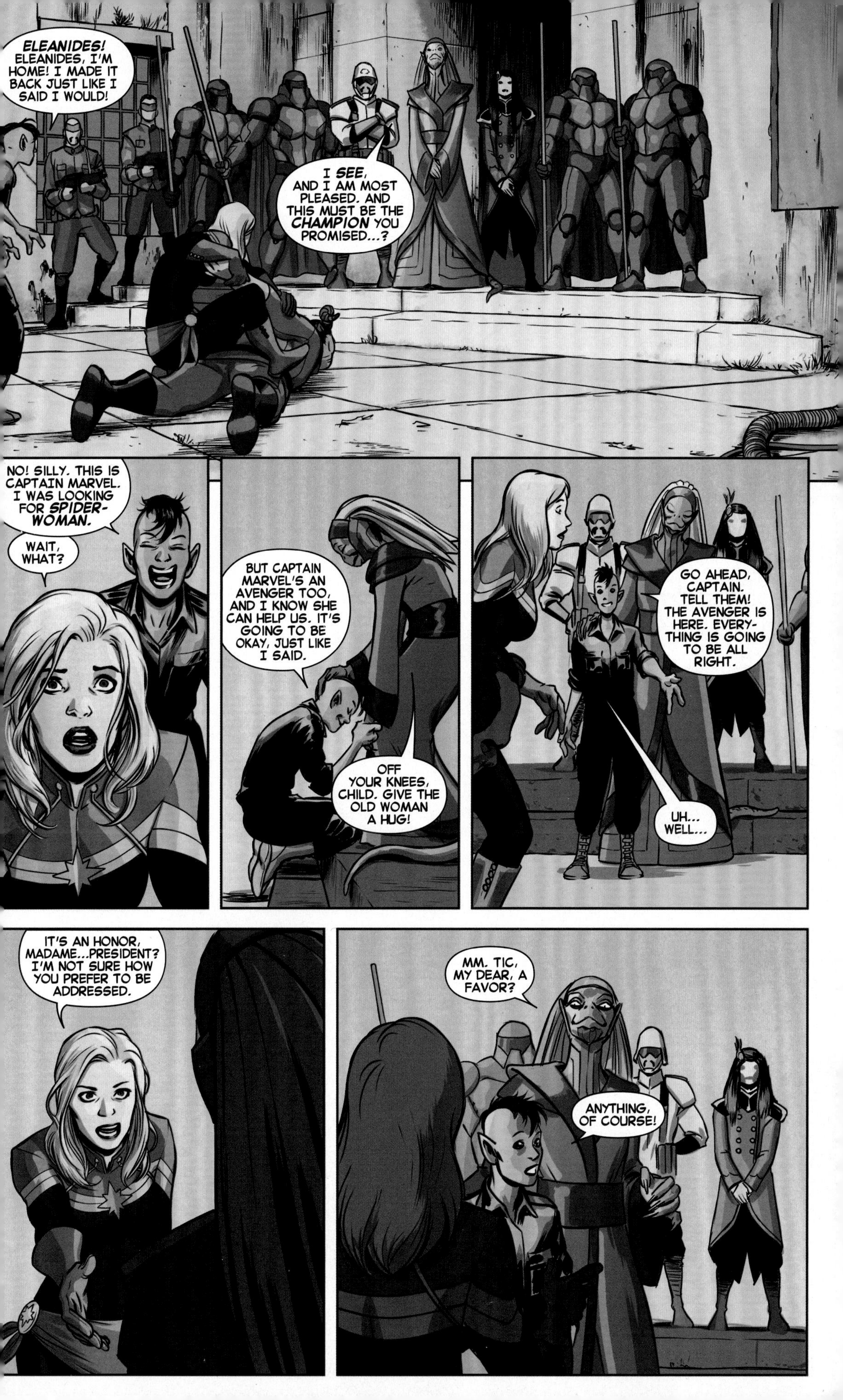
ELEANIDES! ELEANIDES, I'M HOME! I MADE IT BACK JUST LIKE I SAID I WOULD!
I SEE, AND I AM MOST PLEASED. AND THIS MUST BE THE CHAMPION YOU PROMISED...?
NO! SILLY. THIS IS CAPTAIN MARVEL. I WAS LOOKING FOR SPIDER-WOMAN.
WAIT, WHAT?
BUT CAPTAIN MARVEL'S AN AVENGER TOO, AND I KNOW SHE CAN HELP US. IT'S GOING TO BE OKAY, JUST LIKE I SAID.
OFF YOUR KNEES, CHILD. GIVE THE OLD WOMAN A HUG!
GO AHEAD, CAPTAIN. TELL THEM! THE AVENGER IS HERE. EVERY-THING IS GOING TO BE ALL RIGHT.
UH... WELL...
IT'S AN HONOR, MADAME...PRESIDENT? I'M NOT SURE HOW YOU PREFER TO BE ADDRESSED.
MM. TIC, MY DEAR, A FAVOR?
ANYTHING, OF COURSE!

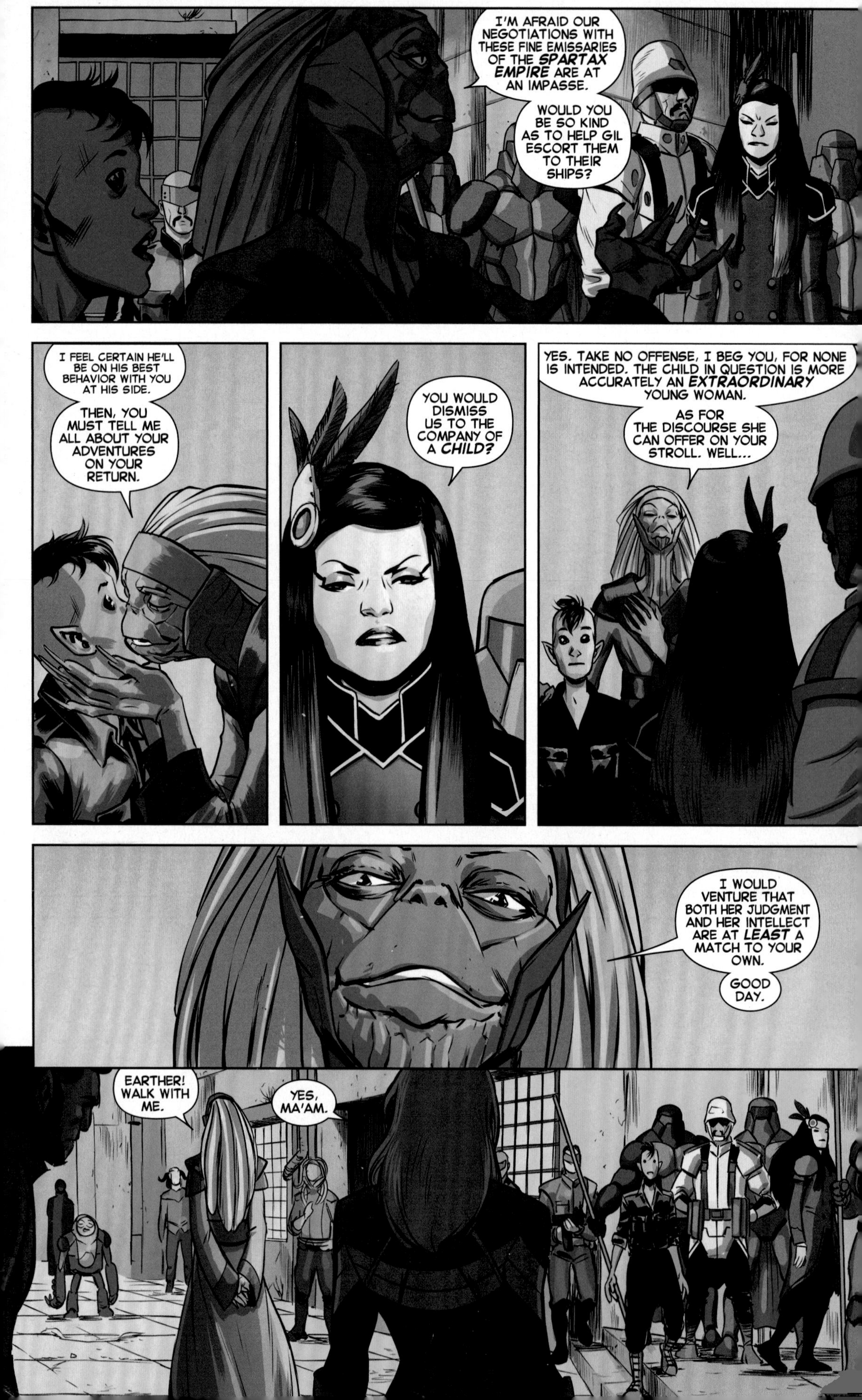

I'M AFRAID OUR NEGOTIATIONS WITH THESE FINE EMISSARIES OF THE *SPARTAX EMPIRE* ARE AT AN IMPASSE.
WOULD YOU BE SO KIND AS TO HELP GIL ESCORT THEM TO THEIR SHIPS?
I FEEL CERTAIN HE'LL BE ON HIS BEST BEHAVIOR WITH YOU AT HIS SIDE.
THEN, YOU MUST TELL ME ALL ABOUT YOUR ADVENTURES ON YOUR RETURN.
YOU WOULD DISMISS US TO THE COMPANY OF A *CHILD?*
YES. TAKE NO OFFENSE, I BEG YOU, FOR NONE IS INTENDED. THE CHILD IN QUESTION IS MORE ACCURATELY AN *EXTRAORDINARY* YOUNG WOMAN.
AS FOR THE DISCOURSE SHE CAN OFFER ON YOUR STROLL. WELL...
I WOULD VENTURE THAT BOTH HER JUDGMENT AND HER INTELLECT ARE AT *LEAST* A MATCH TO YOUR OWN.
GOOD DAY.
EARTHER! WALK WITH ME.
YES, MA'AM.

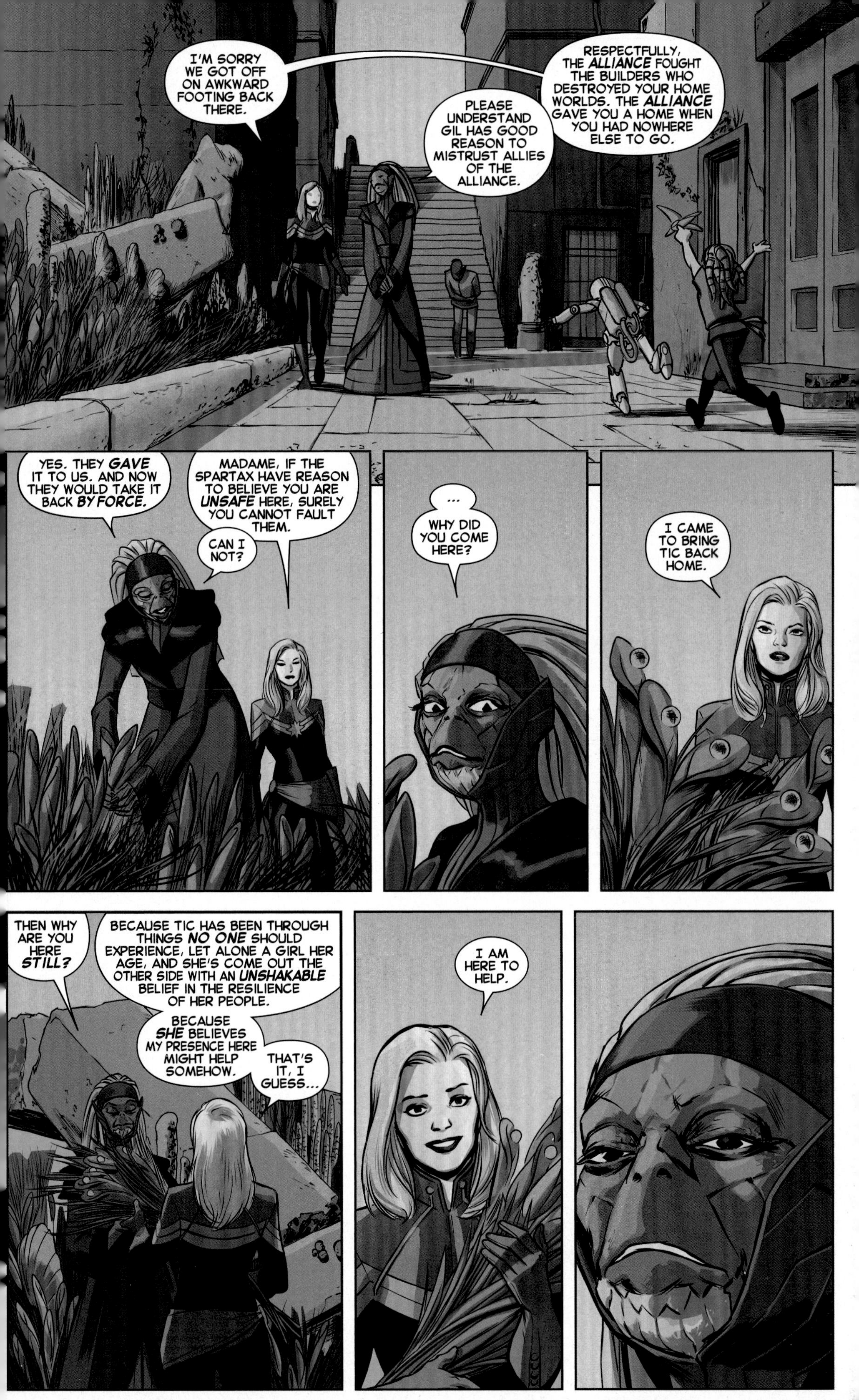
I'M SORRY WE GOT OFF ON AWKWARD FOOTING BACK THERE.
RESPECTFULLY, THE ALLIANCE FOUGHT THE BUILDERS WHO DESTROYED YOUR HOME WORLDS. THE ALLIANCE GAVE YOU A HOME WHEN YOU HAD NOWHERE ELSE TO GO.
PLEASE UNDERSTAND GIL HAS GOOD REASON TO MISTRUST ALLIES OF THE ALLIANCE.
YES. THEY GAVE IT TO US. AND NOW THEY WOULD TAKE IT BACK BY FORCE.
MADAME, IF THE SPARTAX HAVE REASON TO BELIEVE YOU ARE UNSAFE HERE, SURELY YOU CANNOT FAULT THEM.
CAN I NOT?
...
WHY DID YOU COME HERE?
I CAME TO BRING TIC BACK HOME.
THEN WHY ARE YOU HERE STILL?
BECAUSE TIC HAS BEEN THROUGH THINGS NO ONE SHOULD EXPERIENCE, LET ALONE A GIRL HER AGE, AND SHE'S COME OUT THE OTHER SIDE WITH AN UNSHAKABLE BELIEF IN THE RESILIENCE OF HER PEOPLE.
BECAUSE SHE BELIEVES MY PRESENCE HERE MIGHT HELP SOMEHOW.
THAT'S IT, I GUESS...
I AM HERE TO HELP.

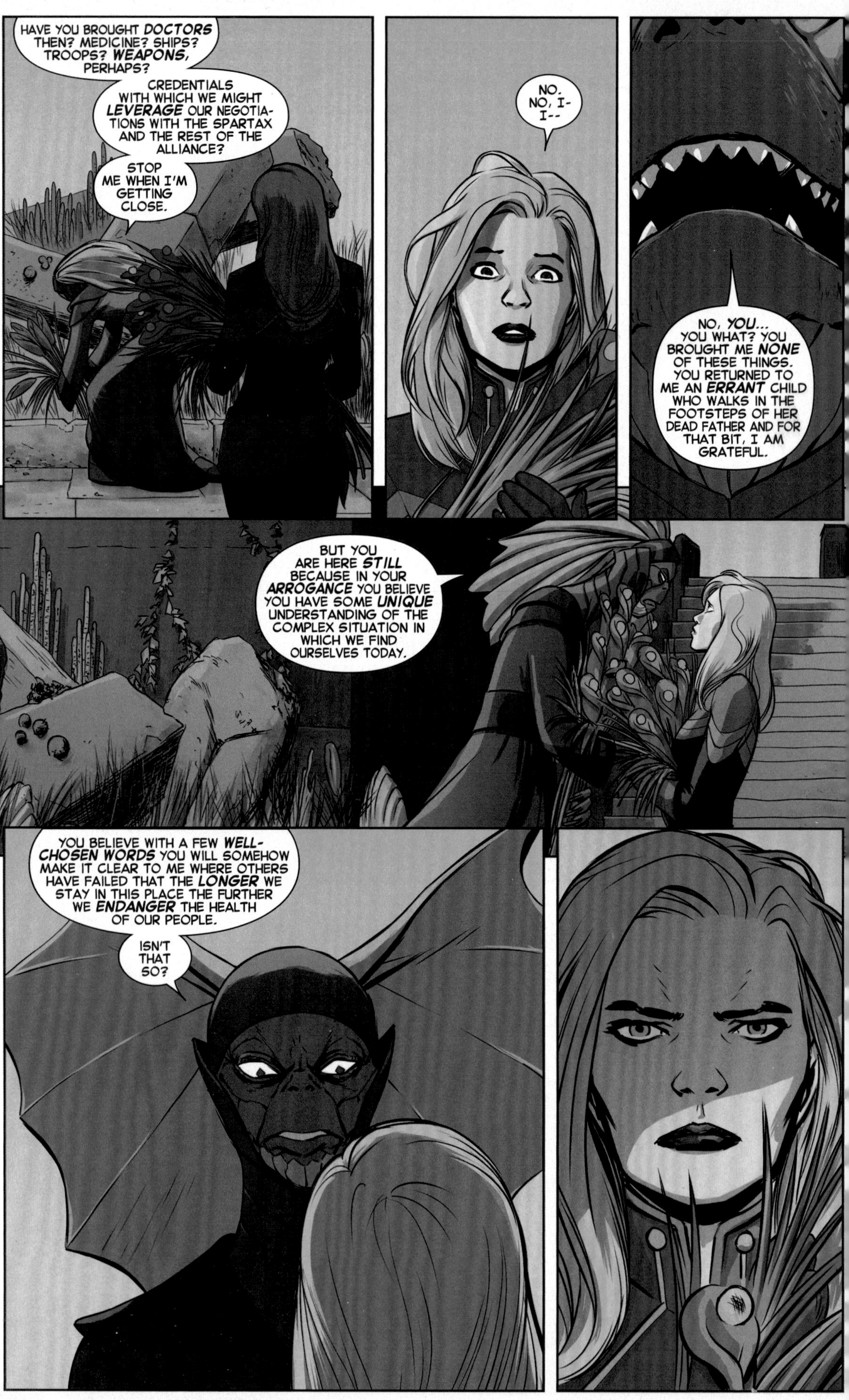
HAVE YOU BROUGHT DOCTORS THEN? MEDICINE? SHIPS? TROOPS? WEAPONS, PERHAPS?
CREDENTIALS WITH WHICH WE MIGHT LEVERAGE OUR NEGOTIATIONS WITH THE SPARTAX AND THE REST OF THE ALLIANCE?
STOP ME WHEN I'M GETTING CLOSE.
NO. NO, I- I--
NO, YOU... YOU WHAT? YOU BROUGHT ME NONE OF THESE THINGS. YOU RETURNED TO ME AN ERRANT CHILD WHO WALKS IN THE FOOTSTEPS OF HER DEAD FATHER AND FOR THAT BIT, I AM GRATEFUL.
BUT YOU ARE HERE STILL BECAUSE IN YOUR ARROGANCE YOU BELIEVE YOU HAVE SOME UNIQUE UNDERSTANDING OF THE COMPLEX SITUATION IN WHICH WE FIND OURSELVES TODAY.
YOU BELIEVE WITH A FEW WELL-CHOSEN WORDS YOU WILL SOMEHOW MAKE IT CLEAR TO ME WHERE OTHERS HAVE FAILED THAT THE LONGER WE STAY IN THIS PLACE THE FURTHER WE ENDANGER THE HEALTH OF OUR PEOPLE.
ISN'T THAT SO?

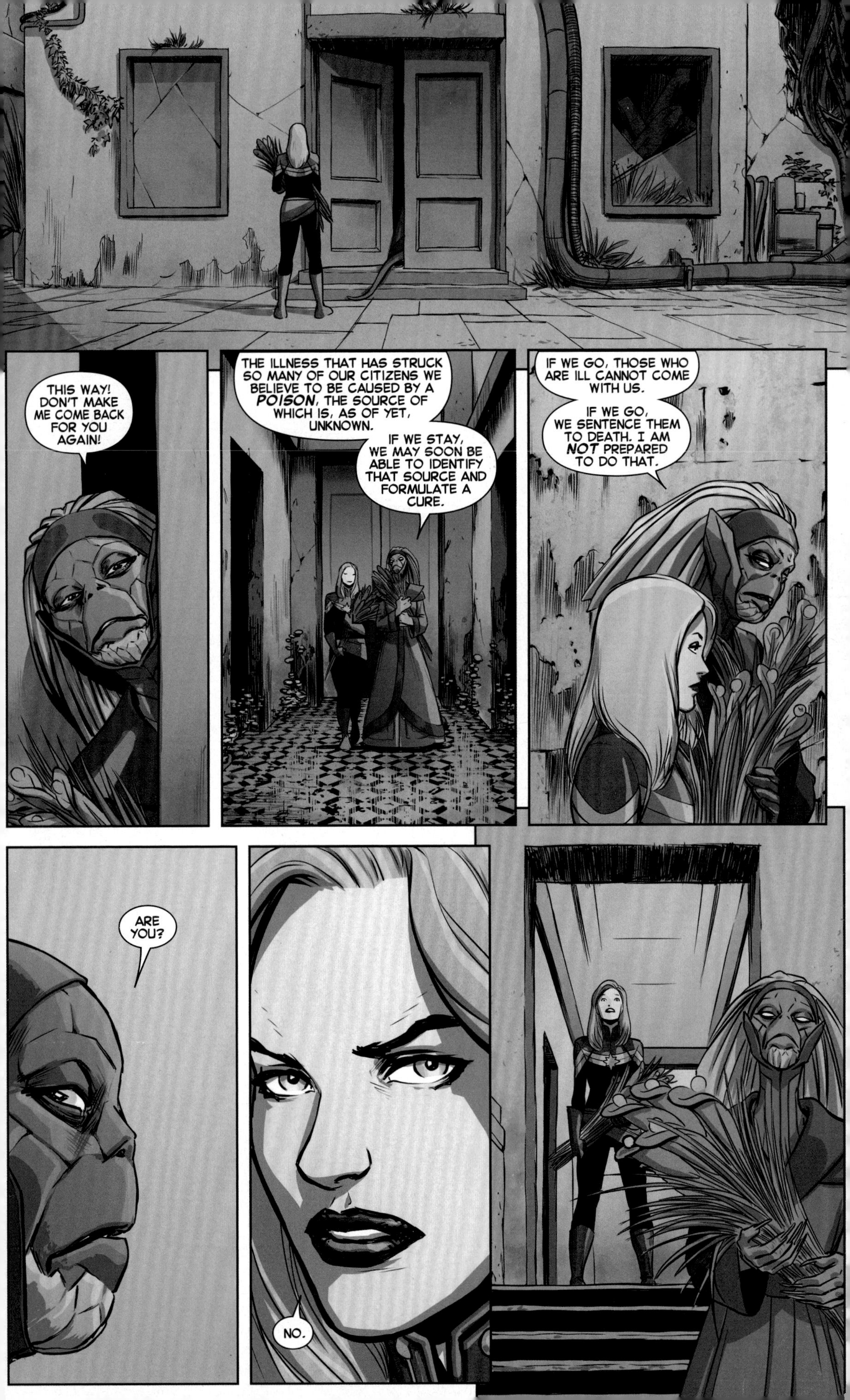
THIS WAY! DON'T MAKE ME COME BACK FOR YOU AGAIN!
THE ILLNESS THAT HAS STRUCK SO MANY OF OUR CITIZENS WE BELIEVE TO BE CAUSED BY A POISON, THE SOURCE OF WHICH IS, AS OF YET, UNKNOWN.
IF WE STAY, WE MAY SOON BE ABLE TO IDENTIFY THAT SOURCE AND FORMULATE A CURE.
IF WE GO, THOSE WHO ARE ILL CANNOT COME WITH US.
IF WE GO, WE SENTENCE THEM TO DEATH. I AM NOT PREPARED TO DO THAT.
ARE YOU?
NO.

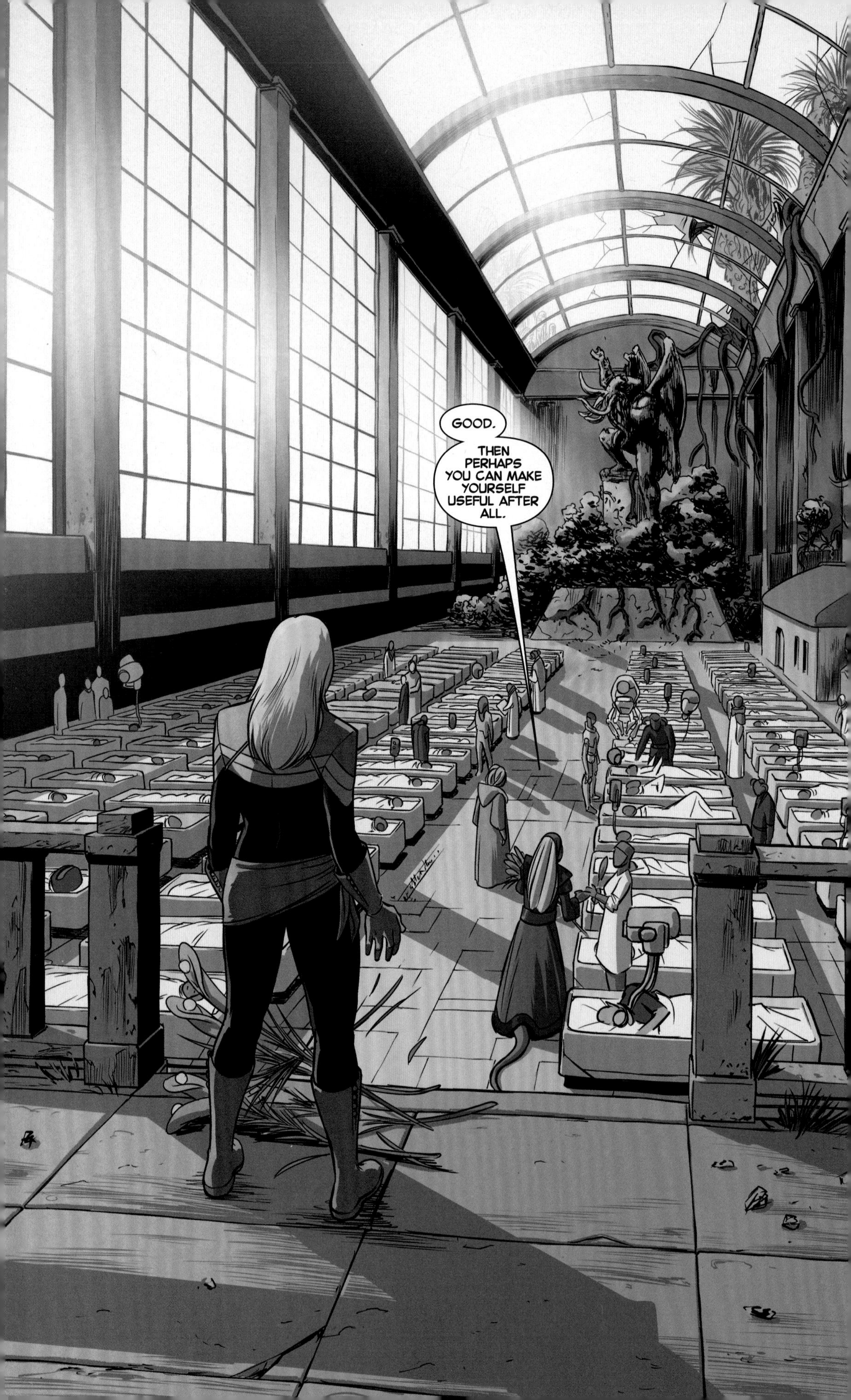
GOOD.
THEN PERHAPS YOU CAN MAKE YOURSELF USEFUL AFTER ALL.

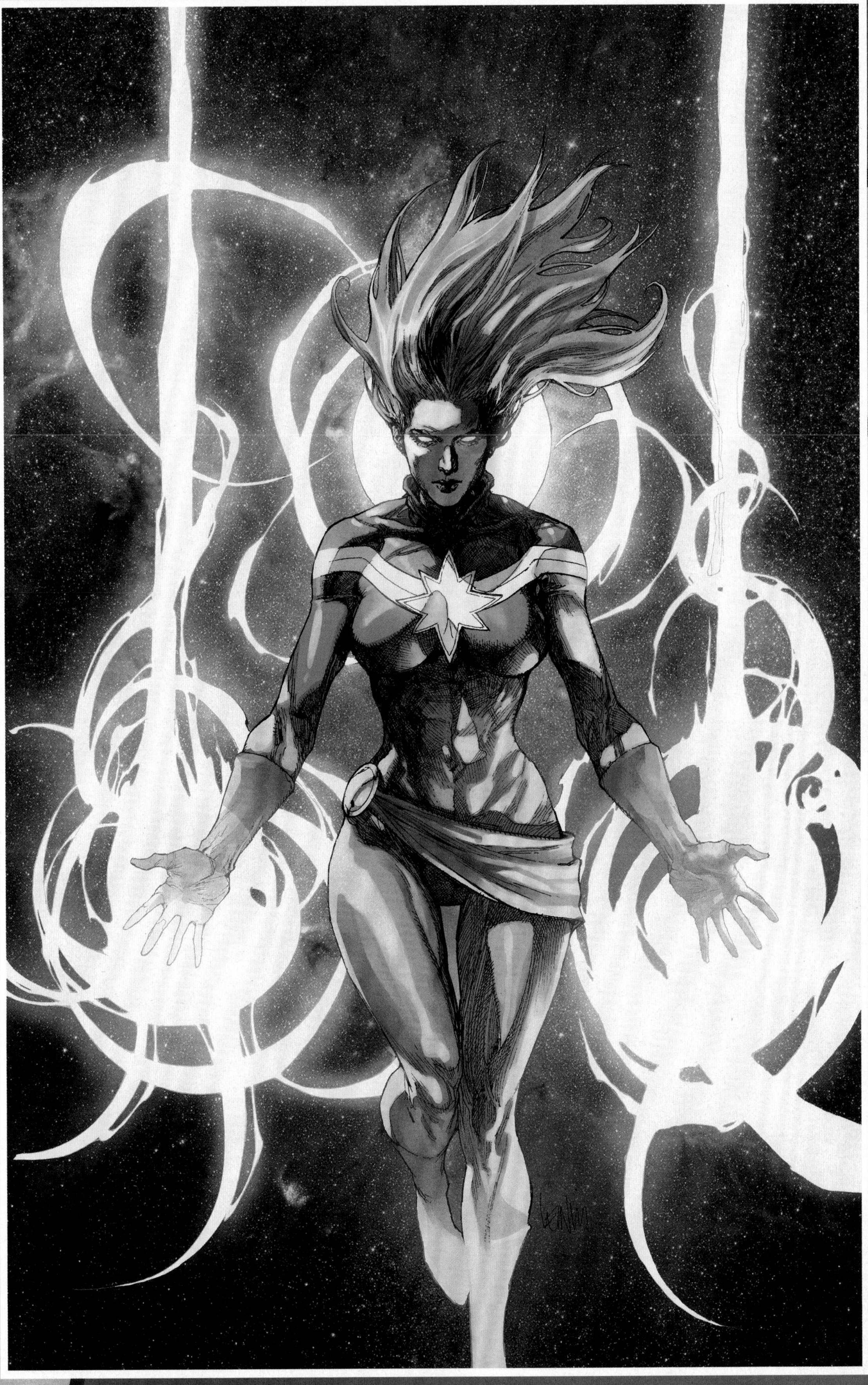

VARIANT BY LEINIL FRANCIS YU & SUNNY GHO ONE

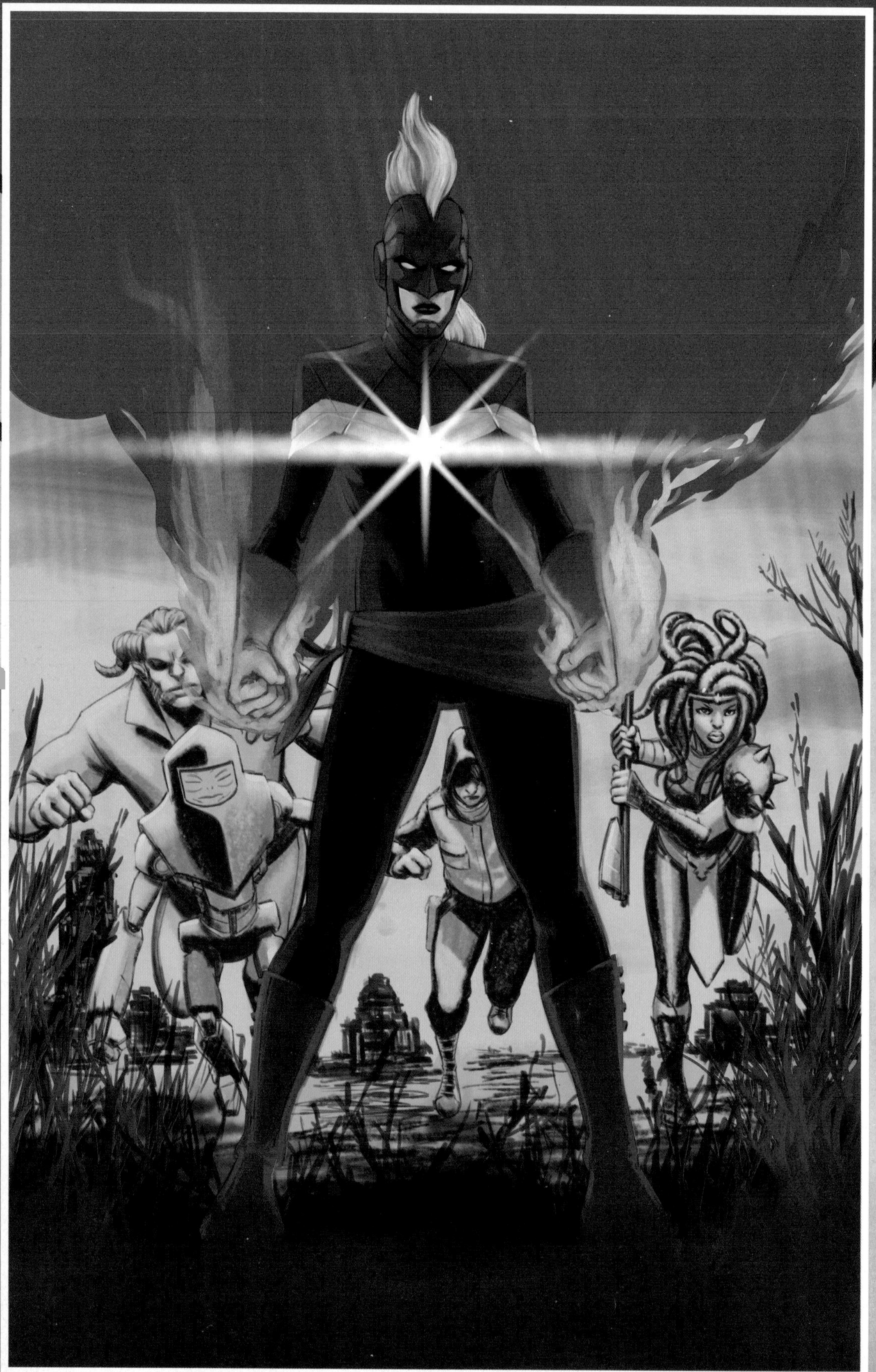

FOUR

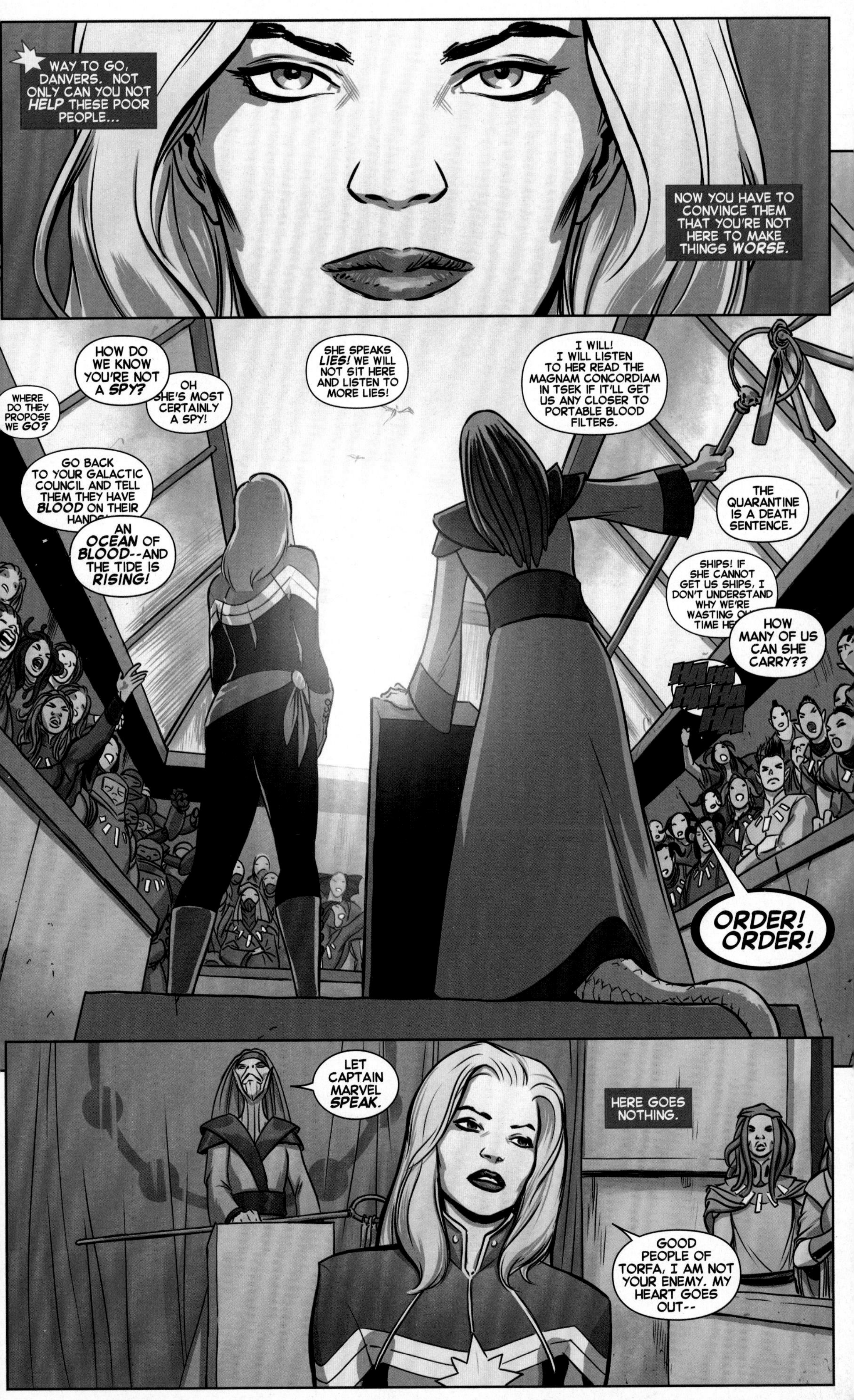

WAY TO GO, DANVERS. NOT ONLY CAN YOU NOT HELP THESE POOR PEOPLE...
NOW YOU HAVE TO CONVINCE THEM THAT YOU'RE NOT HERE TO MAKE THINGS WORSE.
WHERE DO THEY PROPOSE WE GO?
HOW DO WE KNOW YOU'RE NOT A SPY?
OH SHE'S MOST CERTAINLY A SPY!
SHE SPEAKS LIES! WE WILL NOT SIT HERE AND LISTEN TO MORE LIES!
I WILL! I WILL LISTEN TO HER READ THE MAGNAM CONCORDIAM IN TSEK IF IT'LL GET US ANY CLOSER TO PORTABLE BLOOD FILTERS.
GO BACK TO YOUR GALACTIC COUNCIL AND TELL THEM THEY HAVE BLOOD ON THEIR
AN OCEAN OF BLOOD--AND THE TIDE IS RISING!
THE QUARANTINE IS A DEATH SENTENCE.
SHIPS! IF SHE CANNOT GET US SHIPS, I DON'T UNDERSTAND WHY WE'RE WASTING
HOW MANY OF US CAN SHE CARRY??
HAHA HAHA HA
ORDER! ORDER!
LET CAPTAIN MARVEL SPEAK.
HERE GOES NOTHING.
GOOD PEOPLE OF TORFA, I AM NOT YOUR ENEMY. MY HEART GOES OUT--

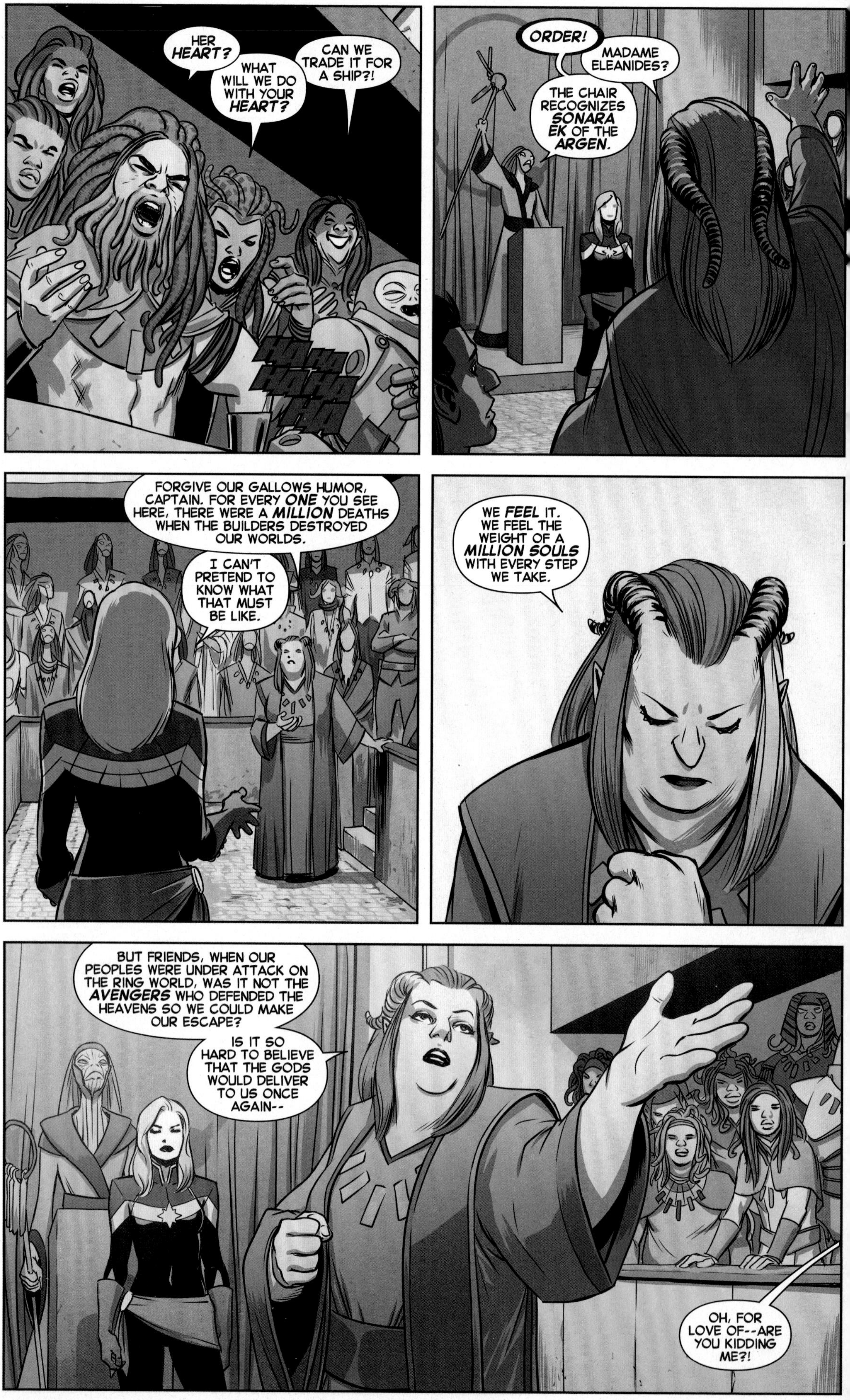

HER HEART?
WHAT WILL WE DO WITH YOUR HEART?
CAN WE TRADE IT FOR A SHIP?!
ORDER!
MADAME ELEANIDES?
THE CHAIR RECOGNIZES SONARA EK OF THE ARGEN.
FORGIVE OUR GALLOWS HUMOR, CAPTAIN. FOR EVERY ONE YOU SEE HERE, THERE WERE A MILLION DEATHS WHEN THE BUILDERS DESTROYED OUR WORLDS.
I CAN'T PRETEND TO KNOW WHAT THAT MUST BE LIKE.
WE FEEL IT. WE FEEL THE WEIGHT OF A MILLION SOULS WITH EVERY STEP WE TAKE.
BUT FRIENDS, WHEN OUR PEOPLES WERE UNDER ATTACK ON THE RING WORLD, WAS IT NOT THE AVENGERS WHO DEFENDED THE HEAVENS SO WE COULD MAKE OUR ESCAPE?
IS IT SO HARD TO BELIEVE THAT THE GODS WOULD DELIVER TO US ONCE AGAIN--
OH, FOR LOVE OF--ARE YOU KIDDING ME?!

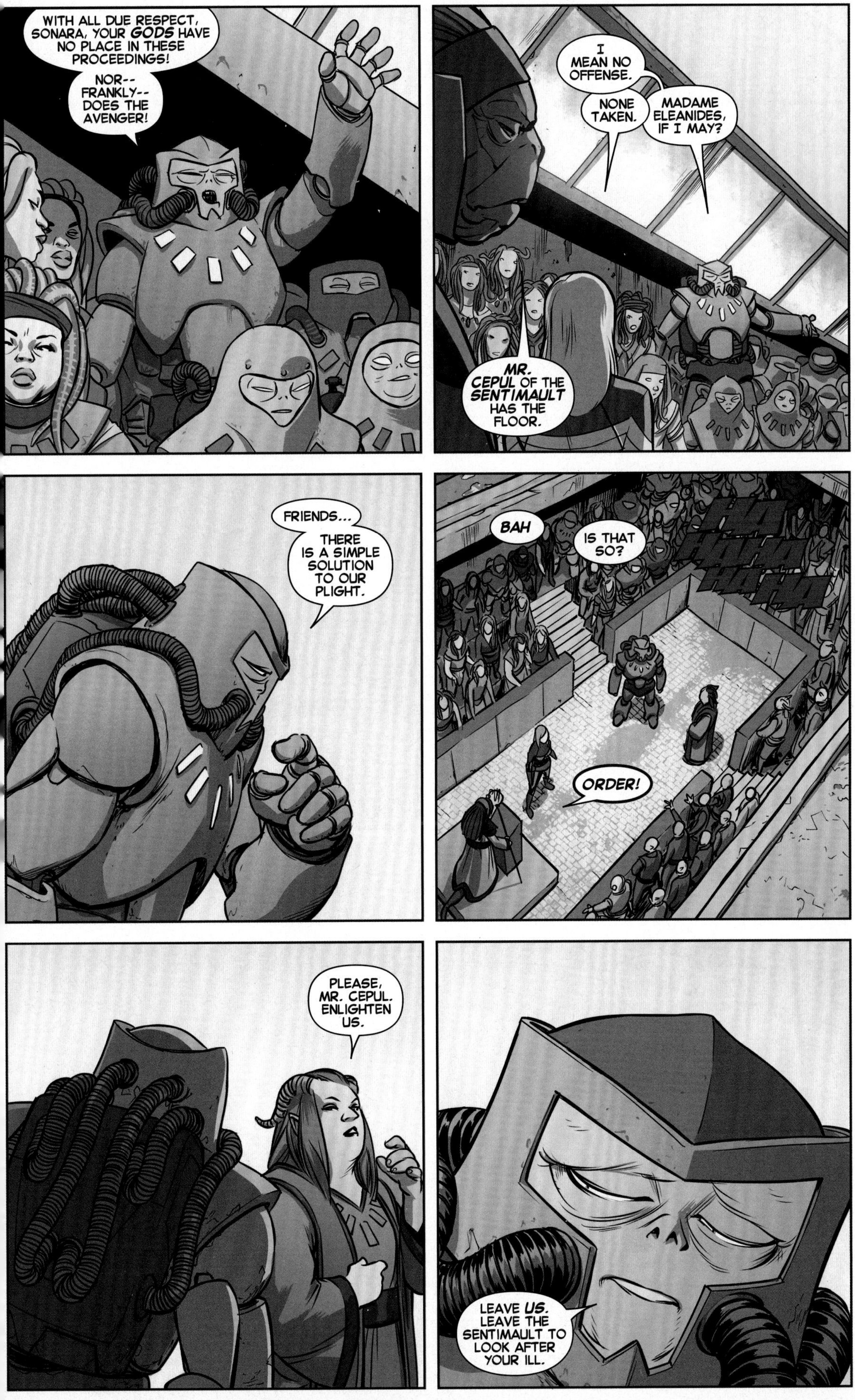
WITH ALL DUE RESPECT, SONARA, YOUR GODS HAVE NO PLACE IN THESE PROCEEDINGS!
NOR-- FRANKLY-- DOES THE AVENGER!
I MEAN NO OFFENSE.
NONE TAKEN.
MADAME ELEANIDES, IF I MAY?
MR. CEPUL OF THE SENTIMAULT HAS THE FLOOR.
FRIENDS...
THERE IS A SIMPLE SOLUTION TO OUR PLIGHT.
BAH
IS THAT SO?
ORDER!
PLEASE, MR. CEPUL. ENLIGHTEN US.
LEAVE US. LEAVE THE SENTIMAULT TO LOOK AFTER YOUR ILL.

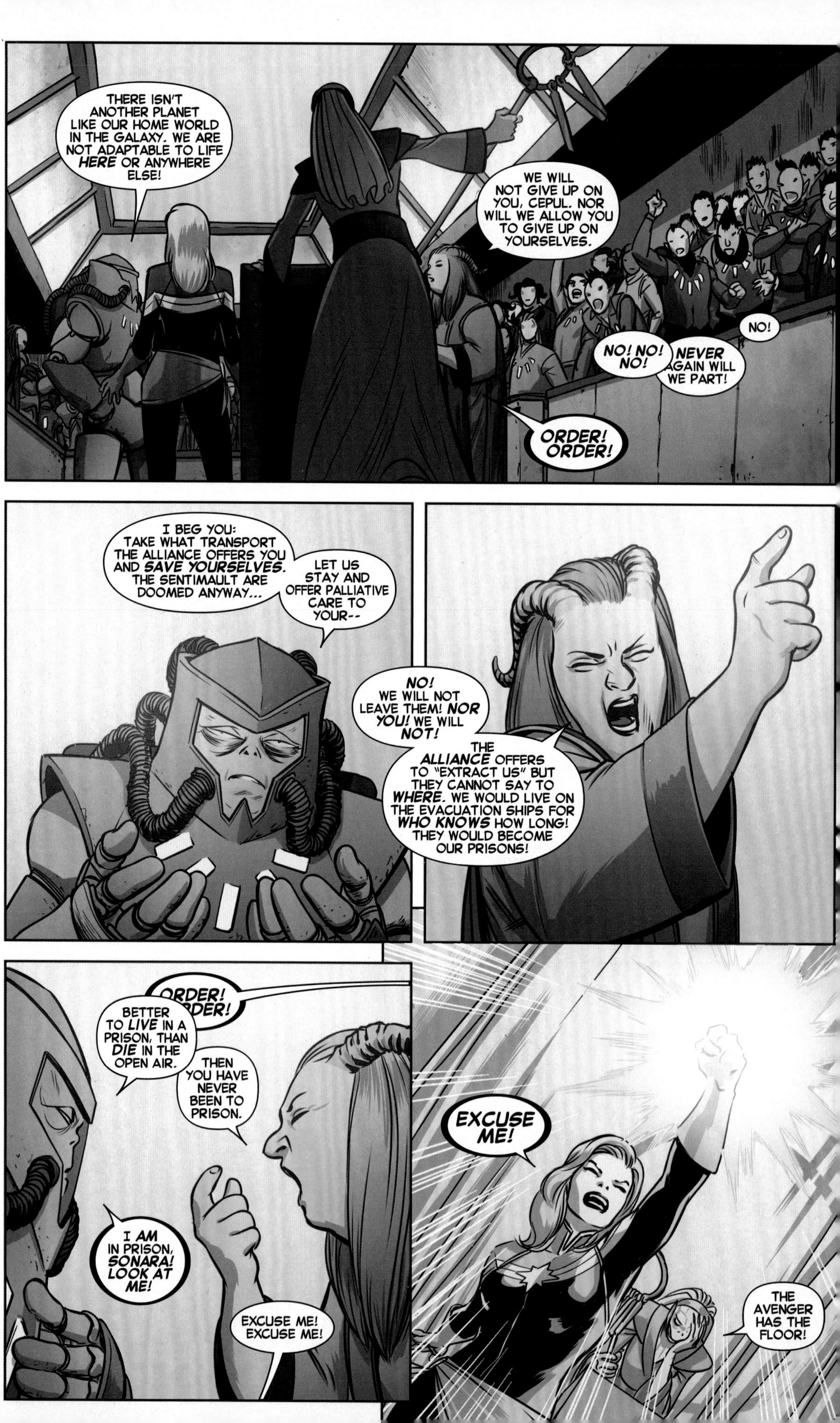
THERE ISN'T ANOTHER PLANET LIKE OUR HOME WORLD IN THE GALAXY. WE ARE NOT ADAPTABLE TO LIFE HERE OR ANYWHERE ELSE!
WE WILL NOT GIVE UP ON YOU, CEPUL. NOR WILL WE ALLOW YOU TO GIVE UP ON YOURSELVES.
NO! NO! NO!
NEVER AGAIN WILL WE PART!
NO!
ORDER! ORDER!
I BEG YOU: TAKE WHAT TRANSPORT THE ALLIANCE OFFERS YOU AND SAVE YOURSELVES. THE SENTIMAULT ARE DOOMED ANYWAY...
LET US STAY AND OFFER PALLIATIVE CARE TO YOUR--
NO! WE WILL NOT LEAVE THEM! NOR YOU! WE WILL NOT!
THE ALLIANCE OFFERS TO "EXTRACT US" BUT THEY CANNOT SAY TO WHERE. WE WOULD LIVE ON THE EVACUATION SHIPS FOR WHO KNOWS HOW LONG! THEY WOULD BECOME OUR PRISONS!
BETTER TO LIVE IN A PRISON, THAN DIE IN THE OPEN AIR.
THEN YOU HAVE NEVER BEEN TO PRISON.
I AM IN PRISON, SONARA! LOOK AT ME!
EXCUSE ME! EXCUSE ME!
EXCUSE ME!
THE AVENGER HAS THE FLOOR!

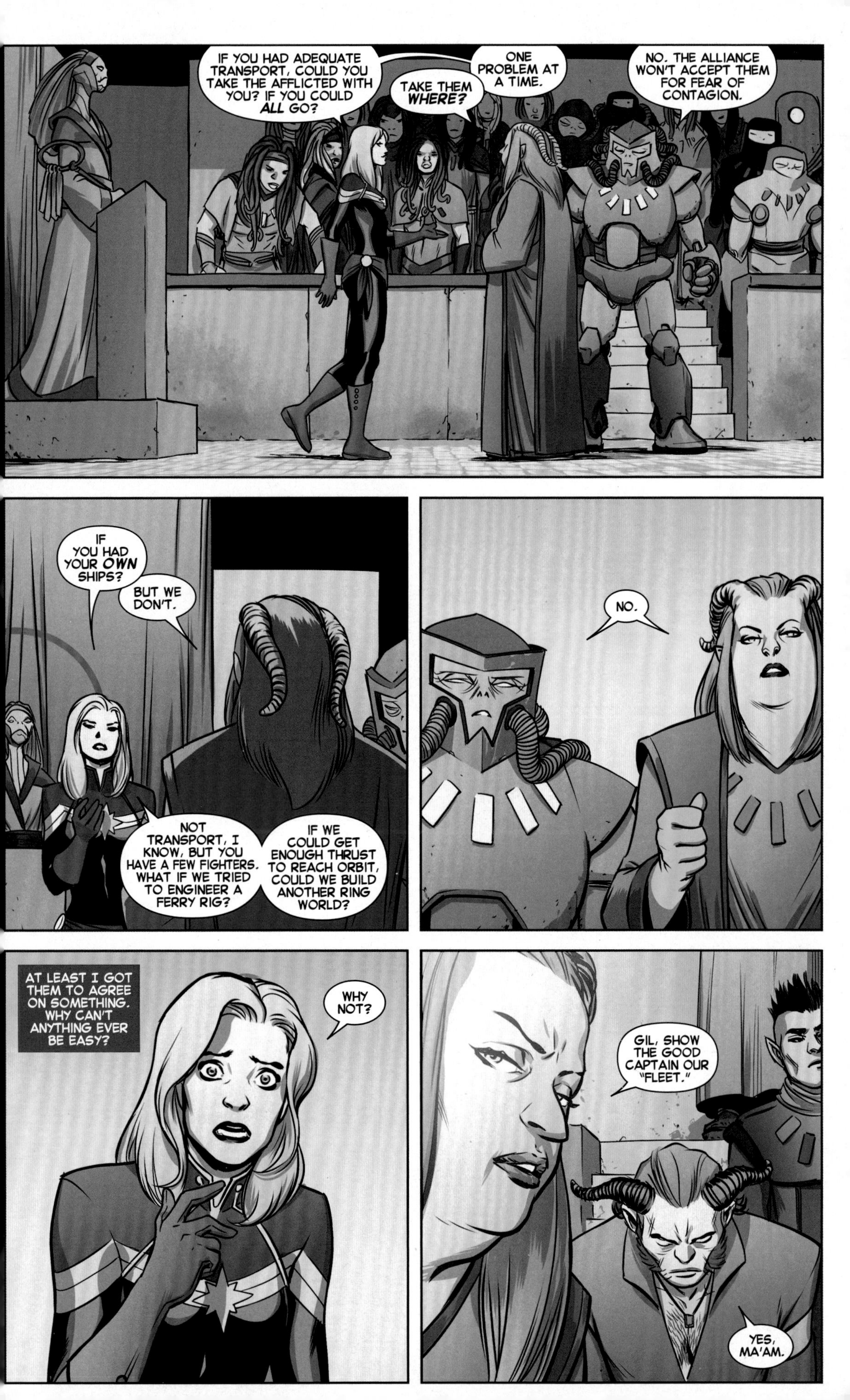
IF YOU HAD ADEQUATE TRANSPORT, COULD YOU TAKE THE AFFLICTED WITH YOU? IF YOU COULD ALL GO?
TAKE THEM WHERE?
ONE PROBLEM AT A TIME.
NO. THE ALLIANCE WON'T ACCEPT THEM FOR FEAR OF CONTAGION.
IF YOU HAD YOUR OWN SHIPS?
BUT WE DON'T.
NOT TRANSPORT, I KNOW, BUT YOU HAVE A FEW FIGHTERS. WHAT IF WE TRIED TO ENGINEER A FERRY RIG?
IF WE COULD GET ENOUGH THRUST TO REACH ORBIT, COULD WE BUILD ANOTHER RING WORLD?
NO.
AT LEAST I GOT THEM TO AGREE ON SOMETHING. WHY CAN'T ANYTHING EVER BE EASY?
WHY NOT?
GIL, SHOW THE GOOD CAPTAIN OUR "FLEET."
YES, MA'AM.

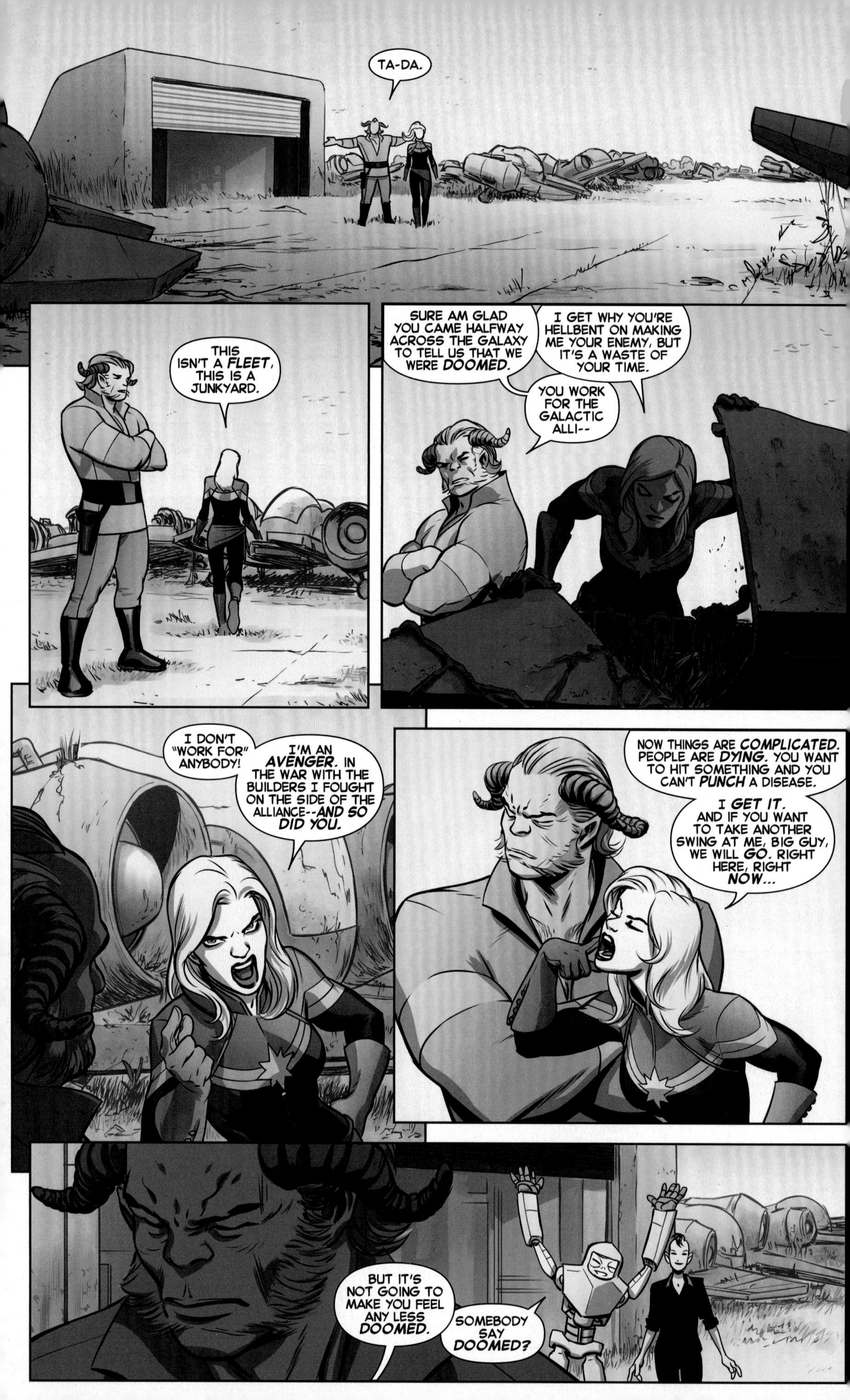
TA-DA.
THIS ISN'T A FLEET, THIS IS A JUNKYARD.
SURE AM GLAD YOU CAME HALFWAY ACROSS THE GALAXY TO TELL US THAT WE WERE DOOMED.
I GET WHY YOU'RE HELLBENT ON MAKING ME YOUR ENEMY, BUT IT'S A WASTE OF YOUR TIME.
YOU WORK FOR THE GALACTIC ALLI--
I DON'T "WORK FOR" ANYBODY!
I'M AN AVENGER. IN THE WAR WITH THE BUILDERS I FOUGHT ON THE SIDE OF THE ALLIANCE--AND SO DID YOU.
NOW THINGS ARE COMPLICATED. PEOPLE ARE DYING. YOU WANT TO HIT SOMETHING AND YOU CAN'T PUNCH A DISEASE.
I GET IT. AND IF YOU WANT TO TAKE ANOTHER SWING AT ME, BIG GUY, WE WILL GO. RIGHT HERE, RIGHT NOW...
BUT IT'S NOT GOING TO MAKE YOU FEEL ANY LESS DOOMED.
SOMEBODY SAY DOOMED?

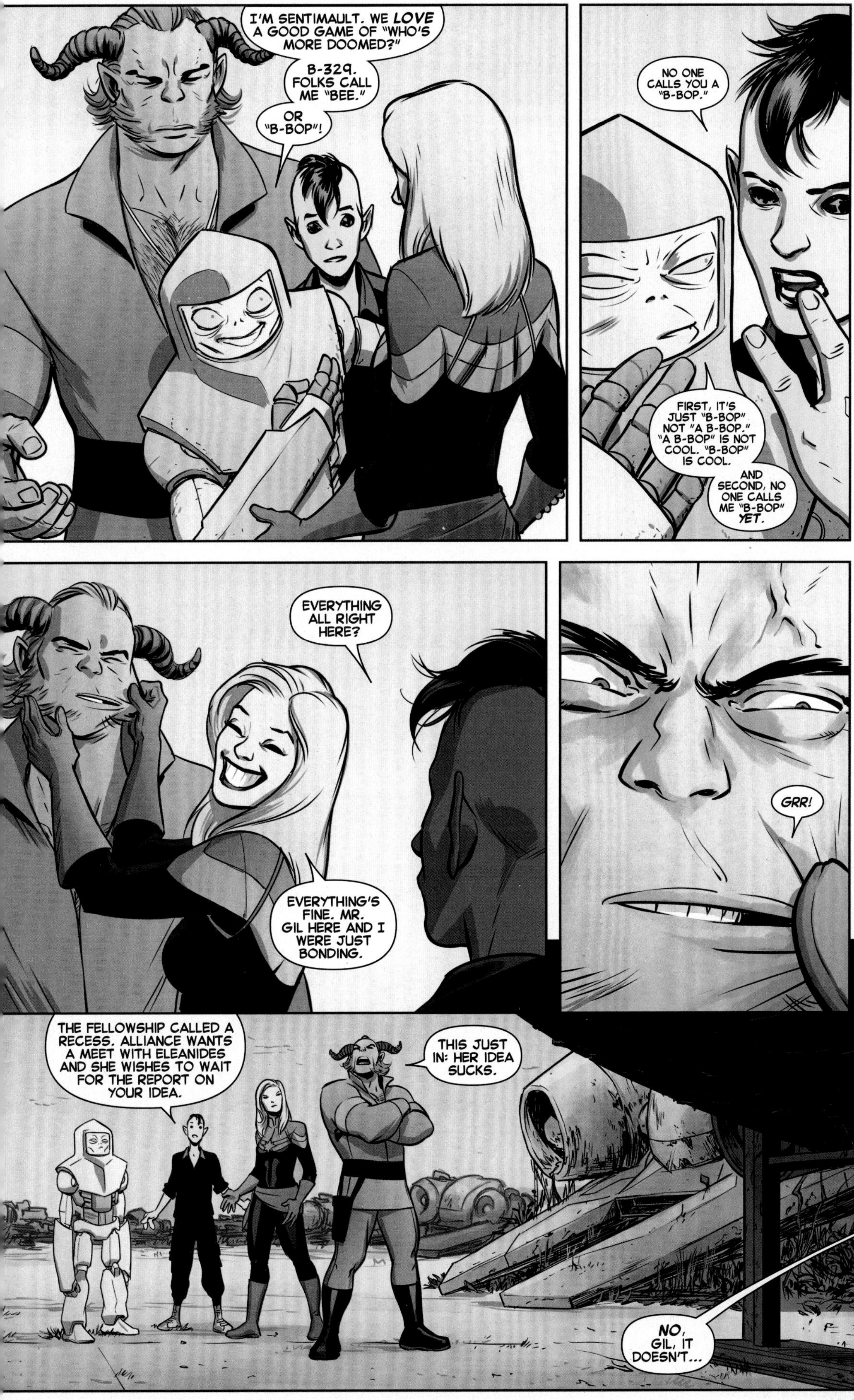

I'M SENTIMAULT. WE LOVE A GOOD GAME OF "WHO'S MORE DOOMED?"
B-329. FOLKS CALL ME "BEE."
OR "B-BOP"!
NO ONE CALLS YOU A "B-BOP."
FIRST, IT'S JUST "B-BOP" NOT "A B-BOP." "A B-BOP" IS NOT COOL. "B-BOP" IS COOL.
AND SECOND, NO ONE CALLS ME "B-BOP" YET.
EVERYTHING ALL RIGHT HERE?
EVERYTHING'S FINE. MR. GIL HERE AND I WERE JUST BONDING.
GRR!
THE FELLOWSHIP CALLED A RECESS. ALLIANCE WANTS A MEET WITH ELEANIDES AND SHE WISHES TO WAIT FOR THE REPORT ON YOUR IDEA.
THIS JUST IN: HER IDEA SUCKS.
NO, GIL, IT DOESN'T...

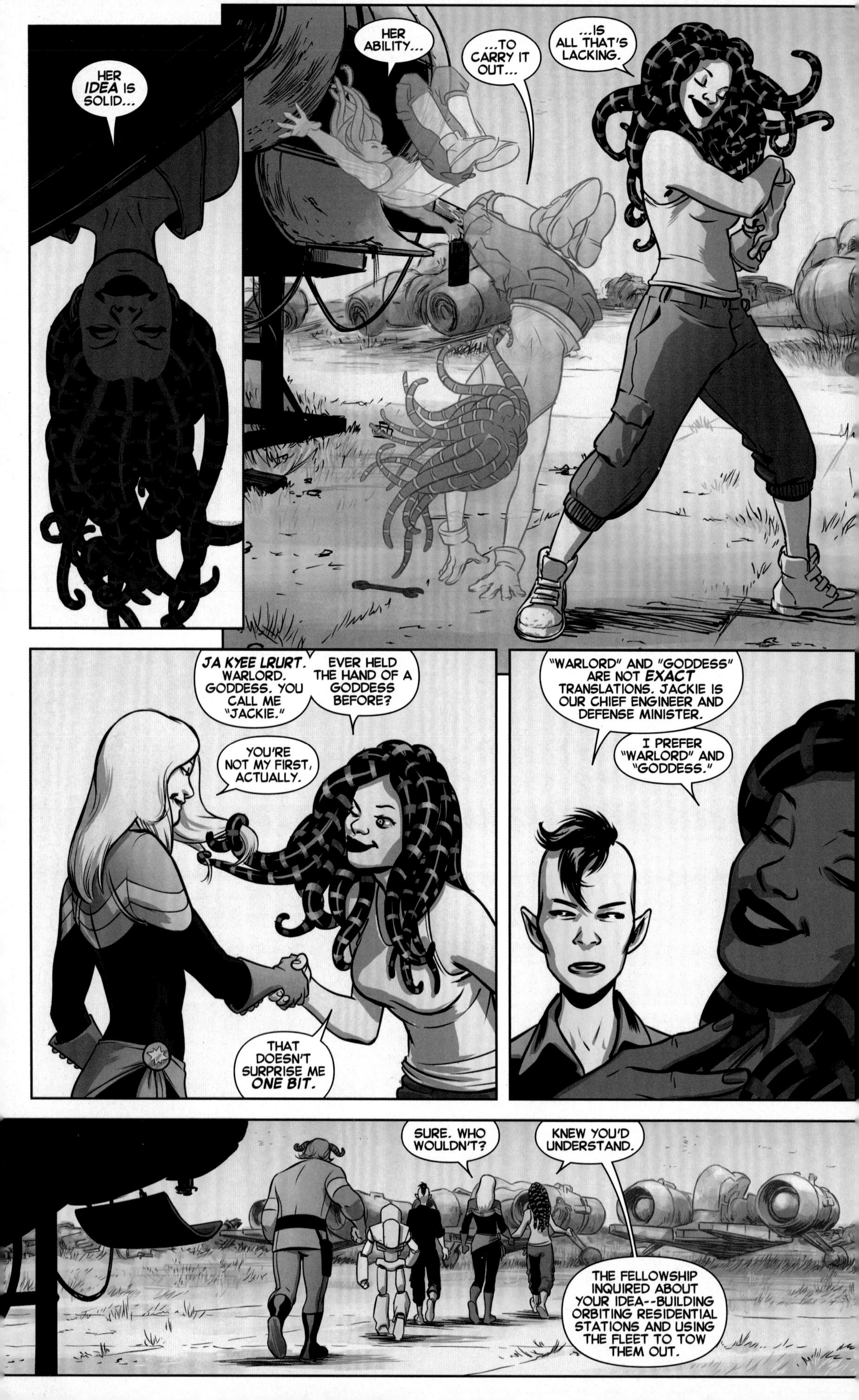
HER IDEA IS SOLID...
HER ABILITY...
...TO CARRY IT OUT...
...IS ALL THAT'S LACKING.
JA KYEE LRURT. WARLORD. GODDESS. YOU CALL ME "JACKIE."
EVER HELD THE HAND OF A GODDESS BEFORE?
YOU'RE NOT MY FIRST, ACTUALLY.
THAT DOESN'T SURPRISE ME ONE BIT.
"WARLORD" AND "GODDESS" ARE NOT EXACT TRANSLATIONS. JACKIE IS OUR CHIEF ENGINEER AND DEFENSE MINISTER.
I PREFER "WARLORD" AND "GODDESS."
SURE. WHO WOULDN'T?
KNEW YOU'D UNDERSTAND.
THE FELLOWSHIP INQUIRED ABOUT YOUR IDEA--BUILDING ORBITING RESIDENTIAL STATIONS AND USING THE FLEET TO TOW THEM OUT.

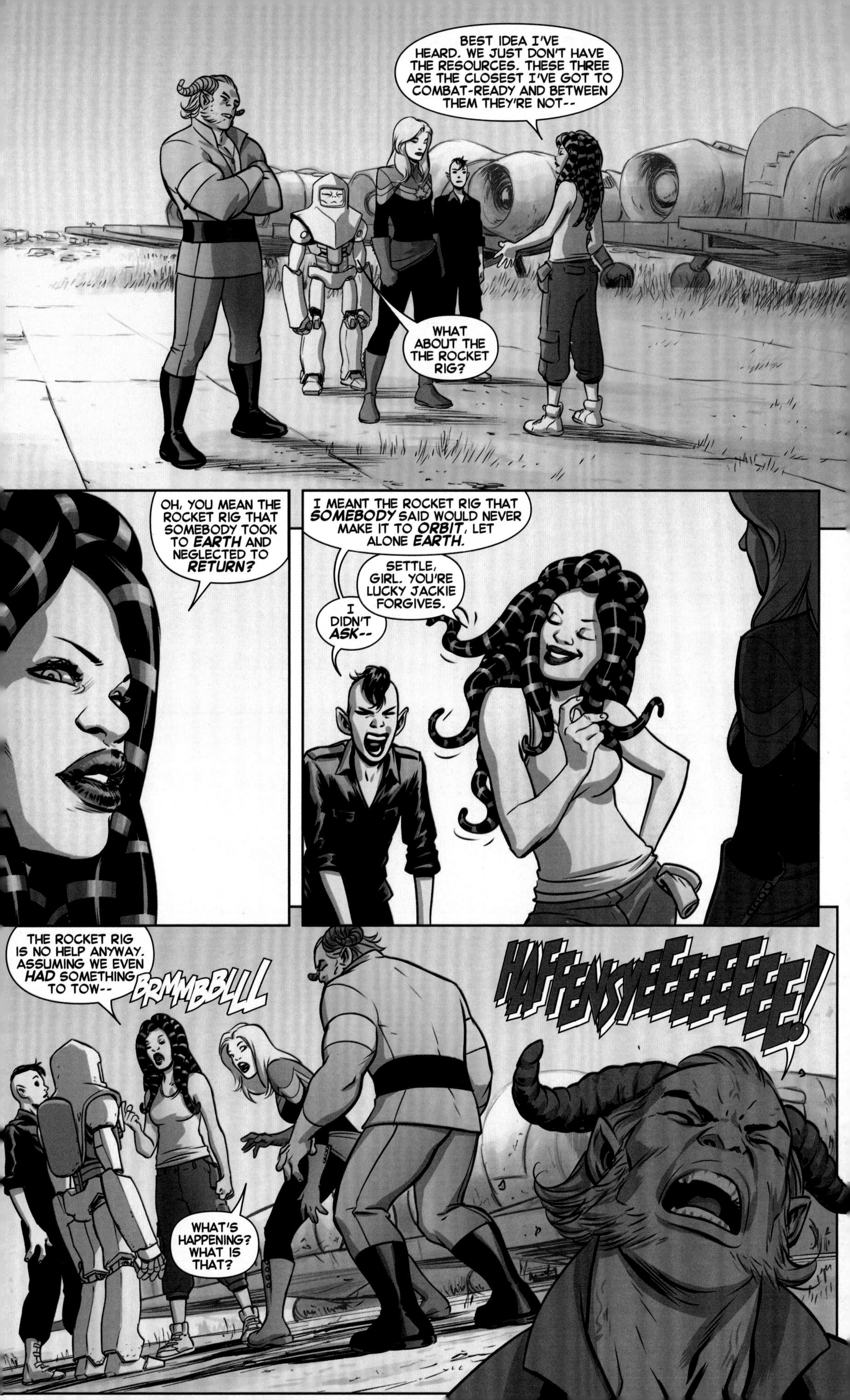
BEST IDEA I'VE HEARD. WE JUST DON'T HAVE THE RESOURCES. THESE THREE ARE THE CLOSEST I'VE GOT TO COMBAT-READY AND BETWEEN THEM THEY'RE NOT--
WHAT ABOUT THE THE ROCKET RIG?
OH, YOU MEAN THE ROCKET RIG THAT SOMEBODY TOOK TO EARTH AND NEGLECTED TO RETURN?
I MEANT THE ROCKET RIG THAT SOMEBODY SAID WOULD NEVER MAKE IT TO ORBIT, LET ALONE EARTH.
SETTLE, GIRL. YOU'RE LUCKY JACKIE FORGIVES.
I DIDN'T ASK--
THE ROCKET RIG IS NO HELP ANYWAY. ASSUMING WE EVEN HAD SOMETHING TO TOW--
BRMMBBLLL
HAFFENSYEEEEEEEEE!
WHAT'S HAPPENING? WHAT IS THAT?

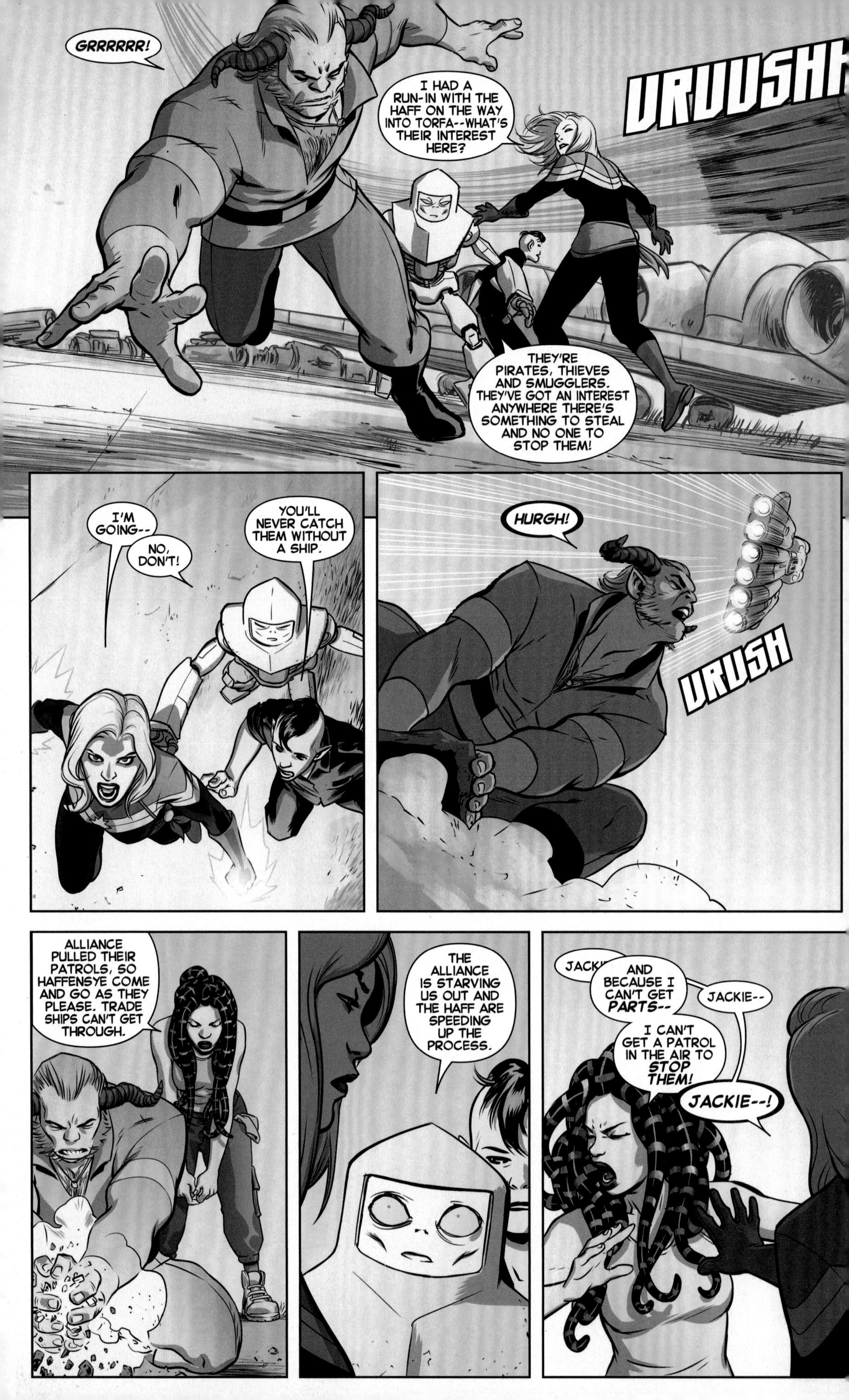
GRRRRRR!
I HAD A RUN-IN WITH THE HAFF ON THE WAY INTO TORFA--WHAT'S THEIR INTEREST HERE?
VRUUSHH
THEY'RE PIRATES, THIEVES AND SMUGGLERS. THEY'VE GOT AN INTEREST ANYWHERE THERE'S SOMETHING TO STEAL AND NO ONE TO STOP THEM!
I'M GOING--
NO, DON'T!
YOU'LL NEVER CATCH THEM WITHOUT A SHIP.
HURGH!
VRUSH
ALLIANCE PULLED THEIR PATROLS, SO HAFFENSYE COME AND GO AS THEY PLEASE. TRADE SHIPS CAN'T GET THROUGH.
THE ALLIANCE IS STARVING US OUT AND THE HAFF ARE SPEEDING UP THE PROCESS.
AND BECAUSE I CAN'T GET PARTS--
JACKIE--
I CAN'T GET A PATROL IN THE AIR TO STOP THEM!
JACKIE--!

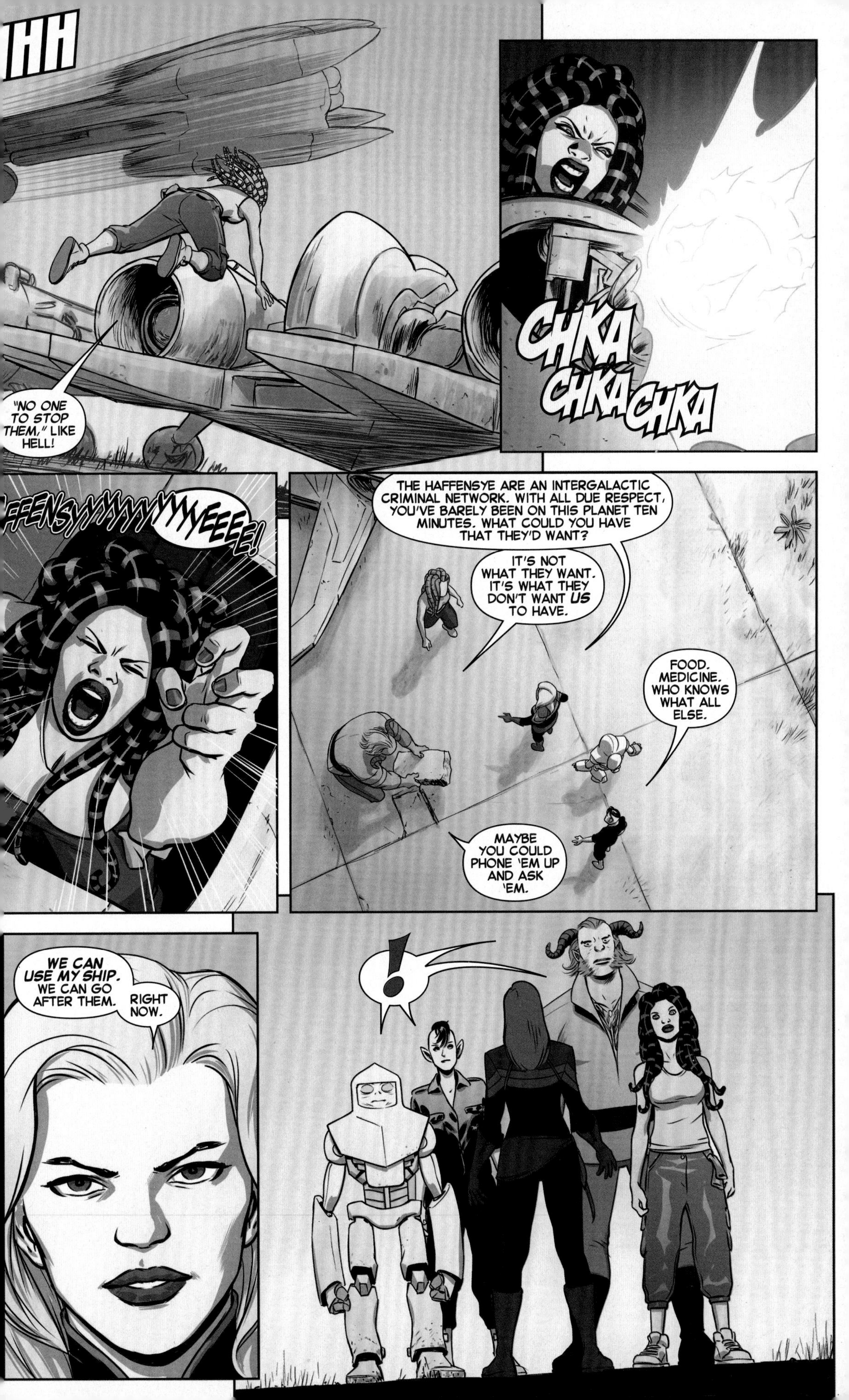

HH
"NO ONE TO STOP THEM," LIKE HELL!
CHKA CHKA CHKA
FFENSYYYYYYYYYYYEEEE!
THE HAFFENSYE ARE AN INTERGALACTIC CRIMINAL NETWORK. WITH ALL DUE RESPECT, YOU'VE BARELY BEEN ON THIS PLANET TEN MINUTES. WHAT COULD YOU HAVE THAT THEY'D WANT?
IT'S NOT WHAT THEY WANT. IT'S WHAT THEY DON'T WANT US TO HAVE.
FOOD. MEDICINE. WHO KNOWS WHAT ALL ELSE.
MAYBE YOU COULD PHONE 'EM UP AND ASK 'EM.
WE CAN USE MY SHIP. WE CAN GO AFTER THEM.
RIGHT NOW.
!

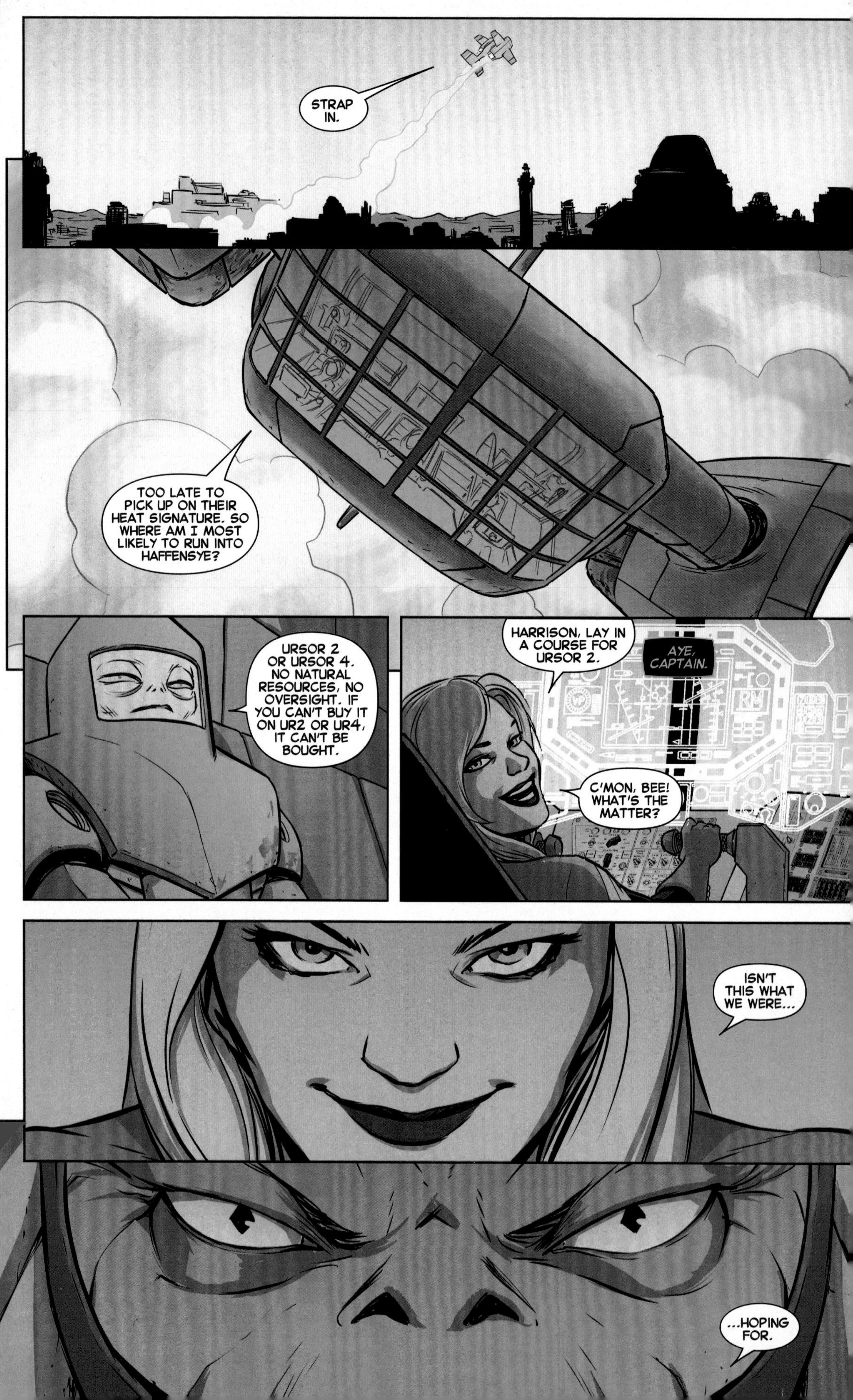
STRAP IN.
TOO LATE TO PICK UP ON THEIR HEAT SIGNATURE. SO WHERE AM I MOST LIKELY TO RUN INTO HAFFENSYE?
URSOR 2 OR URSOR 4. NO NATURAL RESOURCES, NO OVERSIGHT. IF YOU CAN'T BUY IT ON UR2 OR UR4, IT CAN'T BE BOUGHT.
HARRISON, LAY IN A COURSE FOR URSOR 2.
AYE, CAPTAIN.
C'MON, BEE! WHAT'S THE MATTER?
ISN'T THIS WHAT WE WERE...
...HOPING FOR.

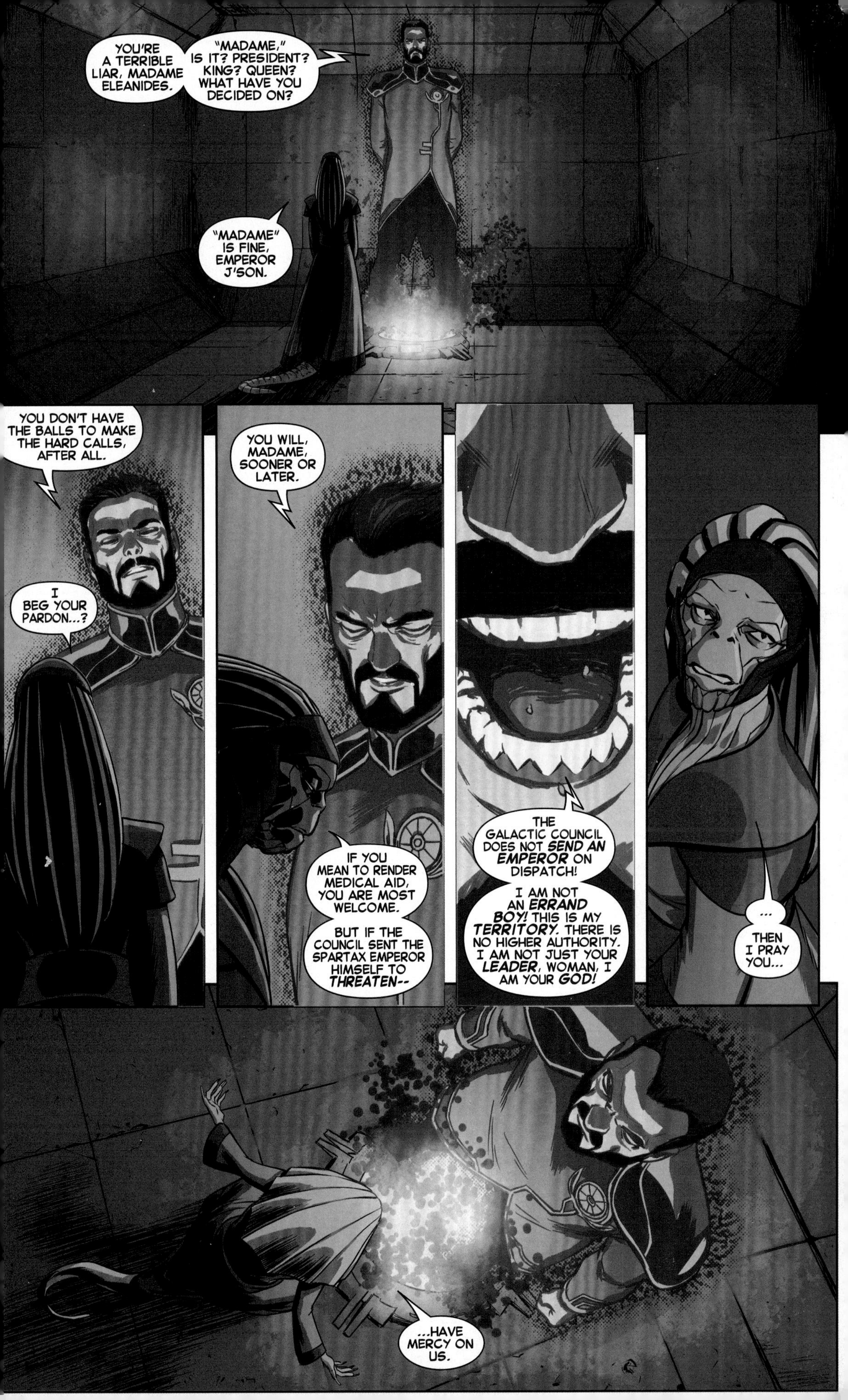

YOU'RE A TERRIBLE LIAR, MADAME ELEANIDES.
"MADAME," IS IT? PRESIDENT? KING? QUEEN? WHAT HAVE YOU DECIDED ON?
"MADAME" IS FINE, EMPEROR J'SON.
YOU DON'T HAVE THE BALLS TO MAKE THE HARD CALLS, AFTER ALL.
I BEG YOUR PARDON...?
YOU WILL, MADAME, SOONER OR LATER.
IF YOU MEAN TO RENDER MEDICAL AID, YOU ARE MOST WELCOME.
BUT IF THE COUNCIL SENT THE SPARTAX EMPEROR HIMSELF TO *THREATEN--*
THE GALACTIC COUNCIL DOES NOT *SEND AN EMPEROR* ON DISPATCH!
I AM NOT AN *ERRAND BOY!* THIS IS MY *TERRITORY*. THERE IS NO HIGHER AUTHORITY. I AM NOT JUST YOUR *LEADER*, WOMAN, I AM YOUR *GOD!*
...
THEN I PRAY YOU...
...HAVE MERCY ON US.

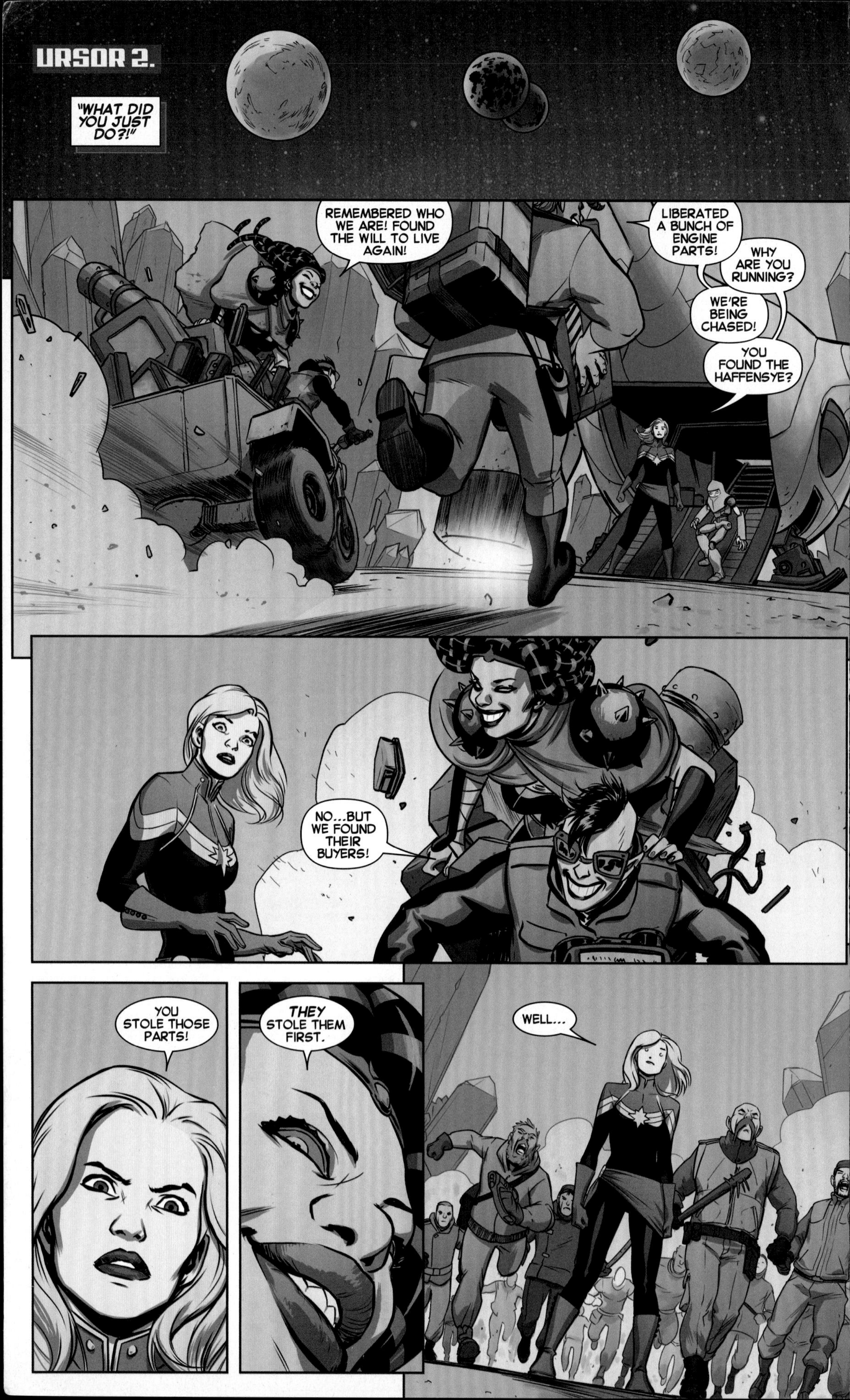
URSOR 2.
"WHAT DID YOU JUST DO?!"
REMEMBERED WHO WE ARE! FOUND THE WILL TO LIVE AGAIN!
LIBERATED A BUNCH OF ENGINE PARTS!
WHY ARE YOU RUNNING?
WE'RE BEING CHASED!
YOU FOUND THE HAFFENSYE?
NO...BUT WE FOUND THEIR BUYERS!
YOU STOLE THOSE PARTS!
THEY STOLE THEM FIRST.
WELL...

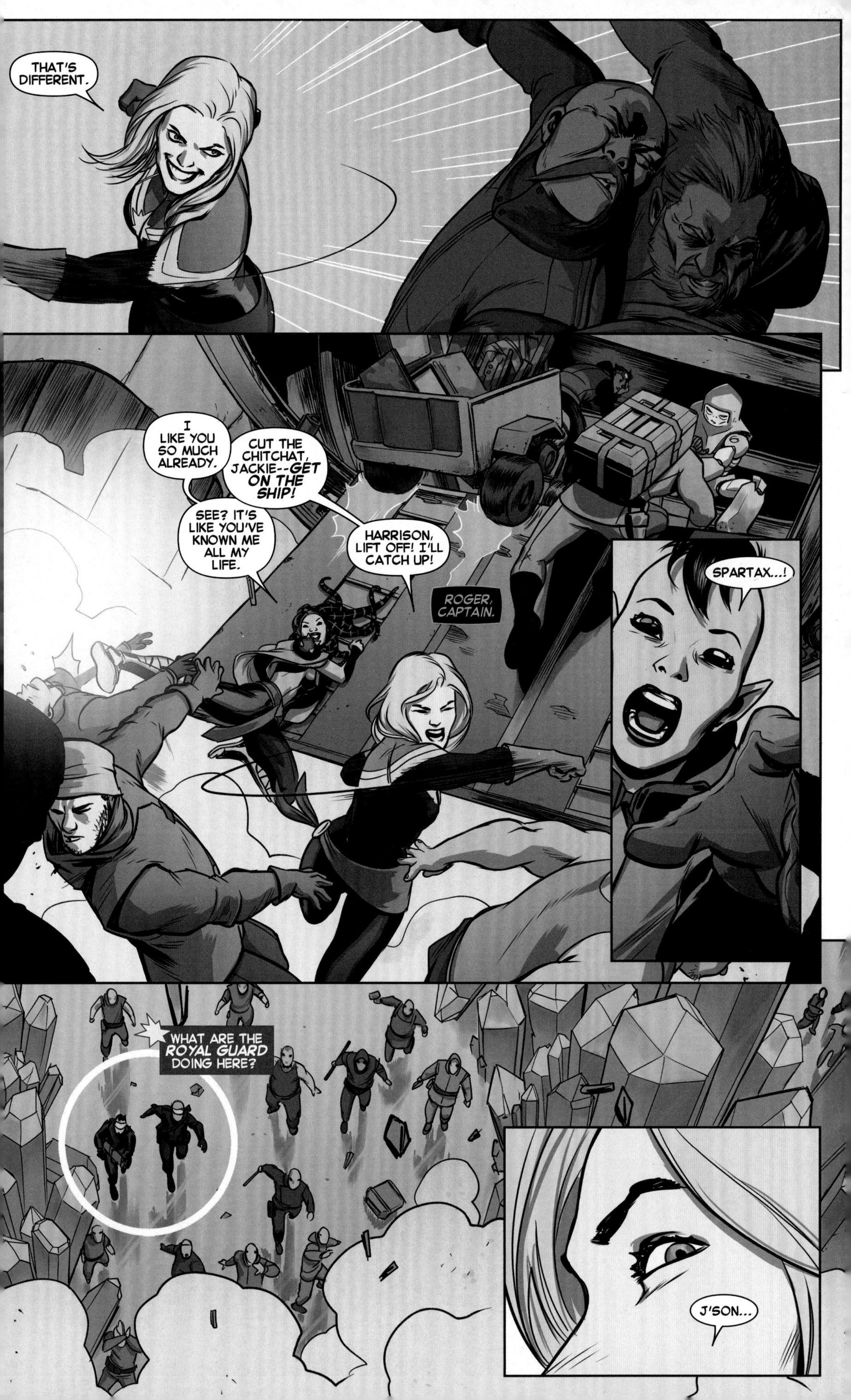
THAT'S DIFFERENT.
I LIKE YOU SO MUCH ALREADY.
CUT THE CHITCHAT, JACKIE--GET ON THE SHIP!
SEE? IT'S LIKE YOU'VE KNOWN ME ALL MY LIFE.
HARRISON, LIFT OFF! I'LL CATCH UP!
ROGER, CAPTAIN.
SPARTAX...!
WHAT ARE THE ROYAL GUARD DOING HERE?
J'SON...

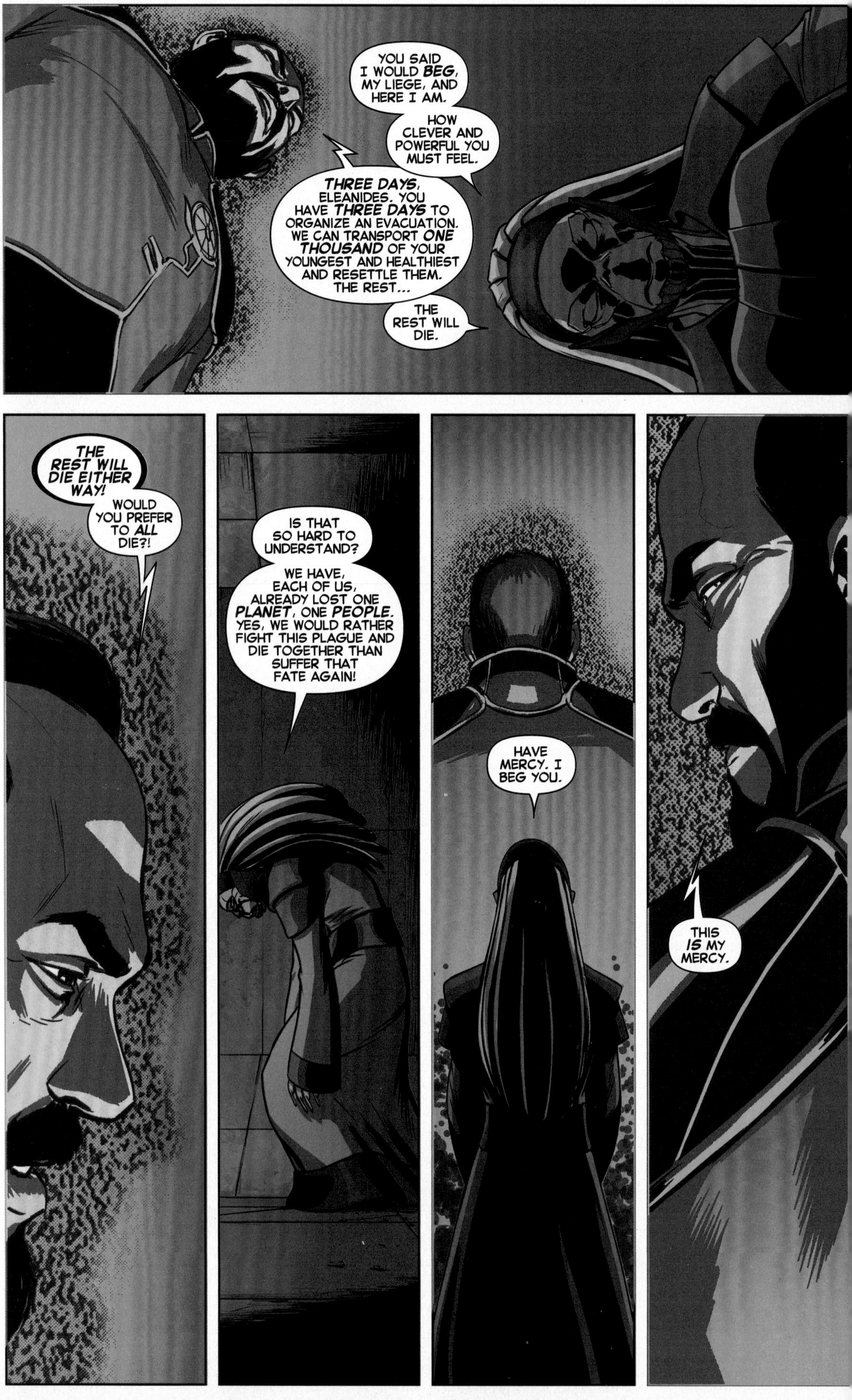

YOU SAID I WOULD BEG, MY LIEGE, AND HERE I AM.
HOW CLEVER AND POWERFUL YOU MUST FEEL.
THREE DAYS, ELEANIDES. YOU HAVE THREE DAYS TO ORGANIZE AN EVACUATION. WE CAN TRANSPORT ONE THOUSAND OF YOUR YOUNGEST AND HEALTHIEST AND RESETTLE THEM. THE REST...
THE REST WILL DIE.
THE REST WILL DIE EITHER WAY!
WOULD YOU PREFER TO ALL DIE?!
IS THAT SO HARD TO UNDERSTAND?
WE HAVE, EACH OF US, ALREADY LOST ONE PLANET, ONE PEOPLE. YES, WE WOULD RATHER FIGHT THIS PLAGUE AND DIE TOGETHER THAN SUFFER THAT FATE AGAIN!
HAVE MERCY. I BEG YOU.
THIS IS MY MERCY.

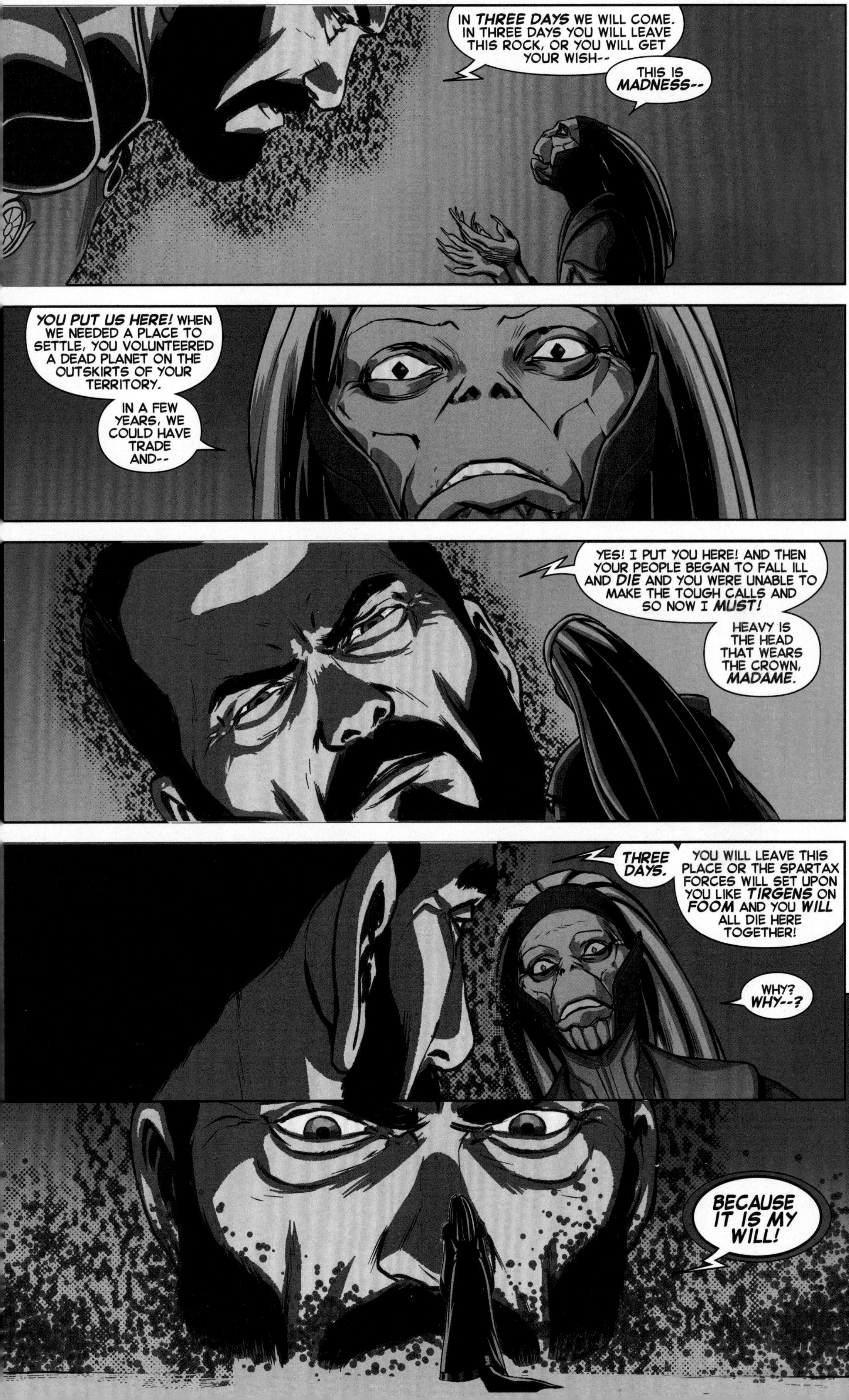

IN THREE DAYS WE WILL COME. IN THREE DAYS YOU WILL LEAVE THIS ROCK, OR YOU WILL GET YOUR WISH--
THIS IS MADNESS--
YOU PUT US HERE! WHEN WE NEEDED A PLACE TO SETTLE, YOU VOLUNTEERED A DEAD PLANET ON THE OUTSKIRTS OF YOUR TERRITORY.
IN A FEW YEARS, WE COULD HAVE TRADE AND--
YES! I PUT YOU HERE! AND THEN YOUR PEOPLE BEGAN TO FALL ILL AND DIE AND YOU WERE UNABLE TO MAKE THE TOUGH CALLS AND SO NOW I MUST!
HEAVY IS THE HEAD THAT WEARS THE CROWN, MADAME.
THREE DAYS.
YOU WILL LEAVE THIS PLACE OR THE SPARTAX FORCES WILL SET UPON YOU LIKE TIRGENS ON FOOM AND YOU WILL ALL DIE HERE TOGETHER!
WHY? WHY--?
BECAUSE IT IS MY WILL!

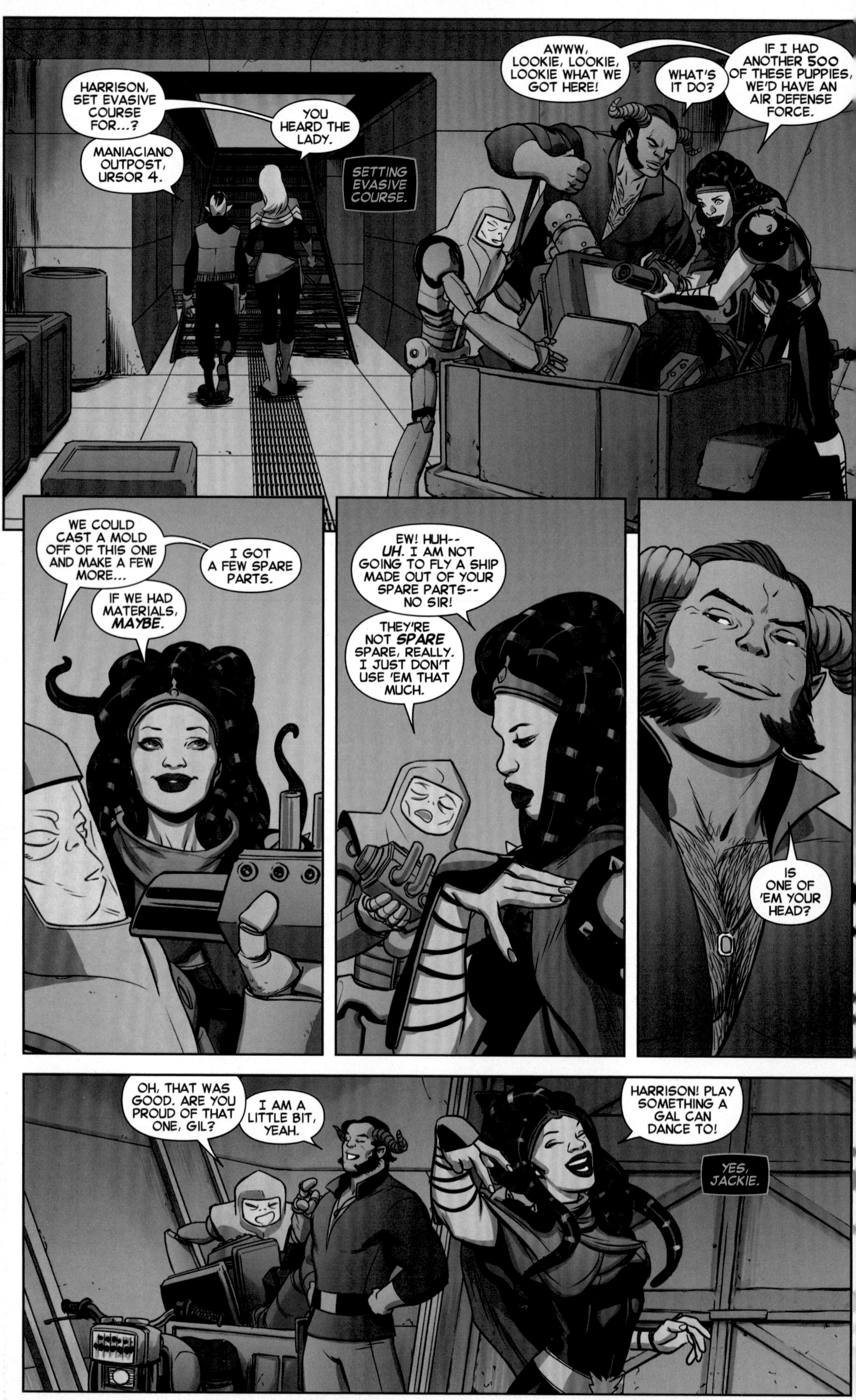
HARRISON, SET EVASIVE COURSE FOR...?
YOU HEARD THE LADY.
MANIACIANO OUTPOST, URSOR 4.
SETTING EVASIVE COURSE.
AWWW, LOOKIE, LOOKIE, LOOKIE WHAT WE GOT HERE!
WHAT'S IT DO?
IF I HAD ANOTHER 500 OF THESE PUPPIES, WE'D HAVE AN AIR DEFENSE FORCE.
WE COULD CAST A MOLD OFF OF THIS ONE AND MAKE A FEW MORE...
I GOT A FEW SPARE PARTS.
IF WE HAD MATERIALS, MAYBE.
EW! HUH--UH. I AM NOT GOING TO FLY A SHIP MADE OUT OF YOUR SPARE PARTS--NO SIR!
THEY'RE NOT SPARE SPARE, REALLY. I JUST DON'T USE 'EM THAT MUCH.
IS ONE OF 'EM YOUR HEAD?
OH, THAT WAS GOOD. ARE YOU PROUD OF THAT ONE, GIL?
I AM A LITTLE BIT, YEAH.
HARRISON! PLAY SOMETHING A GAL CAN DANCE TO!
YES, JACKIE.

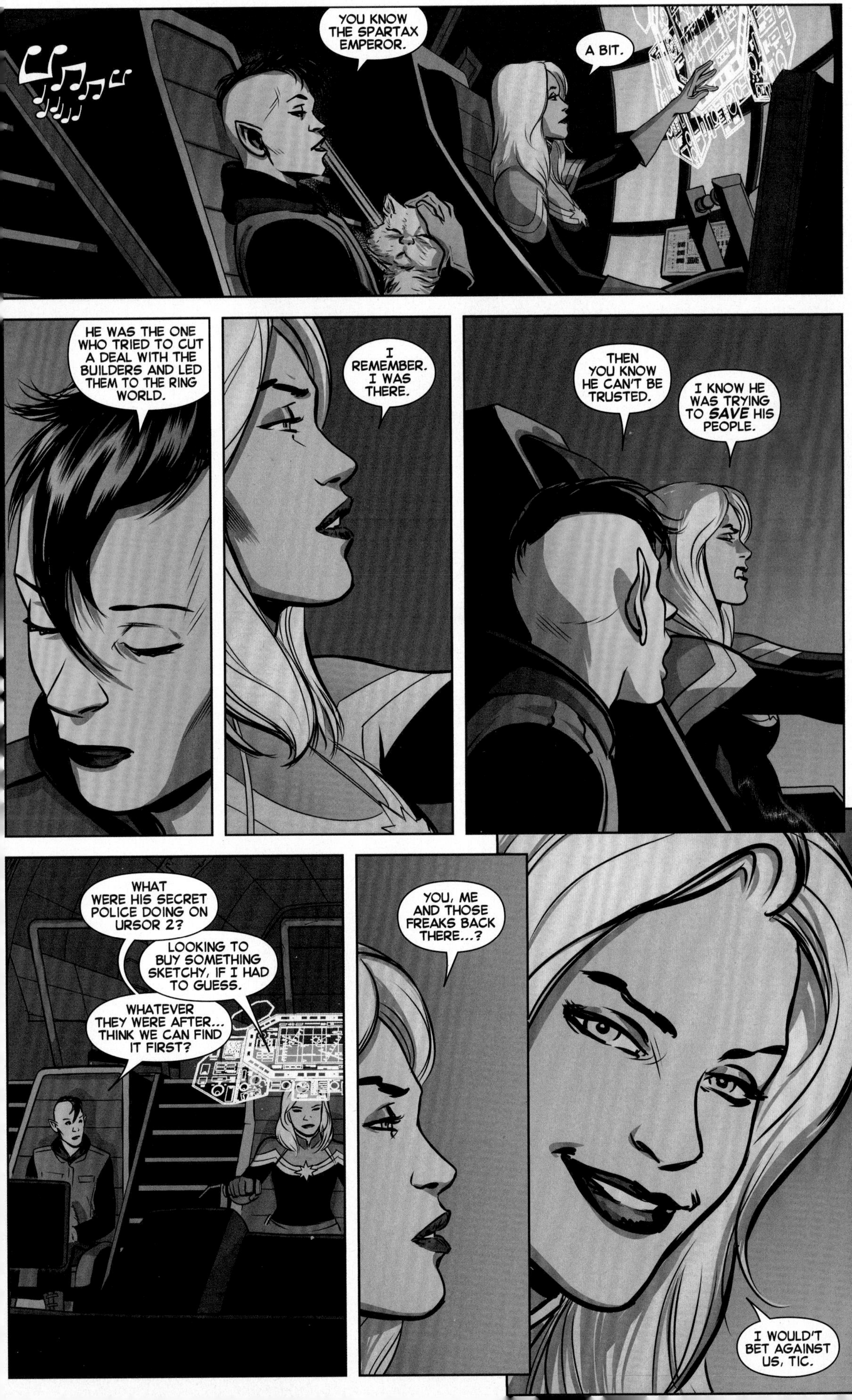
YOU KNOW THE SPARTAX EMPEROR.
A BIT.
HE WAS THE ONE WHO TRIED TO CUT A DEAL WITH THE BUILDERS AND LED THEM TO THE RING WORLD.
I REMEMBER. I WAS THERE.
THEN YOU KNOW HE CAN'T BE TRUSTED.
I KNOW HE WAS TRYING TO *SAVE* HIS PEOPLE.
WHAT WERE HIS SECRET POLICE DOING ON URSOR 2?
LOOKING TO BUY SOMETHING SKETCHY, IF I HAD TO GUESS.
WHATEVER THEY WERE AFTER... THINK WE CAN FIND IT FIRST?
YOU, ME AND THOSE FREAKS BACK THERE...?
I WOULD'T BET AGAINST US, TIC.

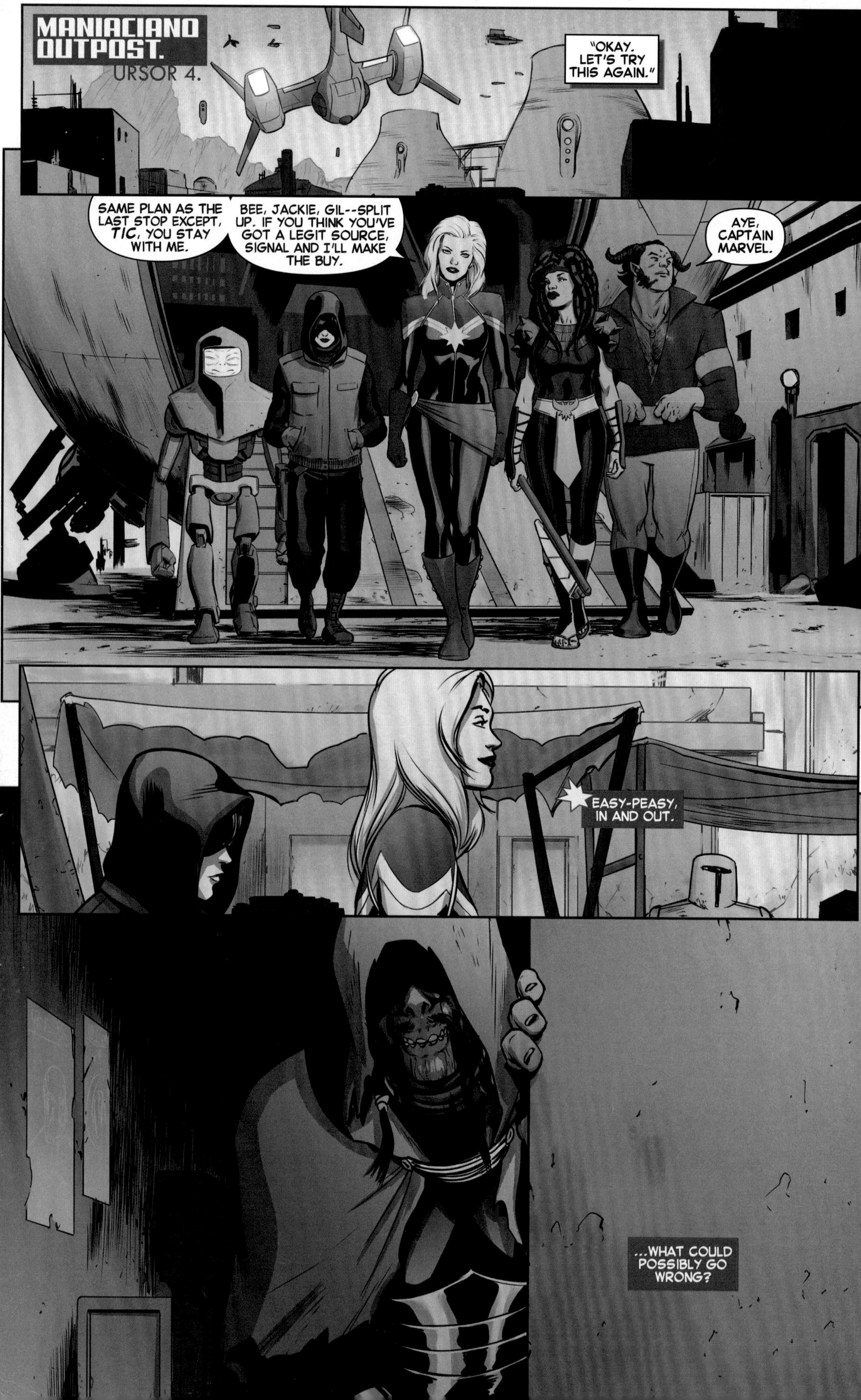
MANIACIANO OUTPOST.
URSOR 4.
"OKAY. LET'S TRY THIS AGAIN."
SAME PLAN AS THE LAST STOP EXCEPT, TIC, YOU STAY WITH ME.
BEE, JACKIE, GIL--SPLIT UP. IF YOU THINK YOU'VE GOT A LEGIT SOURCE, SIGNAL AND I'LL MAKE THE BUY.
AYE, CAPTAIN MARVEL.
EASY-PEASY, IN AND OUT.
...WHAT COULD POSSIBLY GO WRONG?

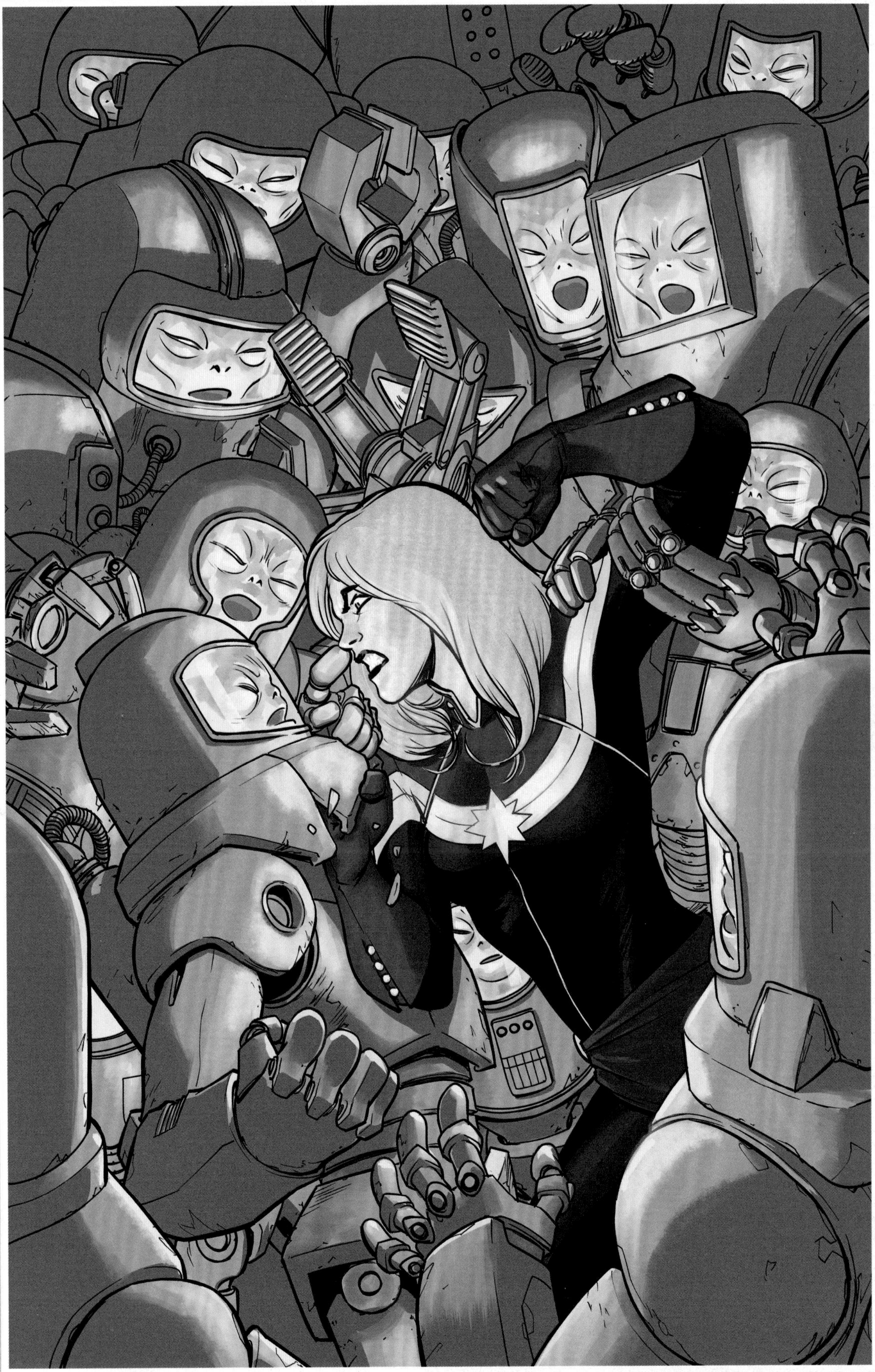

FIVE

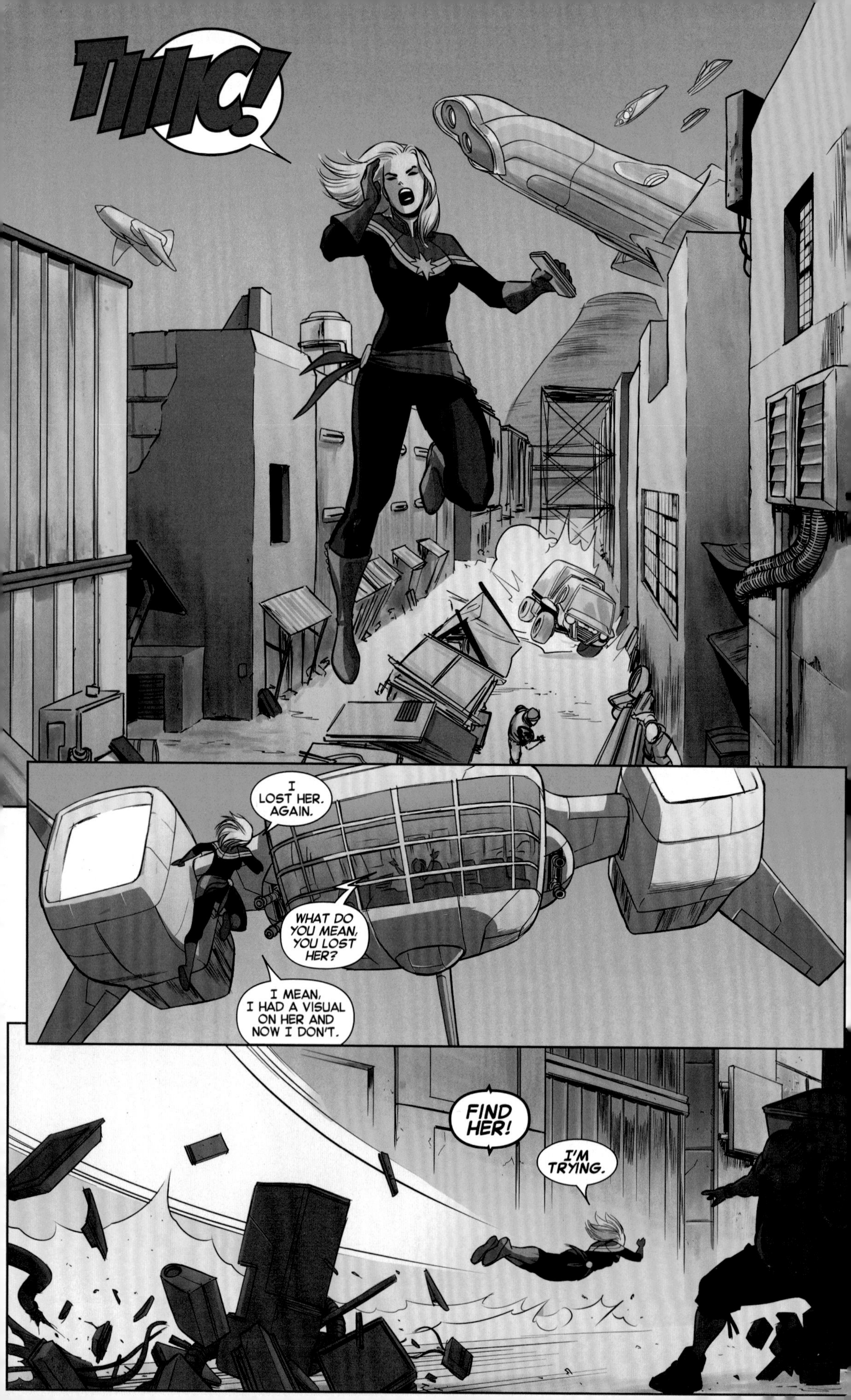
THIIC!
I LOST HER. AGAIN.
WHAT DO YOU MEAN, YOU LOST HER?
I MEAN, I HAD A VISUAL ON HER AND NOW I DON'T.
FIND HER!
I'M TRYING.

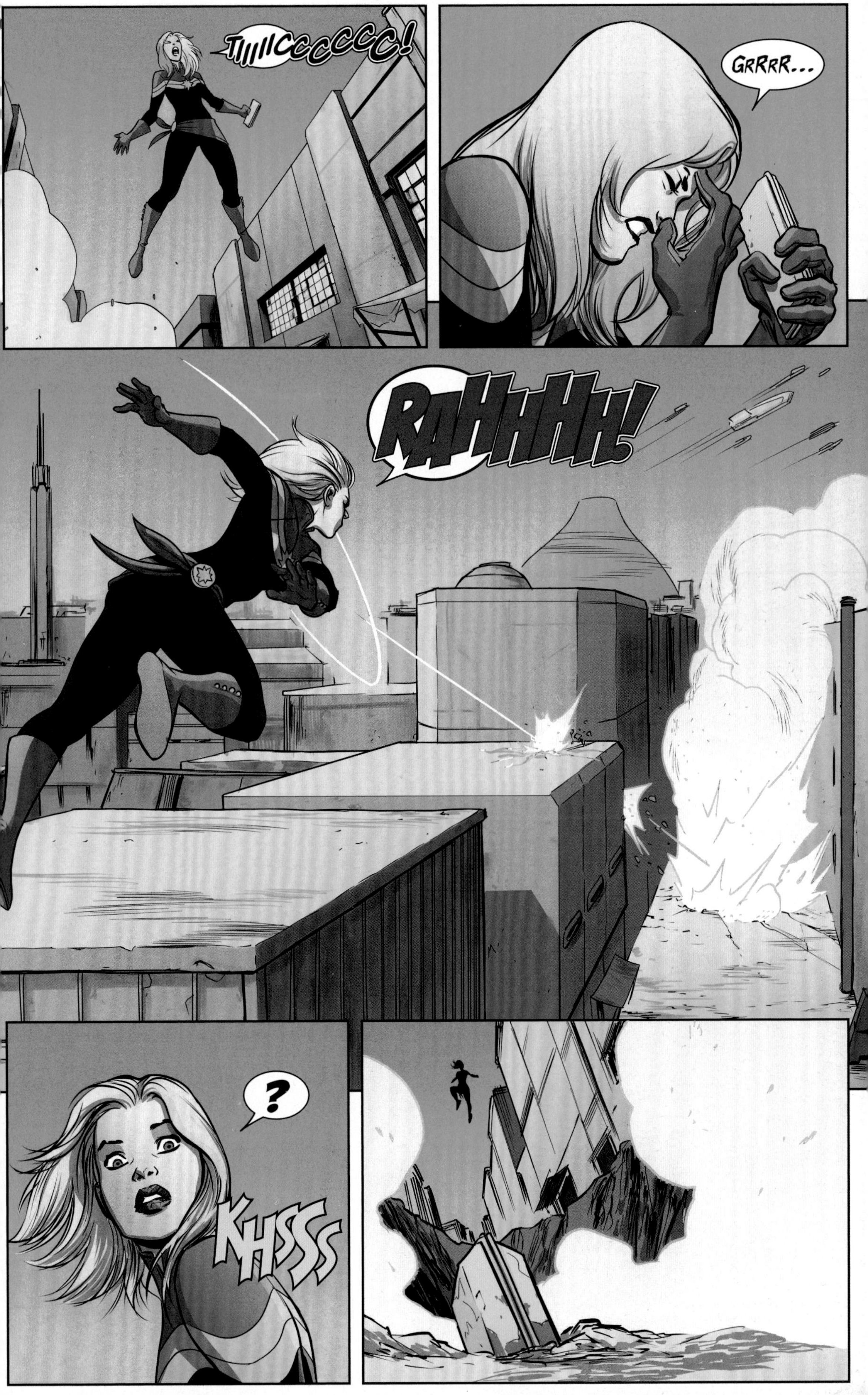
TIIIICCCCCCC!
GRRRR...
RAHHHH!
?
KHSSS

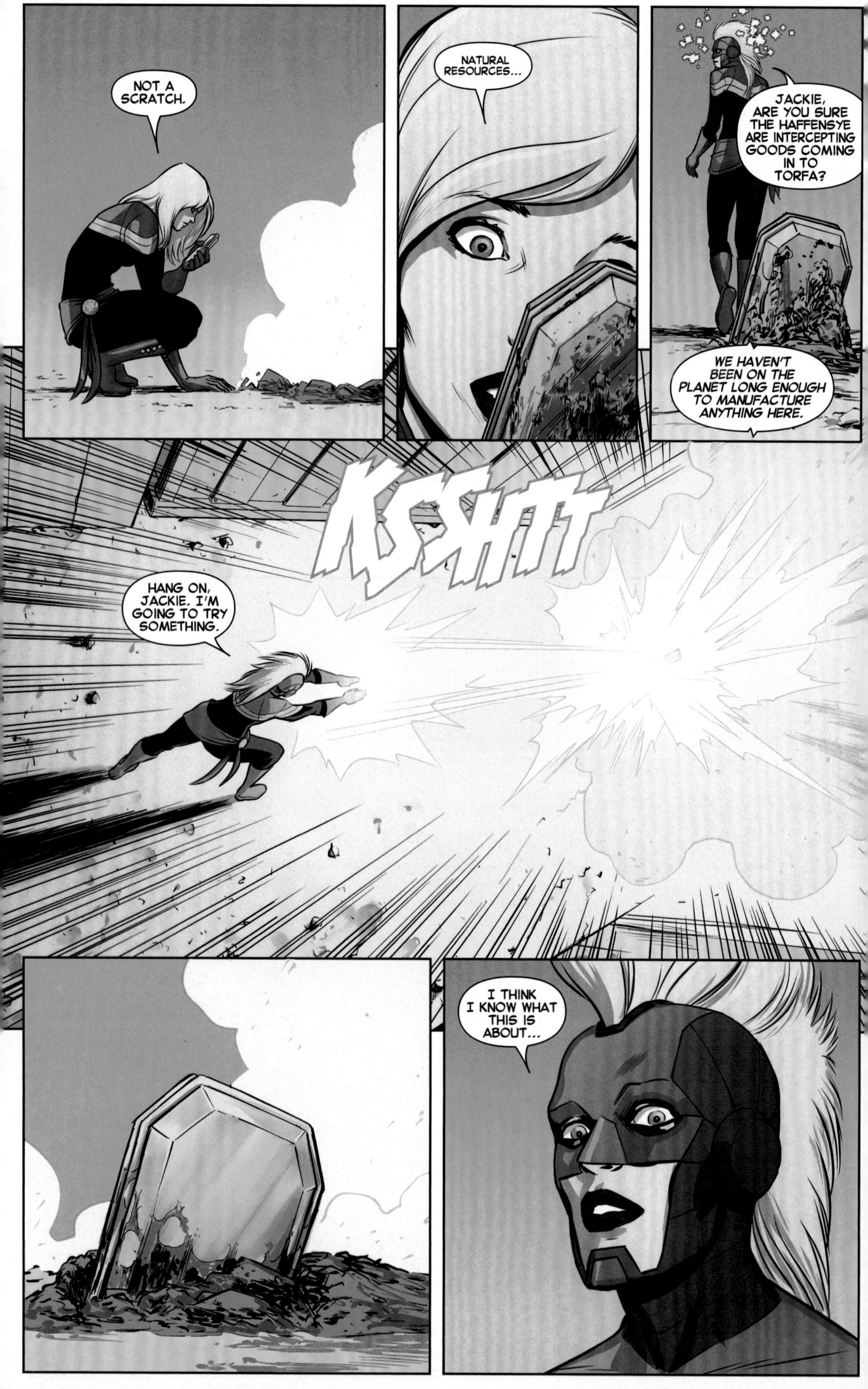
NOT A SCRATCH.
NATURAL RESOURCES...
JACKIE, ARE YOU SURE THE HAFFENSYE ARE INTERCEPTING GOODS COMING IN TO TORFA?
WE HAVEN'T BEEN ON THE PLANET LONG ENOUGH TO MANUFACTURE ANYTHING HERE.
KSSHTT
HANG ON, JACKIE. I'M GOING TO TRY SOMETHING.
I THINK I KNOW WHAT THIS IS ABOUT...

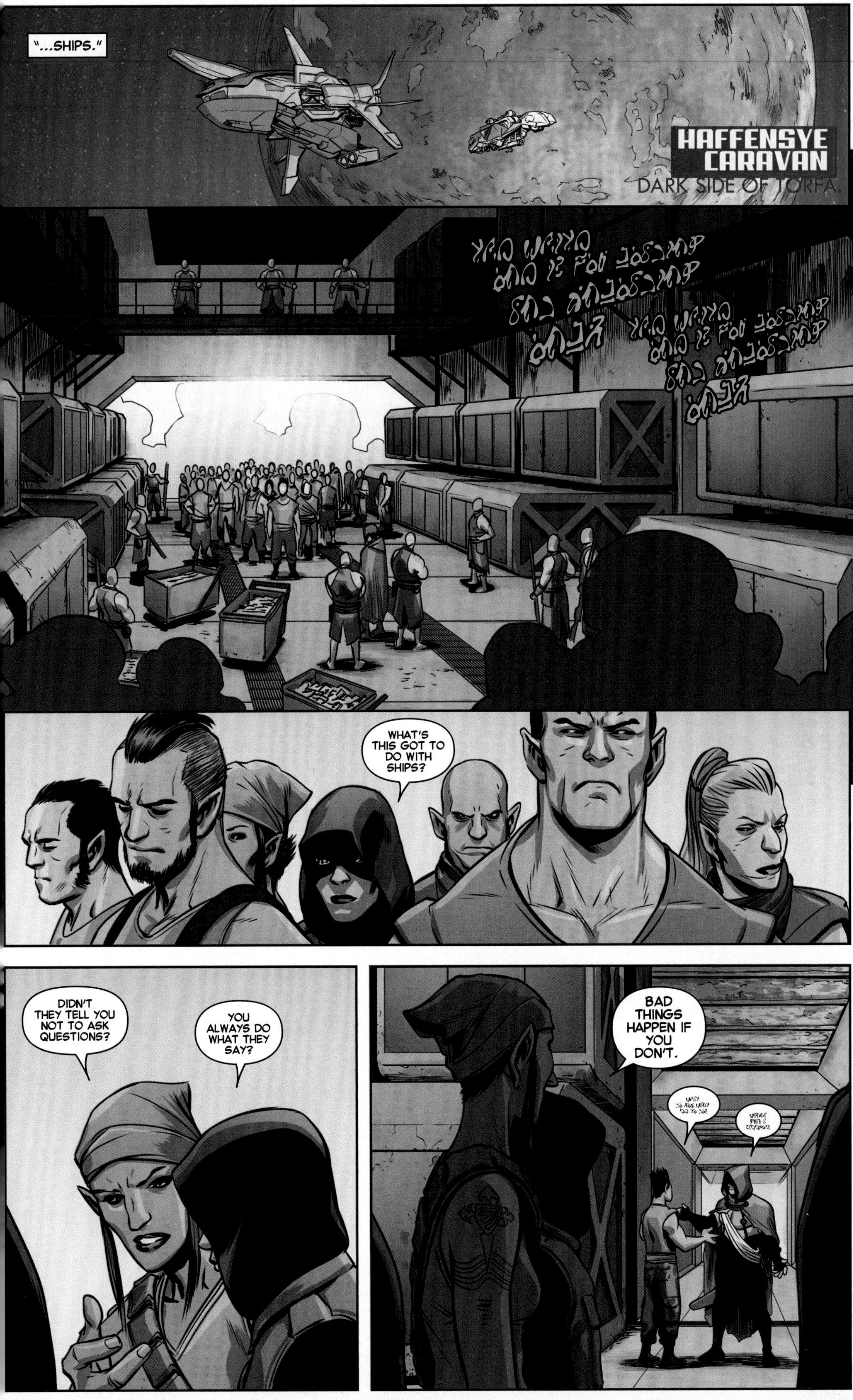
"...SHIPS."
HAFFENSYE CARAVAN
DARK SIDE OF TORFA.
WHAT'S THIS GOT TO DO WITH SHIPS?
DIDN'T THEY TELL YOU NOT TO ASK QUESTIONS?
YOU ALWAYS DO WHAT THEY SAY?
BAD THINGS HAPPEN IF YOU DON'T.

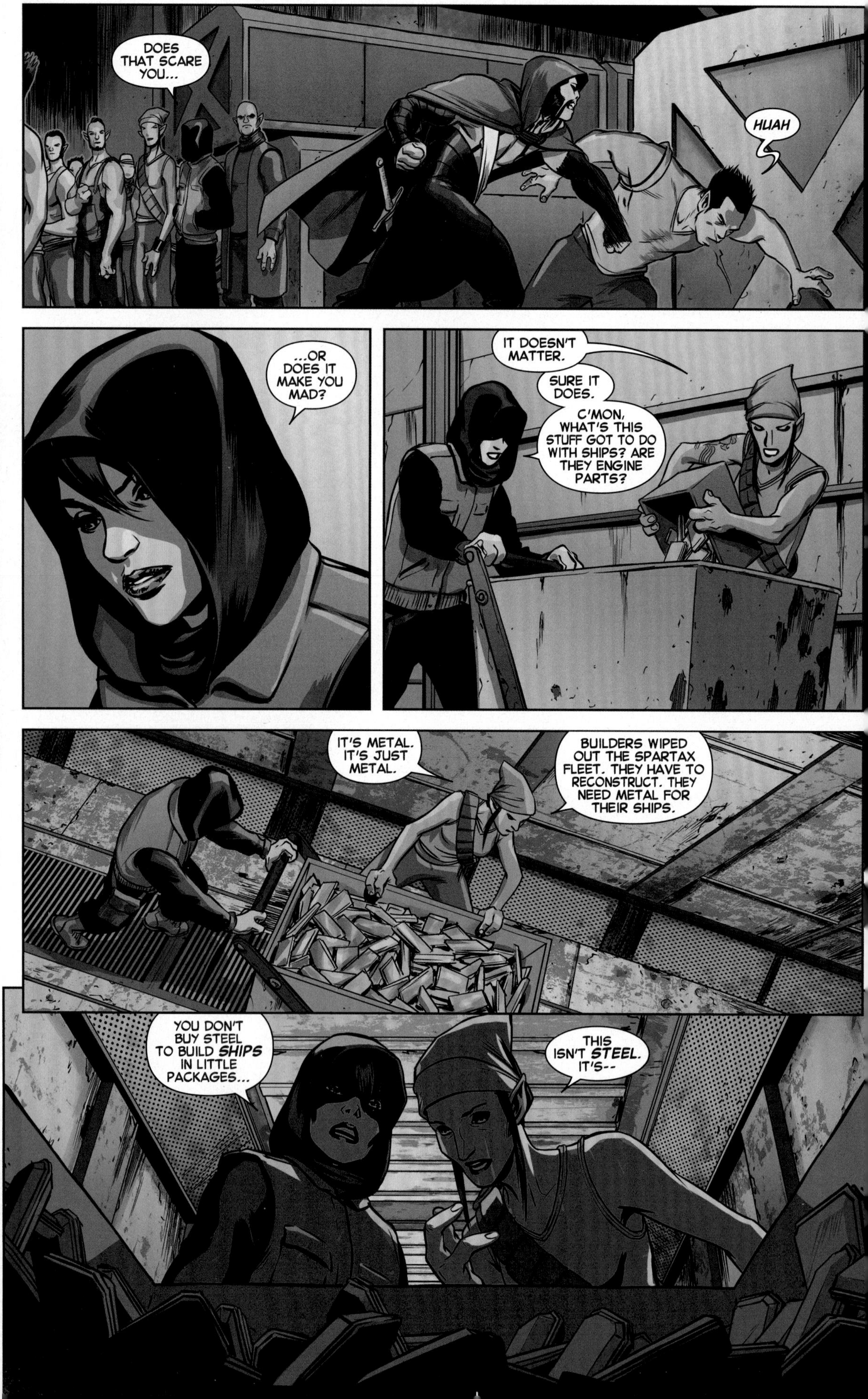
DOES THAT SCARE YOU...
HUAH
...OR DOES IT MAKE YOU MAD?
IT DOESN'T MATTER.
SURE IT DOES.
C'MON, WHAT'S THIS STUFF GOT TO DO WITH SHIPS? ARE THEY ENGINE PARTS?
IT'S METAL. IT'S JUST METAL.
BUILDERS WIPED OUT THE SPARTAX FLEET. THEY HAVE TO RECONSTRUCT. THEY NEED METAL FOR THEIR SHIPS.
YOU DON'T BUY STEEL TO BUILD SHIPS IN LITTLE PACKAGES...
THIS ISN'T STEEL. IT'S--

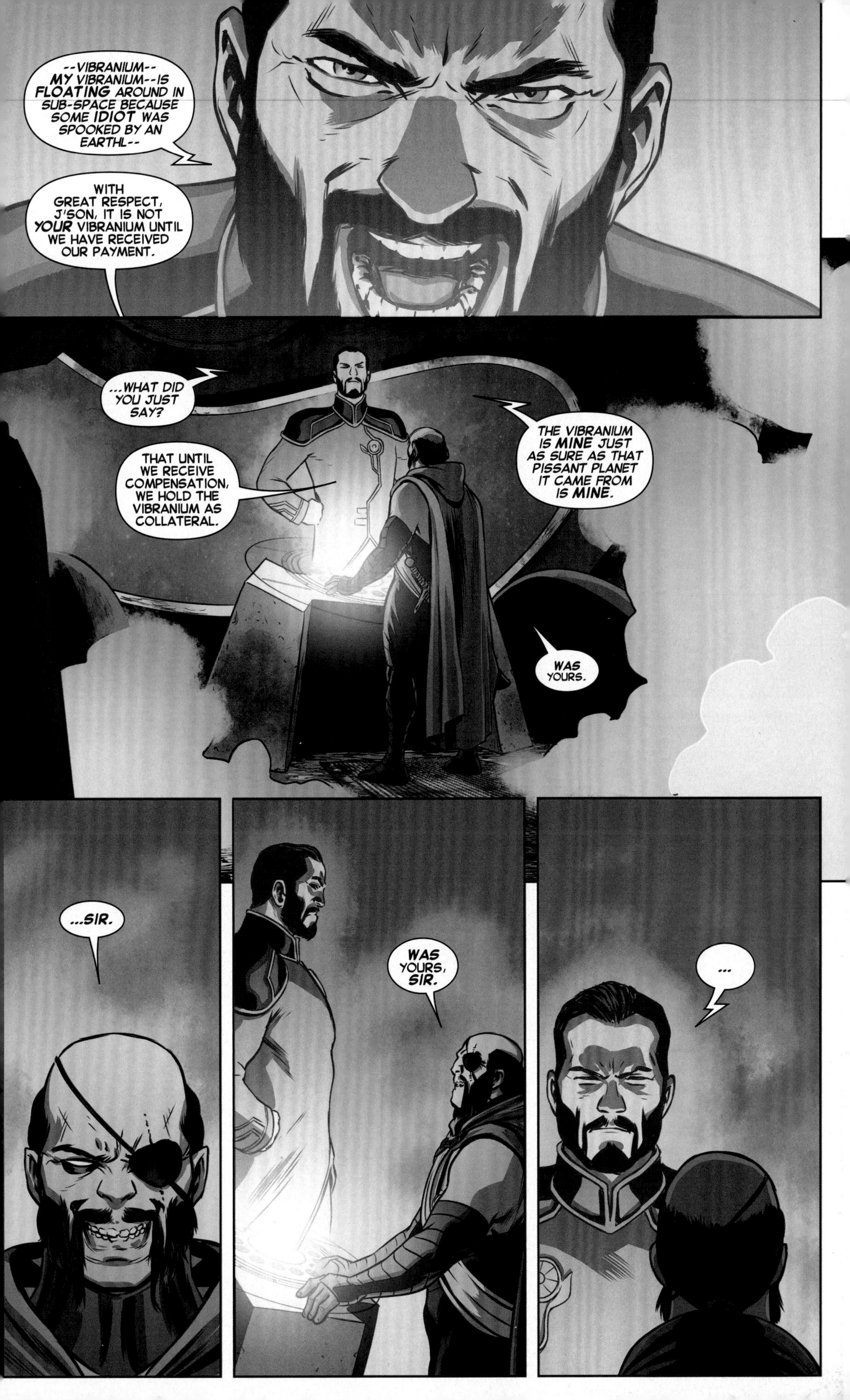
--VIBRANIUM-- MY VIBRANIUM--IS FLOATING AROUND IN SUB-SPACE BECAUSE SOME IDIOT WAS SPOOKED BY AN EARTHL--
WITH GREAT RESPECT, J'SON, IT IS NOT YOUR VIBRANIUM UNTIL WE HAVE RECEIVED OUR PAYMENT.
...WHAT DID YOU JUST SAY?
THAT UNTIL WE RECEIVE COMPENSATION, WE HOLD THE VIBRANIUM AS COLLATERAL.
THE VIBRANIUM IS MINE JUST AS SURE AS THAT PISSANT PLANET IT CAME FROM IS MINE.
WAS YOURS.
...SIR.
WAS YOURS, SIR.
...

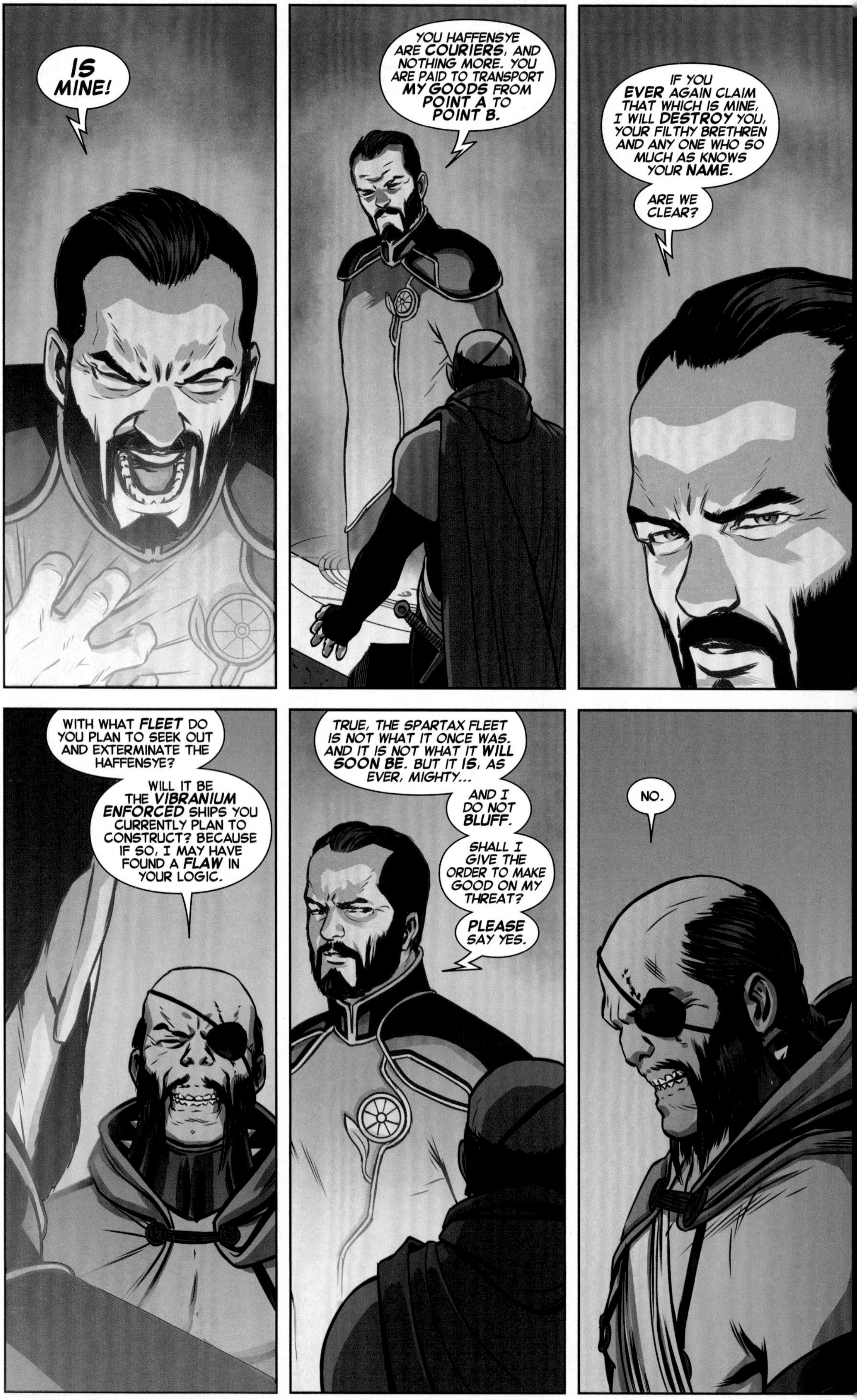
IS MINE!
YOU HAFFENSYE ARE COURIERS, AND NOTHING MORE. YOU ARE PAID TO TRANSPORT MY GOODS FROM POINT A TO POINT B.
IF YOU EVER AGAIN CLAIM THAT WHICH IS MINE, I WILL DESTROY YOU, YOUR FILTHY BRETHREN AND ANY ONE WHO SO MUCH AS KNOWS YOUR NAME.
ARE WE CLEAR?
WITH WHAT FLEET DO YOU PLAN TO SEEK OUT AND EXTERMINATE THE HAFFENSYE?
WILL IT BE THE VIBRANIUM ENFORCED SHIPS YOU CURRENTLY PLAN TO CONSTRUCT? BECAUSE IF SO, I MAY HAVE FOUND A FLAW IN YOUR LOGIC.
TRUE, THE SPARTAX FLEET IS NOT WHAT IT ONCE WAS. AND IT IS NOT WHAT IT WILL SOON BE. BUT IT IS, AS EVER, MIGHTY...
AND I DO NOT BLUFF.
SHALL I GIVE THE ORDER TO MAKE GOOD ON MY THREAT?
PLEASE SAY YES.
NO.

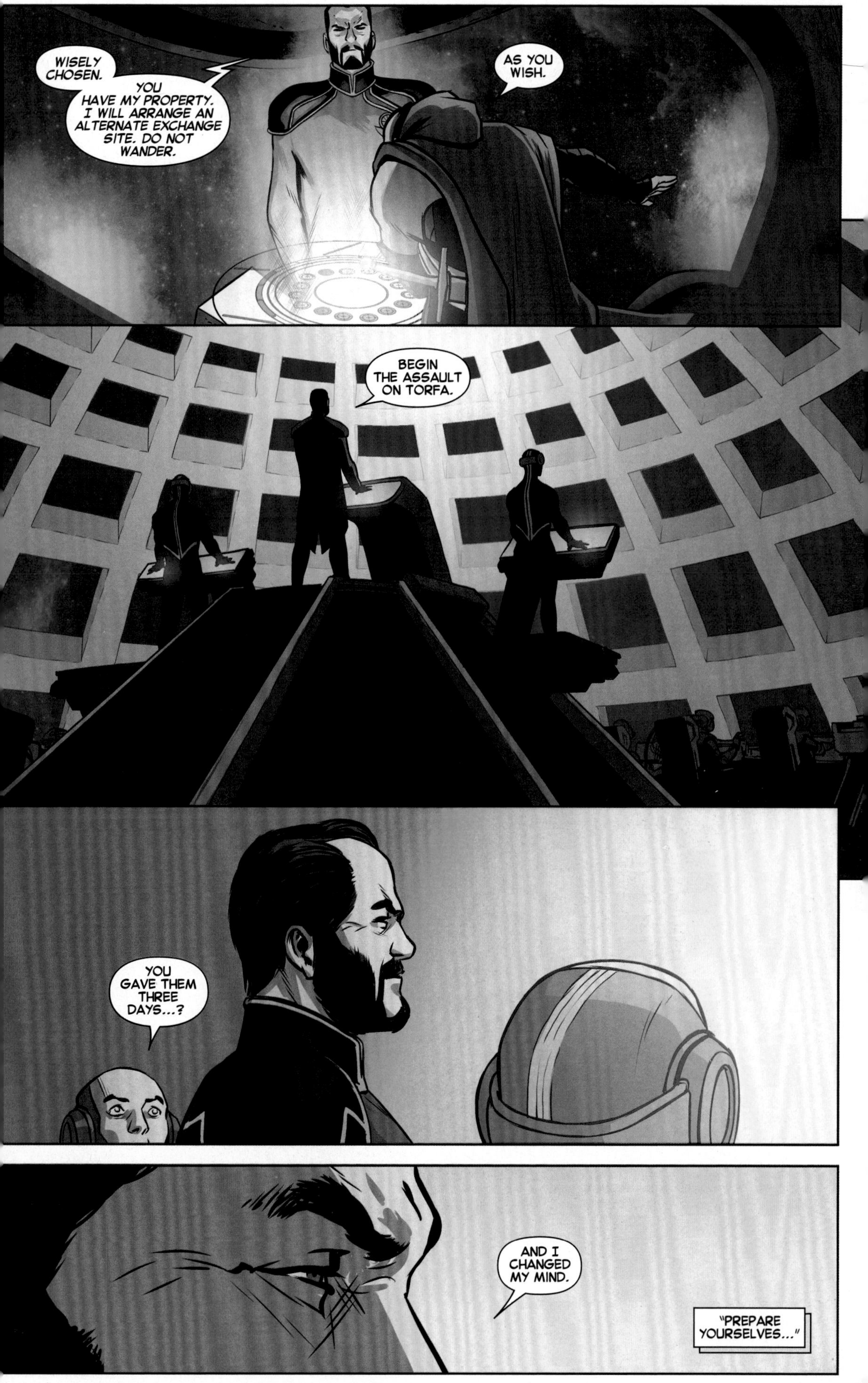
WISELY CHOSEN.
YOU HAVE MY PROPERTY. I WILL ARRANGE AN ALTERNATE EXCHANGE SITE. DO NOT WANDER.
AS YOU WISH.
BEGIN THE ASSAULT ON TORFA.
YOU GAVE THEM THREE DAYS...?
AND I CHANGED MY MIND.
"PREPARE YOURSELVES..."

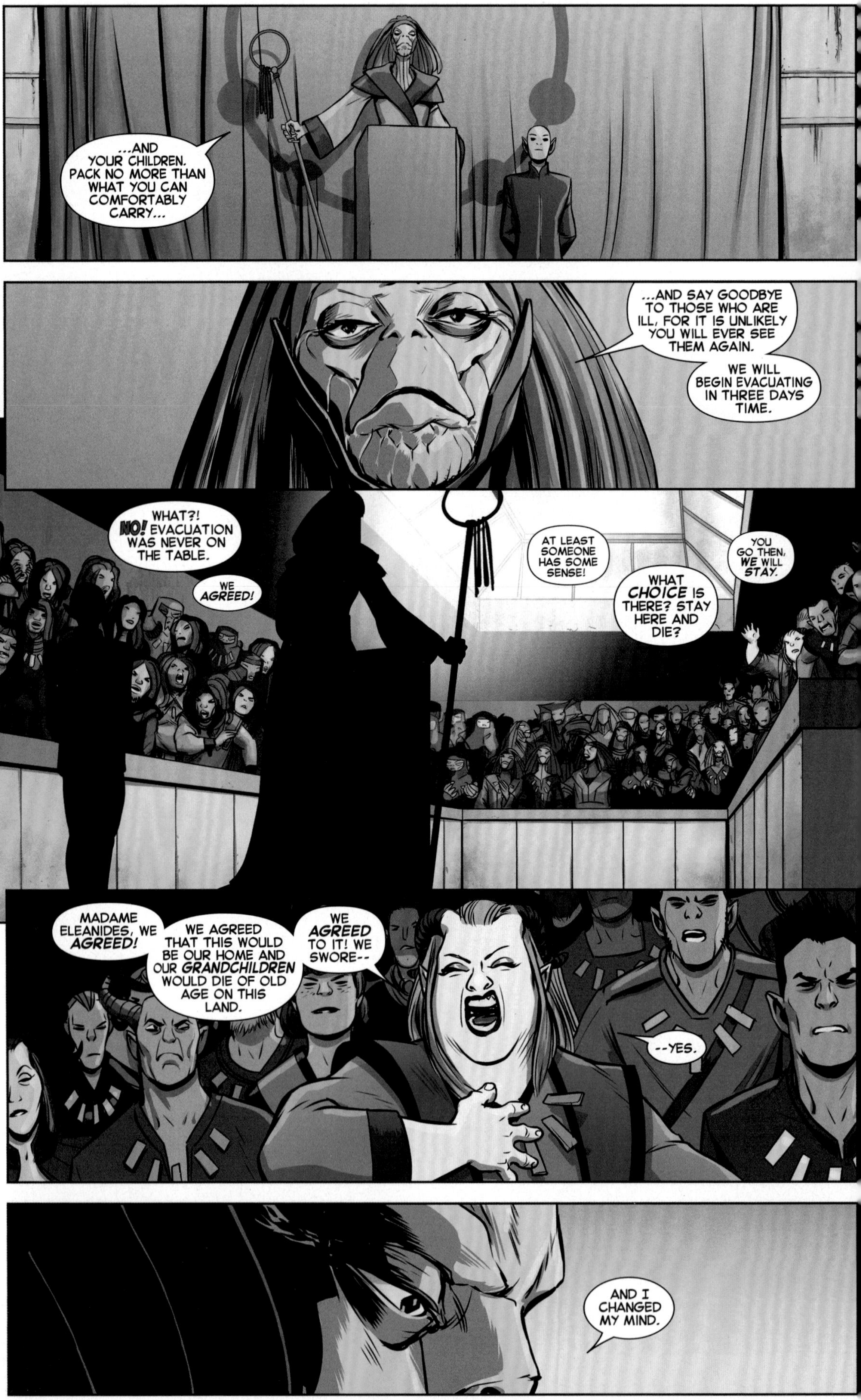
...AND YOUR CHILDREN. PACK NO MORE THAN WHAT YOU CAN COMFORTABLY CARRY...
...AND SAY GOODBYE TO THOSE WHO ARE ILL, FOR IT IS UNLIKELY YOU WILL EVER SEE THEM AGAIN.
WE WILL BEGIN EVACUATING IN THREE DAYS TIME.
WHAT?! NO! EVACUATION WAS NEVER ON THE TABLE.
WE AGREED!
AT LEAST SOMEONE HAS SOME SENSE!
WHAT CHOICE IS THERE? STAY HERE AND DIE?
YOU GO THEN, WE WILL STAY.
MADAME ELEANIDES, WE AGREED!
WE AGREED THAT THIS WOULD BE OUR HOME AND OUR GRANDCHILDREN WOULD DIE OF OLD AGE ON THIS LAND.
WE AGREED TO IT! WE SWORE--
--YES.
AND I CHANGED MY MIND.

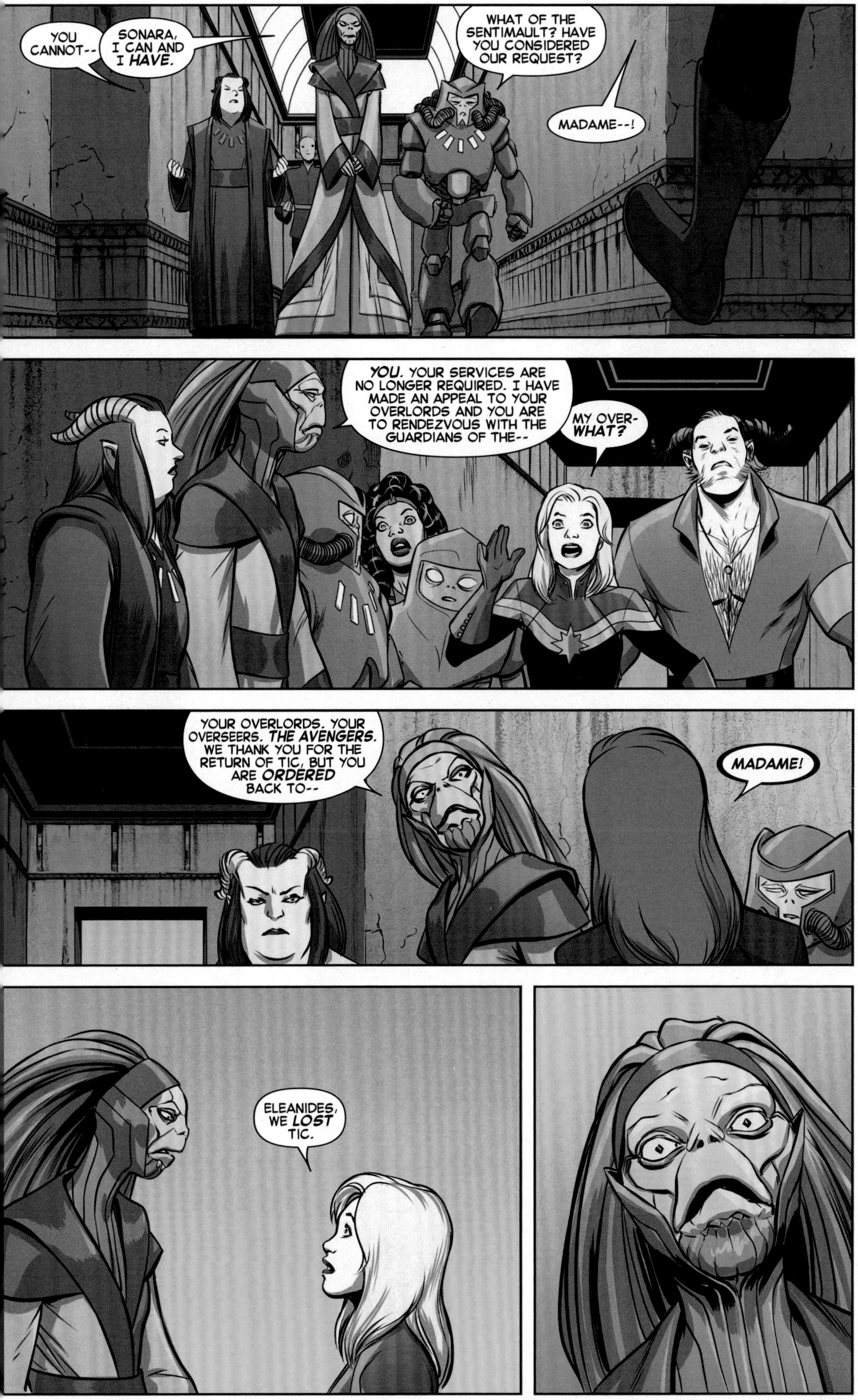
YOU CANNOT--
SONARA, I CAN AND I HAVE.
WHAT OF THE SENTIMAULT? HAVE YOU CONSIDERED OUR REQUEST?
MADAME--!
YOU. YOUR SERVICES ARE NO LONGER REQUIRED. I HAVE MADE AN APPEAL TO YOUR OVERLORDS AND YOU ARE TO RENDEZVOUS WITH THE GUARDIANS OF THE--
MY OVER-WHAT?
YOUR OVERLORDS. YOUR OVERSEERS. THE AVENGERS. WE THANK YOU FOR THE RETURN OF TIC, BUT YOU ARE ORDERED BACK TO--
MADAME!
ELEANIDES, WE LOST TIC.

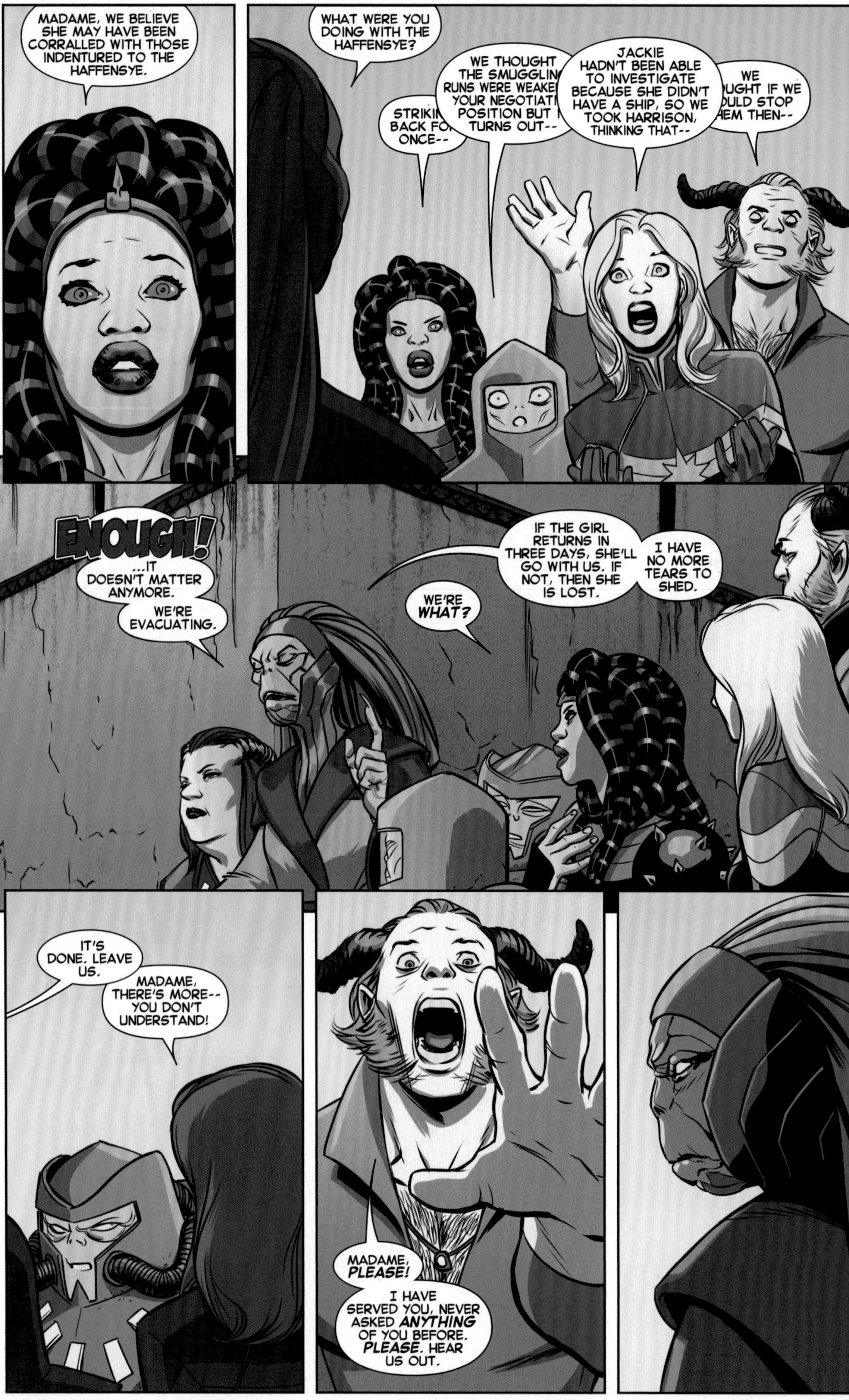
MADAME, WE BELIEVE SHE MAY HAVE BEEN CORRALLED WITH THOSE INDENTURED TO THE HAFFENSYE.
WHAT WERE YOU DOING WITH THE HAFFENSYE?
STRIKIN BACK FO ONCE--
WE THOUGHT THE SMUGGLIN RUNS WERE WEAKE YOUR NEGOTIATI POSITION BUT TURNS OUT--
JACKIE HADN'T BEEN ABLE TO INVESTIGATE BECAUSE SHE DIDN'T HAVE A SHIP, SO WE TOOK HARRISON, THINKING THAT--
WE OUGHT IF WE OULD STOP HEM THEN--
ENOUGH!
...IT DOESN'T MATTER ANYMORE.
WE'RE EVACUATING.
WE'RE WHAT?
IF THE GIRL RETURNS IN THREE DAYS, SHE'LL GO WITH US. IF NOT, THEN SHE IS LOST.
I HAVE NO MORE TEARS TO SHED.
IT'S DONE. LEAVE US.
MADAME, THERE'S MORE-- YOU DON'T UNDERSTAND!
MADAME, PLEASE!
I HAVE SERVED YOU, NEVER ASKED ANYTHING OF YOU BEFORE. PLEASE. HEAR US OUT.

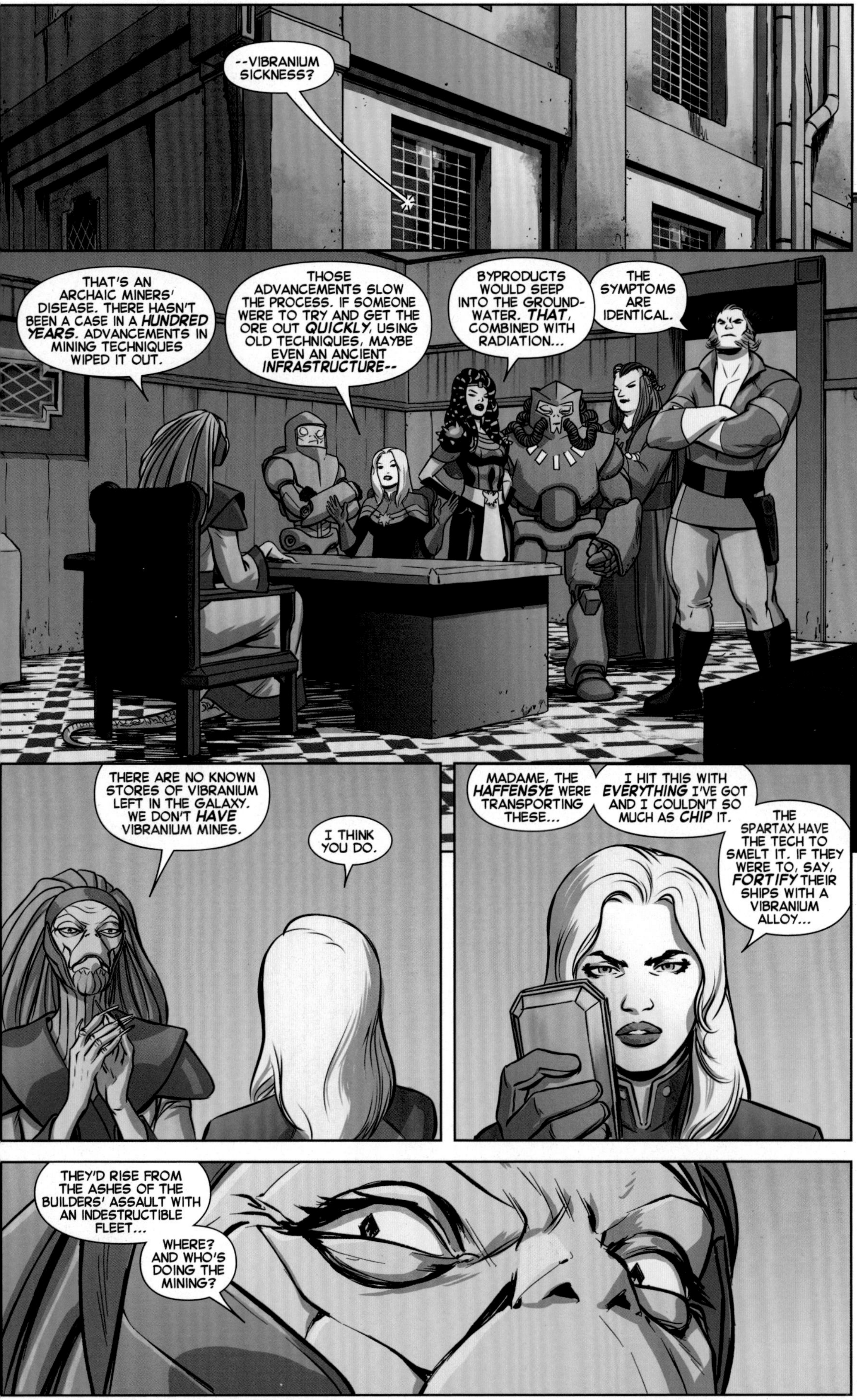
--VIBRANIUM SICKNESS?
THAT'S AN ARCHAIC MINERS' DISEASE. THERE HASN'T BEEN A CASE IN A HUNDRED YEARS. ADVANCEMENTS IN MINING TECHNIQUES WIPED IT OUT.
THOSE ADVANCEMENTS SLOW THE PROCESS. IF SOMEONE WERE TO TRY AND GET THE ORE OUT QUICKLY, USING OLD TECHNIQUES, MAYBE EVEN AN ANCIENT INFRASTRUCTURE--
BYPRODUCTS WOULD SEEP INTO THE GROUND-WATER. THAT, COMBINED WITH RADIATION...
THE SYMPTOMS ARE IDENTICAL.
THERE ARE NO KNOWN STORES OF VIBRANIUM LEFT IN THE GALAXY. WE DON'T HAVE VIBRANIUM MINES.
I THINK YOU DO.
MADAME, THE HAFFENSYE WERE TRANSPORTING THESE...
I HIT THIS WITH EVERYTHING I'VE GOT AND I COULDN'T SO MUCH AS CHIP IT.
THE SPARTAX HAVE THE TECH TO SMELT IT. IF THEY WERE TO, SAY, FORTIFY THEIR SHIPS WITH A VIBRANIUM ALLOY...
THEY'D RISE FROM THE ASHES OF THE BUILDERS' ASSAULT WITH AN INDESTRUCTIBLE FLEET...
WHERE? AND WHO'S DOING THE MINING?

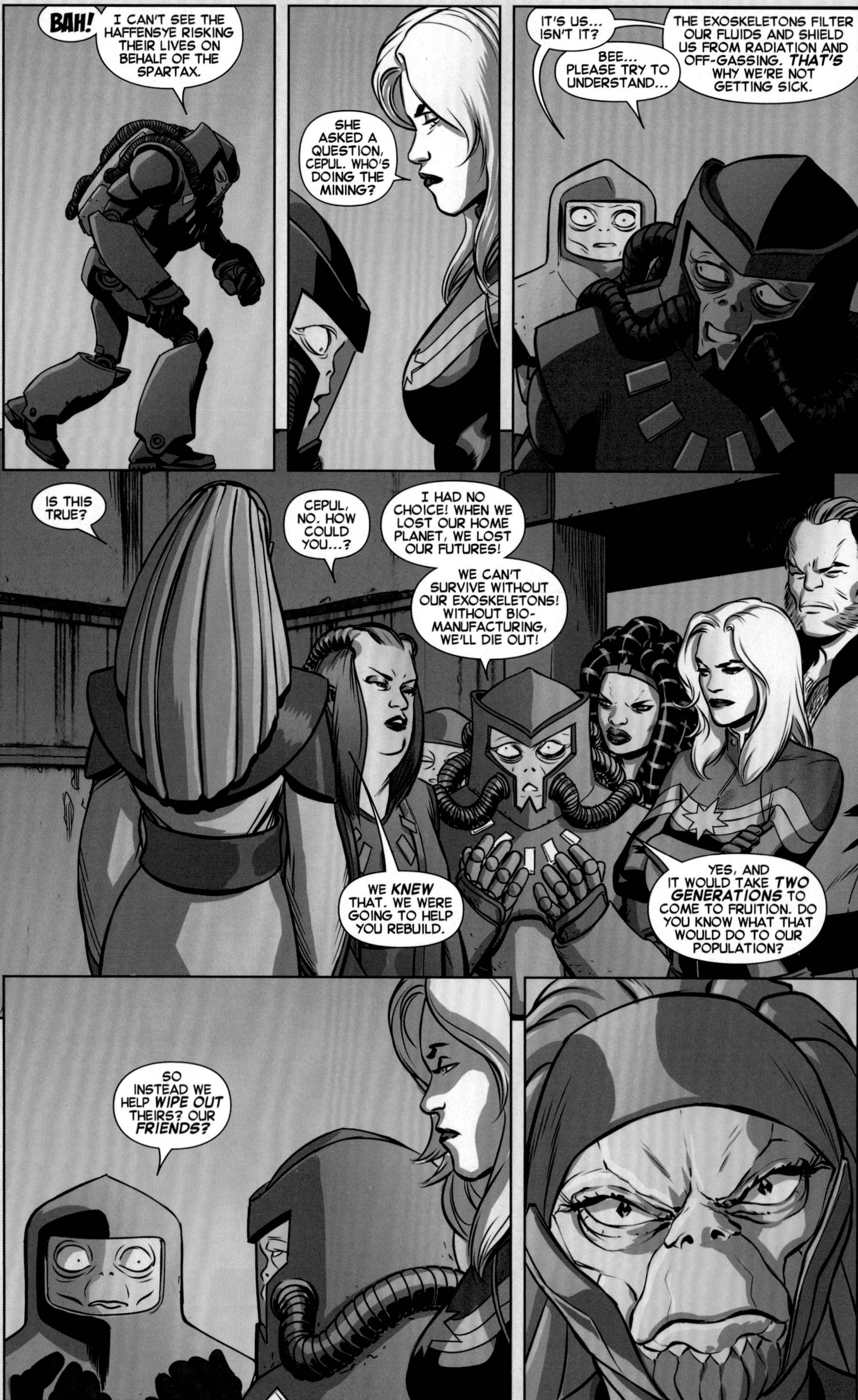
BAH!
I CAN'T SEE THE HAFFENSYE RISKING THEIR LIVES ON BEHALF OF THE SPARTAX.
SHE ASKED A QUESTION, CEPUL. WHO'S DOING THE MINING?
IT'S US... ISN'T IT?
BEE... PLEASE TRY TO UNDERSTAND...
THE EXOSKELETONS FILTER OUR FLUIDS AND SHIELD US FROM RADIATION AND OFF-GASSING. THAT'S WHY WE'RE NOT GETTING SICK.
IS THIS TRUE?
CEPUL, NO. HOW COULD YOU...?
I HAD NO CHOICE! WHEN WE LOST OUR HOME PLANET, WE LOST OUR FUTURES!
WE CAN'T SURVIVE WITHOUT OUR EXOSKELETONS! WITHOUT BIO-MANUFACTURING, WE'LL DIE OUT!
WE KNEW THAT. WE WERE GOING TO HELP YOU REBUILD.
YES, AND IT WOULD TAKE TWO GENERATIONS TO COME TO FRUITION. DO YOU KNOW WHAT THAT WOULD DO TO OUR POPULATION?
SO INSTEAD WE HELP WIPE OUT THEIRS? OUR FRIENDS?

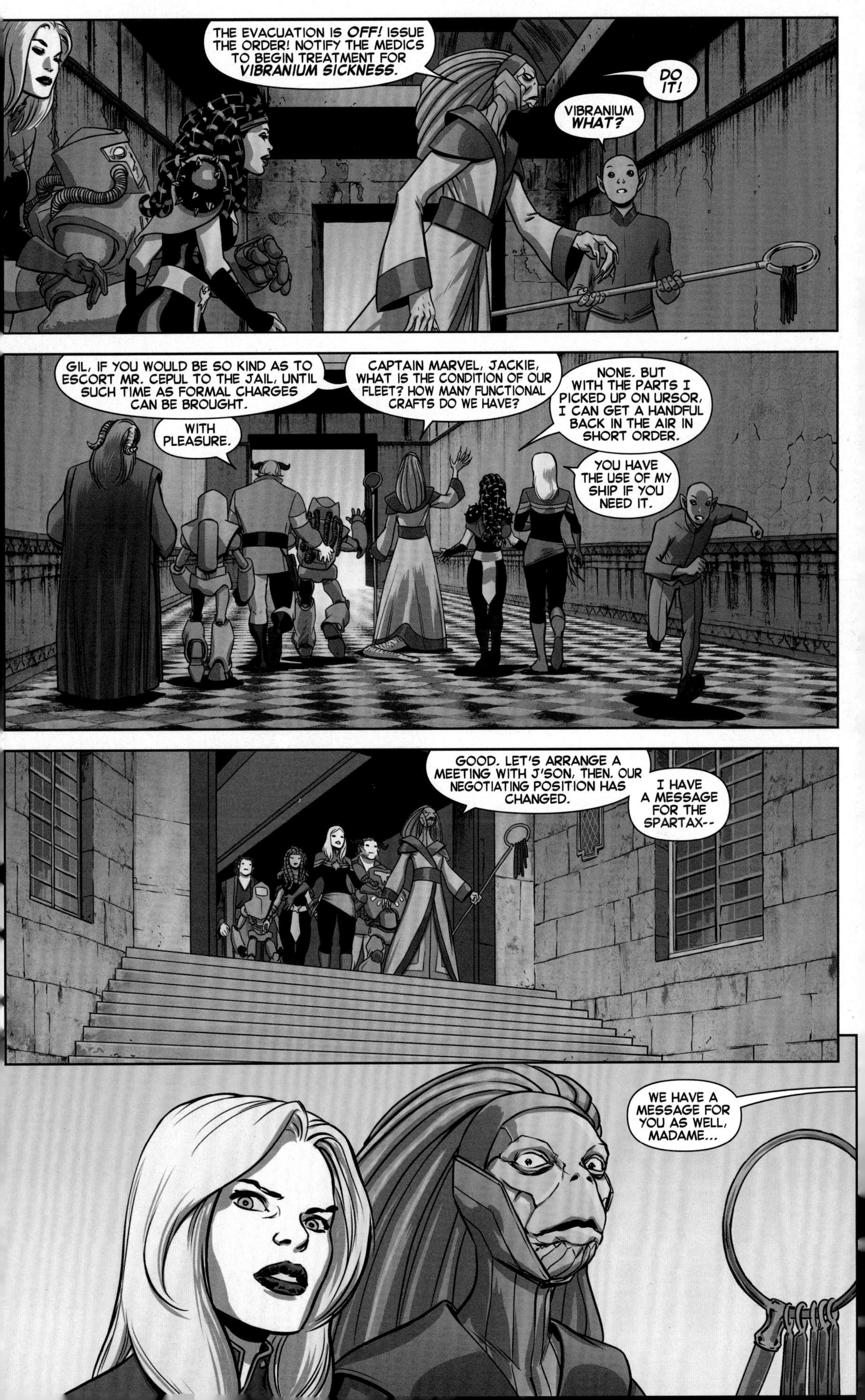
THE EVACUATION IS OFF! ISSUE THE ORDER! NOTIFY THE MEDICS TO BEGIN TREATMENT FOR VIBRANIUM SICKNESS.
DO IT!
VIBRANIUM WHAT?
GIL, IF YOU WOULD BE SO KIND AS TO ESCORT MR. CEPUL TO THE JAIL, UNTIL SUCH TIME AS FORMAL CHARGES CAN BE BROUGHT.
WITH PLEASURE.
CAPTAIN MARVEL, JACKIE, WHAT IS THE CONDITION OF OUR FLEET? HOW MANY FUNCTIONAL CRAFTS DO WE HAVE?
NONE. BUT WITH THE PARTS I PICKED UP ON URSOR, I CAN GET A HANDFUL BACK IN THE AIR IN SHORT ORDER.
YOU HAVE THE USE OF MY SHIP IF YOU NEED IT.
GOOD. LET'S ARRANGE A MEETING WITH J'SON, THEN. OUR NEGOTIATING POSITION HAS CHANGED.
I HAVE A MESSAGE FOR THE SPARTAX--
WE HAVE A MESSAGE FOR YOU AS WELL, MADAME...

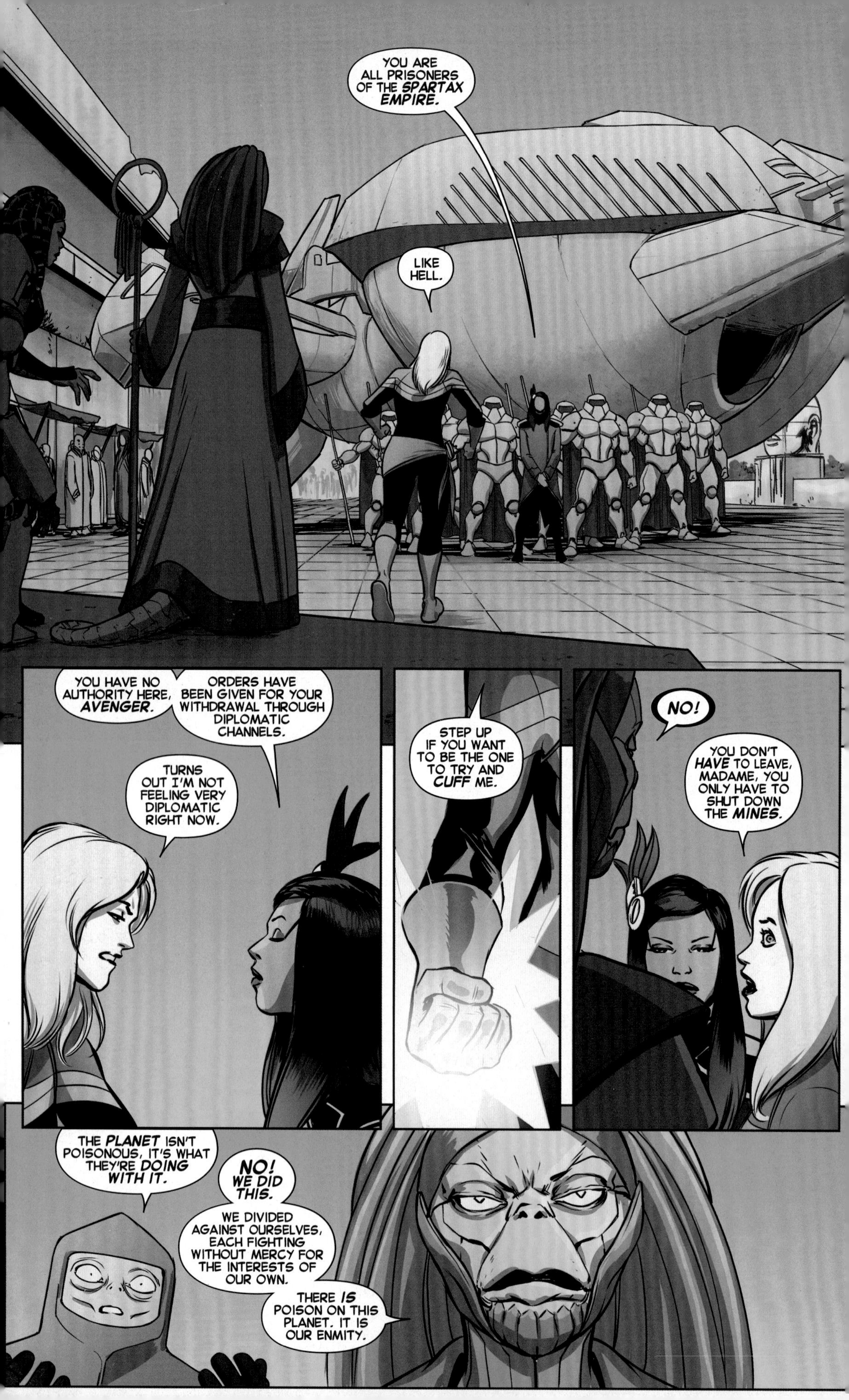

YOU ARE ALL PRISONERS OF THE SPARTAX EMPIRE.
LIKE HELL.
YOU HAVE NO AUTHORITY HERE, AVENGER.
ORDERS HAVE BEEN GIVEN FOR YOUR WITHDRAWAL THROUGH DIPLOMATIC CHANNELS.
TURNS OUT I'M NOT FEELING VERY DIPLOMATIC RIGHT NOW.
STEP UP IF YOU WANT TO BE THE ONE TO TRY AND CUFF ME.
NO!
YOU DON'T HAVE TO LEAVE, MADAME, YOU ONLY HAVE TO SHUT DOWN THE MINES.
THE PLANET ISN'T POISONOUS, IT'S WHAT THEY'RE DOING WITH IT.
NO! WE DID THIS.
WE DIVIDED AGAINST OURSELVES, EACH FIGHTING WITHOUT MERCY FOR THE INTERESTS OF OUR OWN.
THERE IS POISON ON THIS PLANET. IT IS OUR ENMITY.

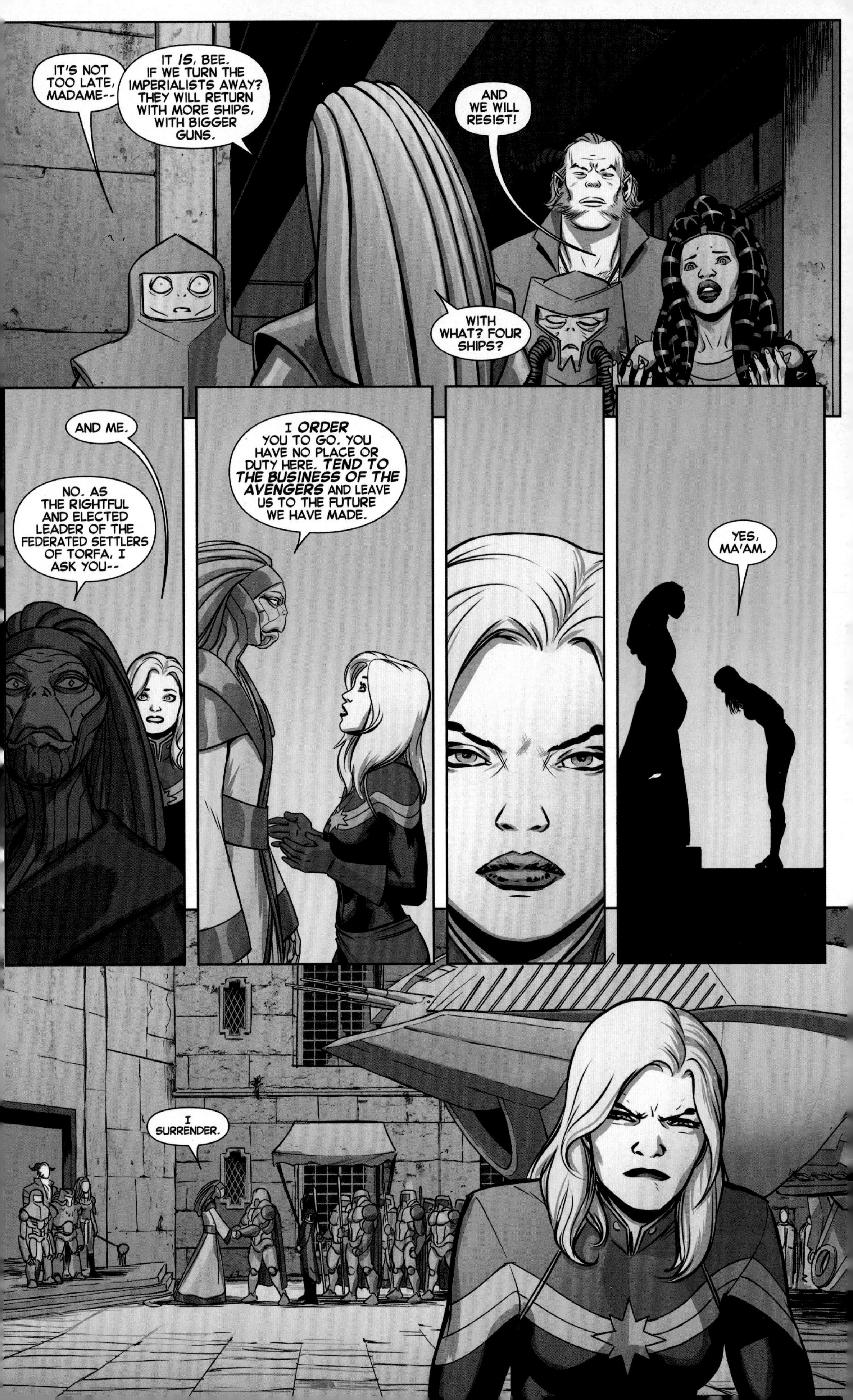
IT'S NOT TOO LATE, MADAME--
IT IS, BEE. IF WE TURN THE IMPERIALISTS AWAY? THEY WILL RETURN WITH MORE SHIPS, WITH BIGGER GUNS.
AND WE WILL RESIST!
WITH WHAT? FOUR SHIPS?
AND ME.
NO. AS THE RIGHTFUL AND ELECTED LEADER OF THE FEDERATED SETTLERS OF TORFA, I ASK YOU--
I ORDER YOU TO GO. YOU HAVE NO PLACE OR DUTY HERE. TEND TO THE BUSINESS OF THE AVENGERS AND LEAVE US TO THE FUTURE WE HAVE MADE.
YES, MA'AM.
I SURRENDER.

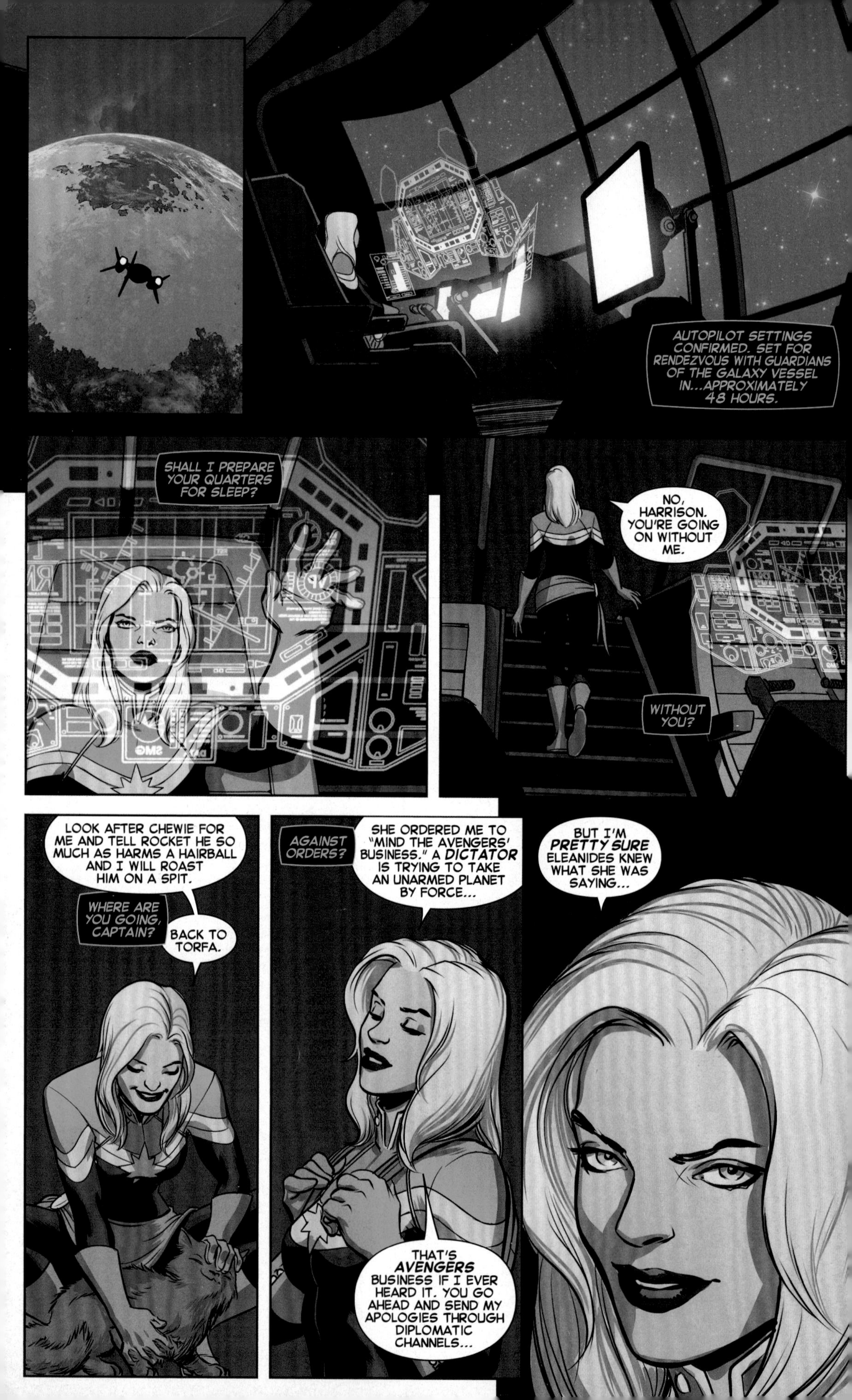
AUTOPILOT SETTINGS CONFIRMED. SET FOR RENDEZVOUS WITH GUARDIANS OF THE GALAXY VESSEL IN...APPROXIMATELY 48 HOURS.
SHALL I PREPARE YOUR QUARTERS FOR SLEEP?
NO, HARRISON. YOU'RE GOING ON WITHOUT ME.
WITHOUT YOU?
LOOK AFTER CHEWIE FOR ME AND TELL ROCKET HE SO MUCH AS HARMS A HAIRBALL AND I WILL ROAST HIM ON A SPIT.
WHERE ARE YOU GOING, CAPTAIN?
BACK TO TORFA.
AGAINST ORDERS?
SHE ORDERED ME TO "MIND THE AVENGERS' BUSINESS." A DICTATOR IS TRYING TO TAKE AN UNARMED PLANET BY FORCE...
THAT'S AVENGERS BUSINESS IF I EVER HEARD IT. YOU GO AHEAD AND SEND MY APOLOGIES THROUGH DIPLOMATIC CHANNELS...
BUT I'M PRETTY SURE ELEANIDES KNEW WHAT SHE WAS SAYING...

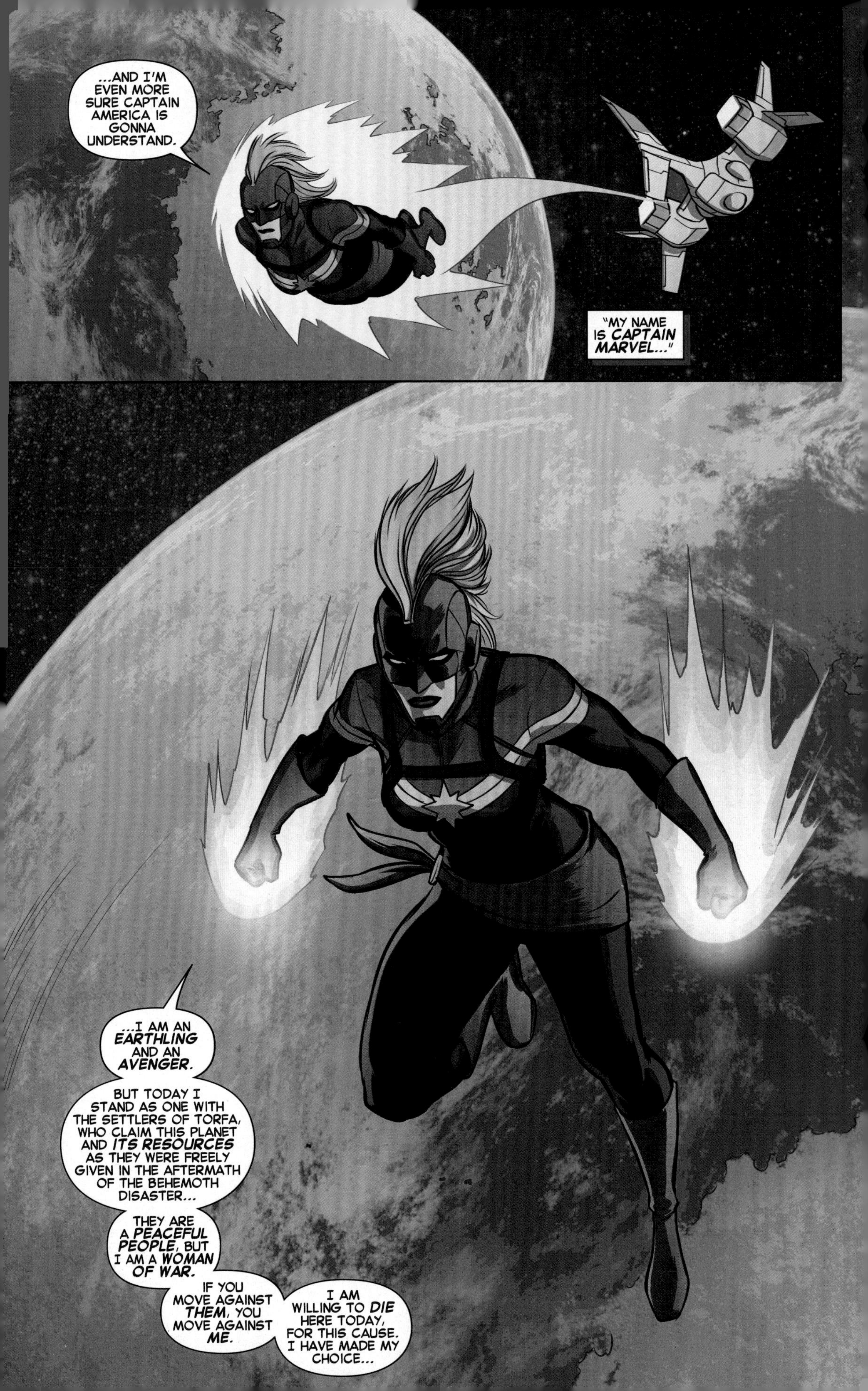
...AND I'M EVEN MORE SURE CAPTAIN AMERICA IS GONNA UNDERSTAND.
"MY NAME IS CAPTAIN MARVEL..."
...I AM AN EARTHLING AND AN AVENGER.
BUT TODAY I STAND AS ONE WITH THE SETTLERS OF TORFA, WHO CLAIM THIS PLANET AND ITS RESOURCES AS THEY WERE FREELY GIVEN IN THE AFTERMATH OF THE BEHEMOTH DISASTER...
THEY ARE A PEACEFUL PEOPLE, BUT I AM A WOMAN OF WAR.
IF YOU MOVE AGAINST THEM, YOU MOVE AGAINST ME.
I AM WILLING TO DIE HERE TODAY, FOR THIS CAUSE. I HAVE MADE MY CHOICE...

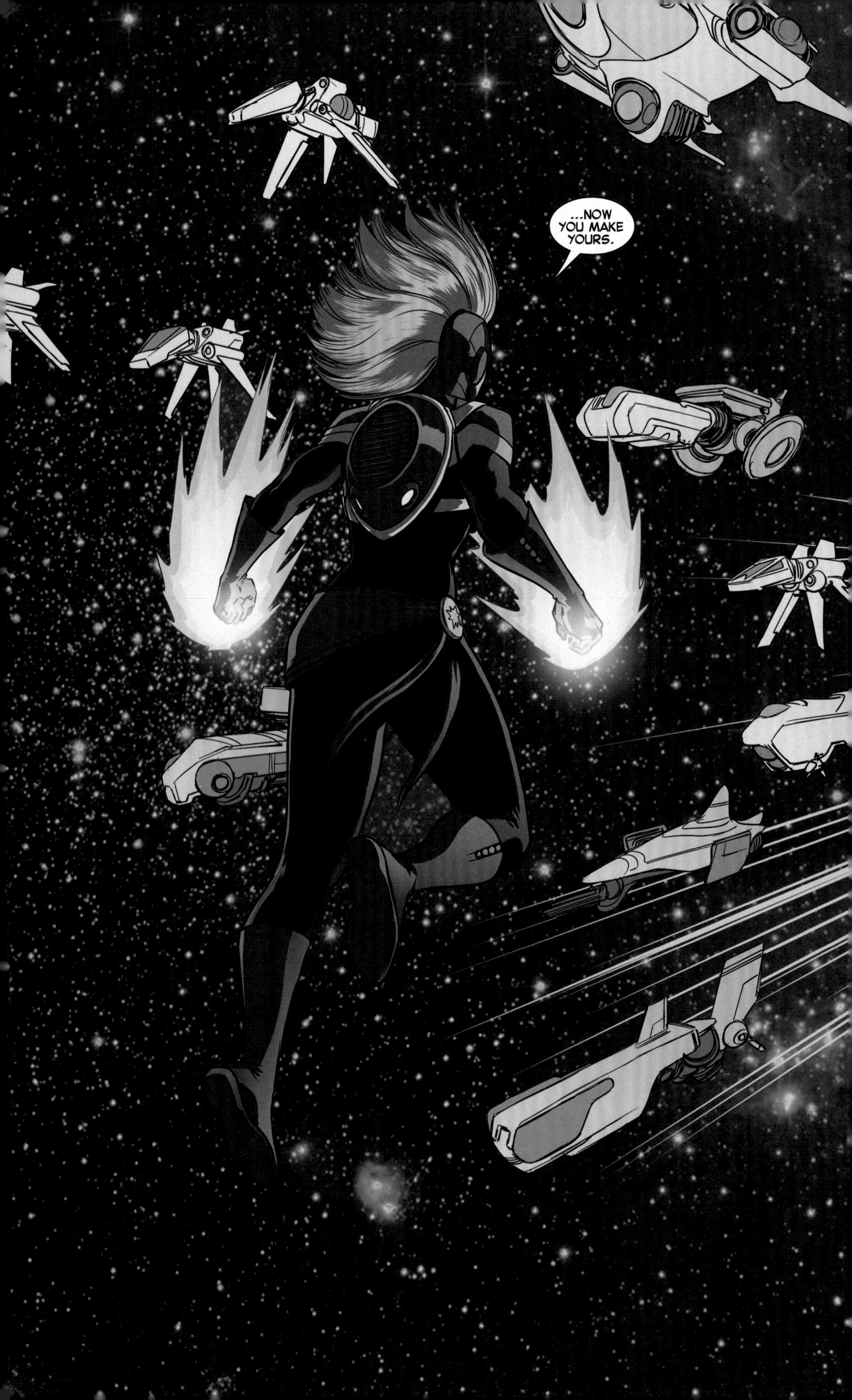
...NOW YOU MAKE YOURS.

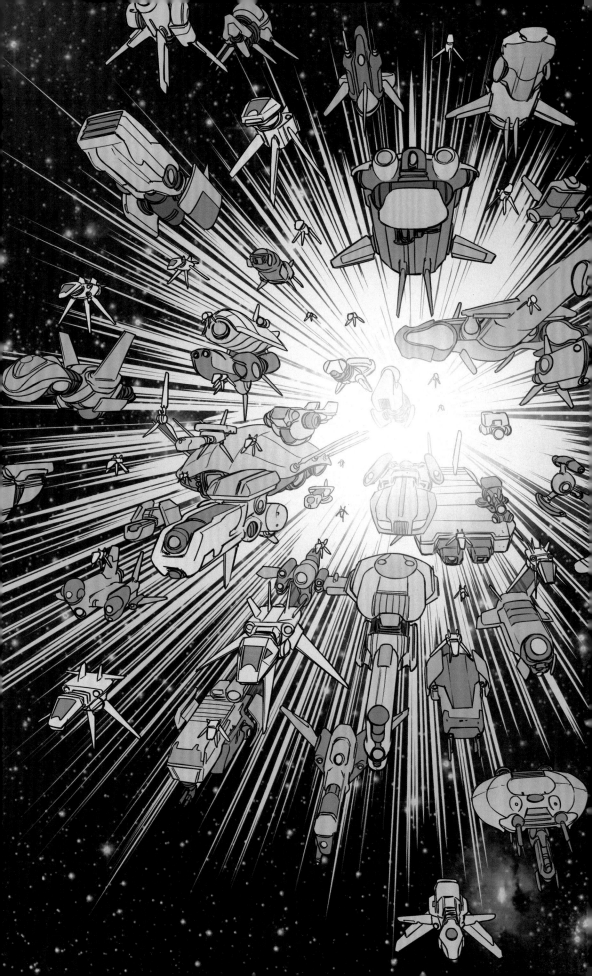

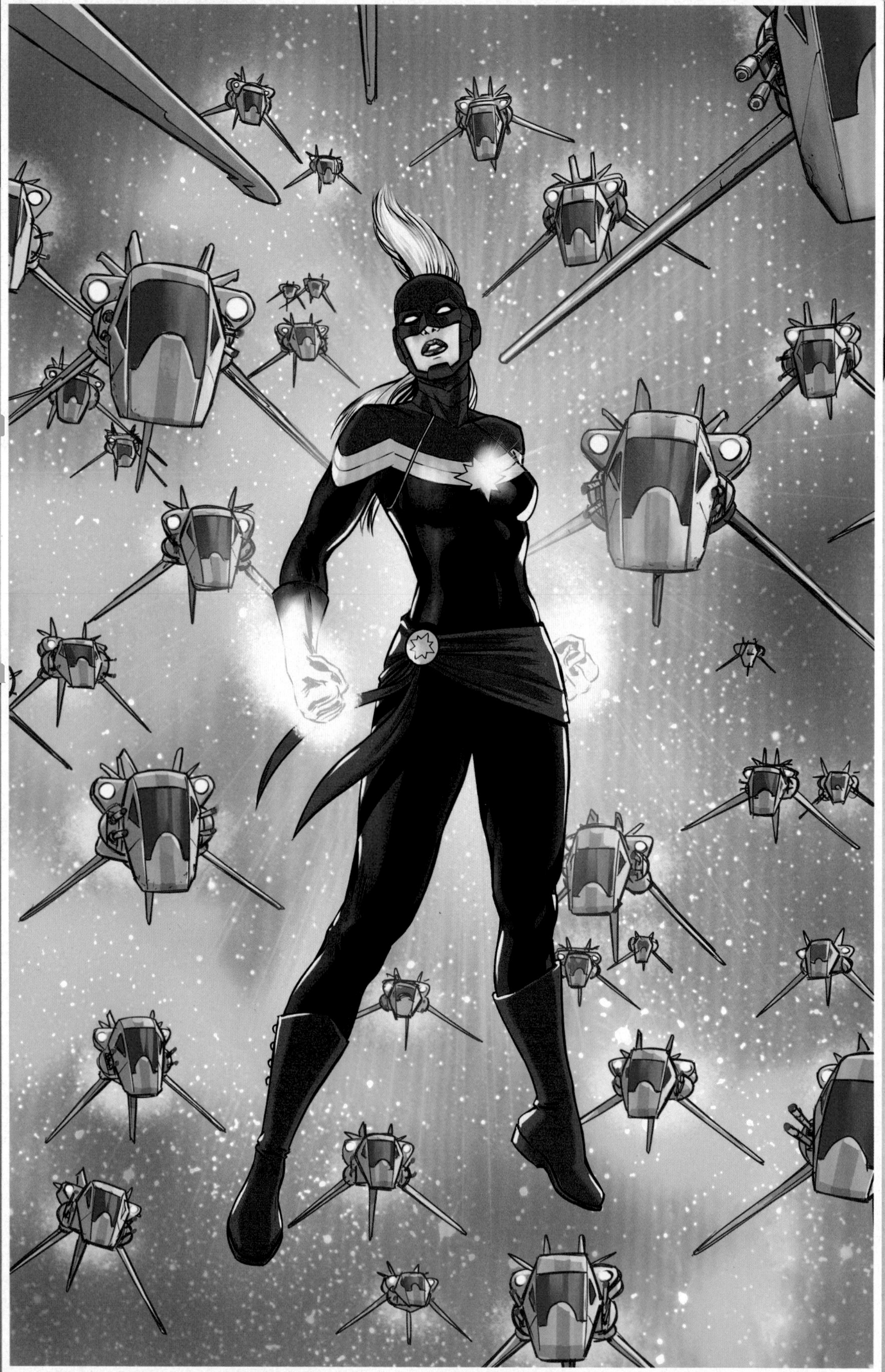

SIX

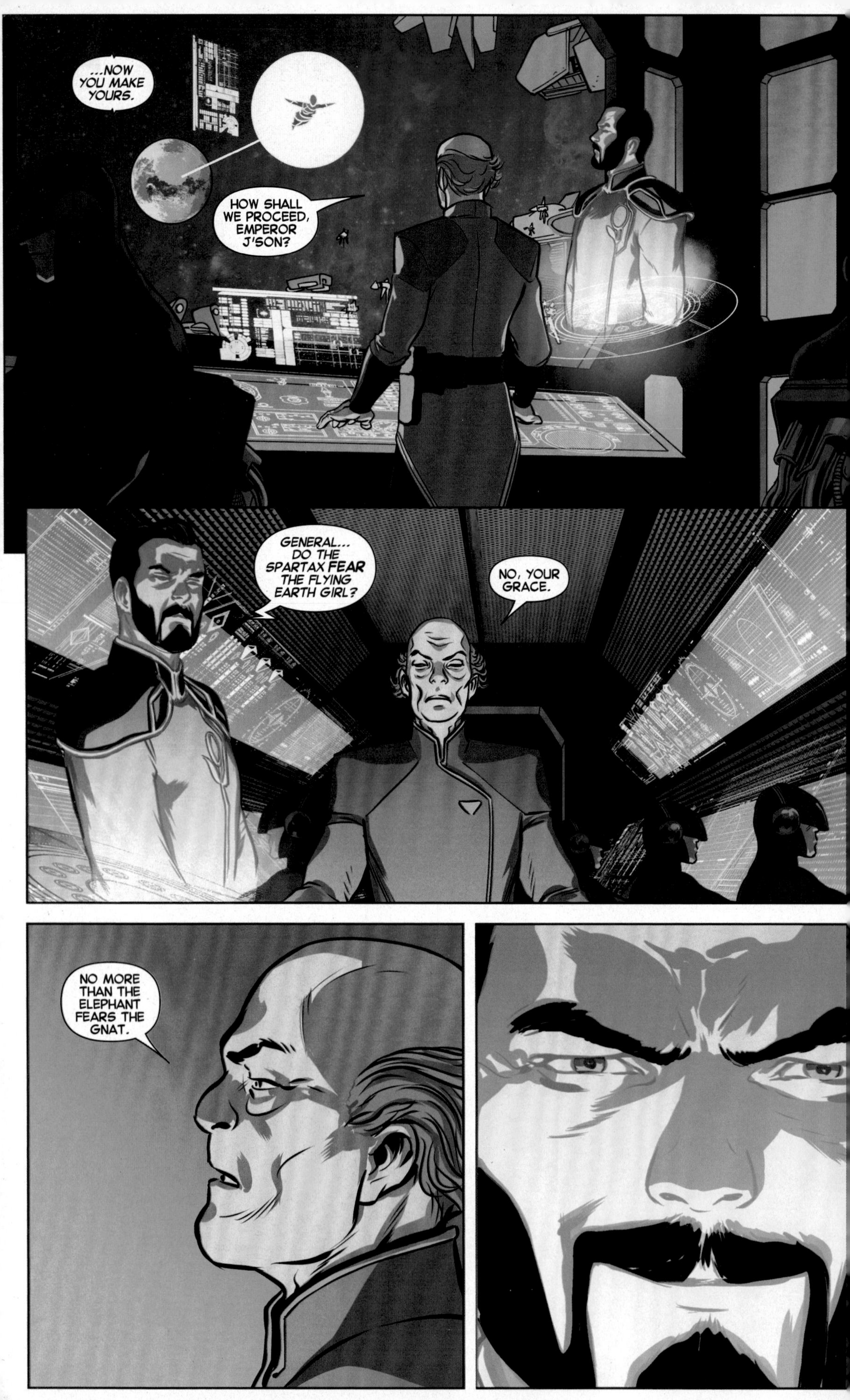
...NOW YOU MAKE YOURS.
HOW SHALL WE PROCEED, EMPEROR J'SON?
GENERAL... DO THE SPARTAX FEAR THE FLYING EARTH GIRL?
NO, YOUR GRACE.
NO MORE THAN THE ELEPHANT FEARS THE GNAT.

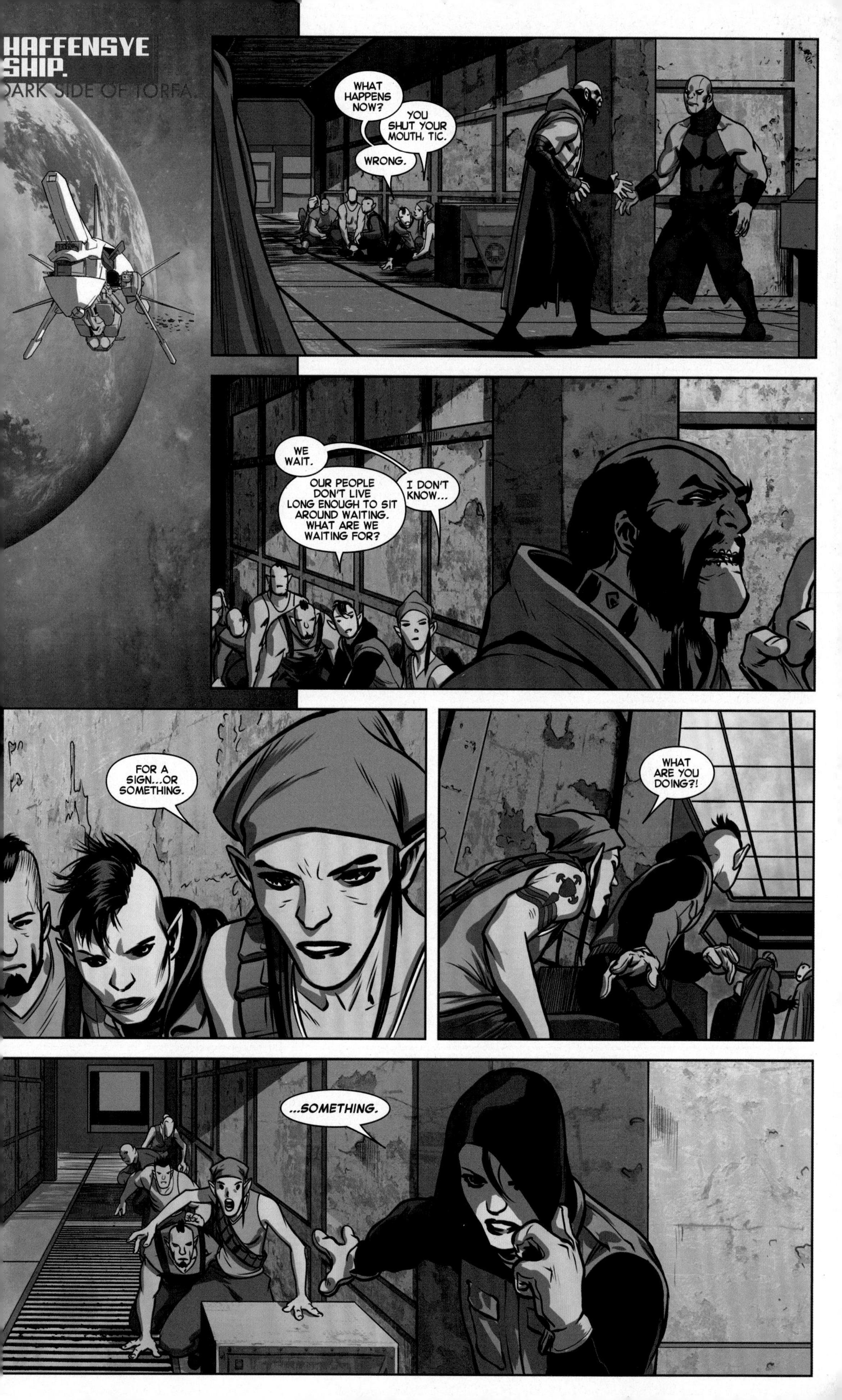

HAFFENSYE SHIP.
DARK SIDE OF TORFA.
WHAT HAPPENS NOW?
YOU SHUT YOUR MOUTH, TIC.
WRONG.
WE WAIT.
I DON'T KNOW...
OUR PEOPLE DON'T LIVE LONG ENOUGH TO SIT AROUND WAITING. WHAT ARE WE WAITING FOR?
FOR A SIGN...OR SOMETHING.
WHAT ARE YOU DOING?!
...SOMETHING.

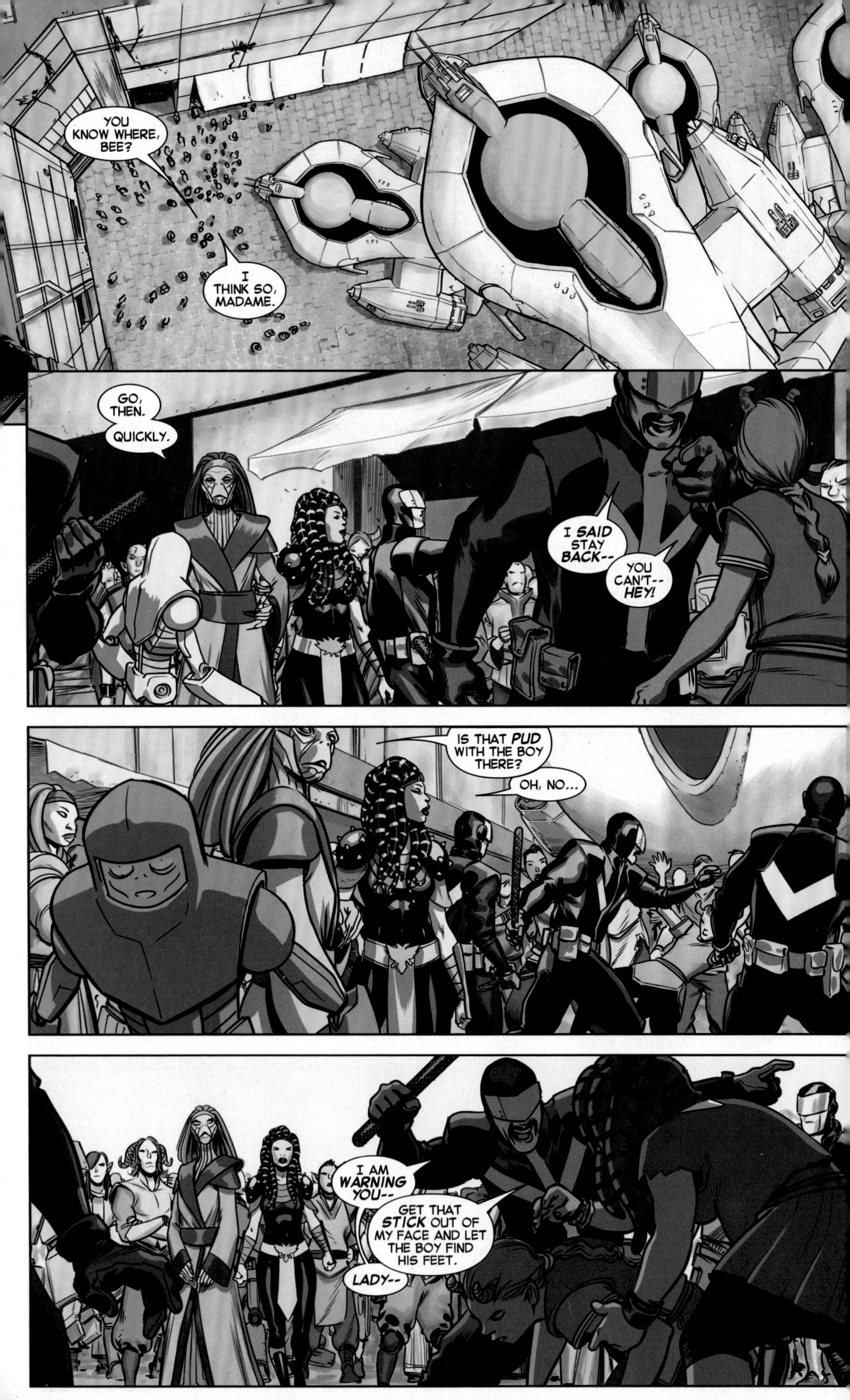
YOU KNOW WHERE, BEE?
I THINK SO, MADAME.
GO, THEN.
QUICKLY.
I SAID STAY BACK--
YOU CAN'T-- HEY!
IS THAT PUD WITH THE BOY THERE?
OH, NO...
I AM WARNING YOU--
GET THAT STICK OUT OF MY FACE AND LET THE BOY FIND HIS FEET.
LADY--

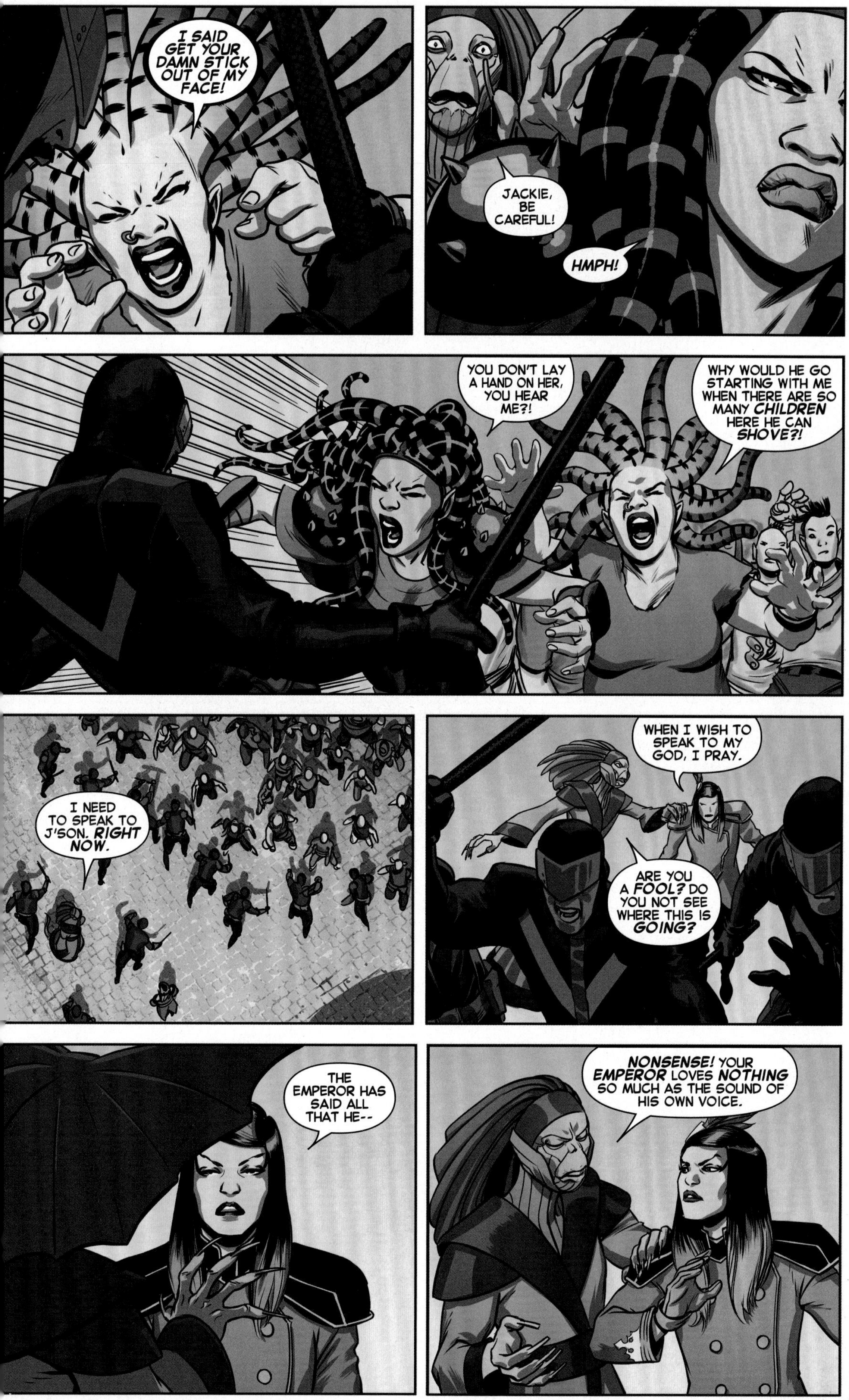
I SAID GET YOUR DAMN STICK OUT OF MY FACE!
JACKIE, BE CAREFUL!
HMPH!
YOU DON'T LAY A HAND ON HER, YOU HEAR ME?!
WHY WOULD HE GO STARTING WITH ME WHEN THERE ARE SO MANY CHILDREN HERE HE CAN SHOVE?!
I NEED TO SPEAK TO J'SON. RIGHT NOW.
WHEN I WISH TO SPEAK TO MY GOD, I PRAY.
ARE YOU A FOOL? DO YOU NOT SEE WHERE THIS IS GOING?
THE EMPEROR HAS SAID ALL THAT HE--
NONSENSE! YOUR EMPEROR LOVES NOTHING SO MUCH AS THE SOUND OF HIS OWN VOICE.

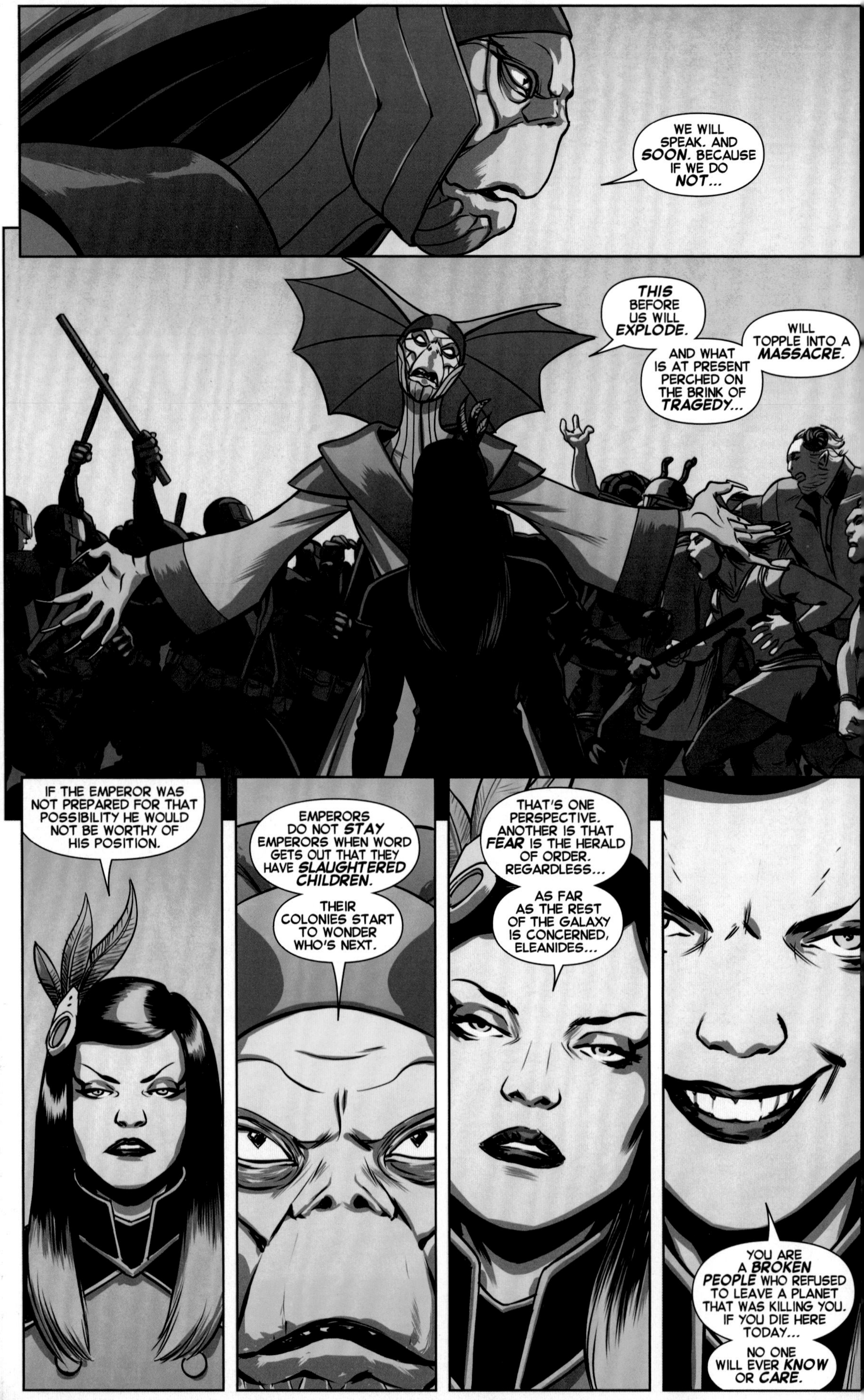
WE WILL SPEAK. AND SOON. BECAUSE IF WE DO NOT...
THIS BEFORE US WILL EXPLODE.
AND WHAT IS AT PRESENT PERCHED ON THE BRINK OF TRAGEDY...
WILL TOPPLE INTO A MASSACRE.
IF THE EMPEROR WAS NOT PREPARED FOR THAT POSSIBILITY HE WOULD NOT BE WORTHY OF HIS POSITION.
EMPERORS DO NOT STAY EMPERORS WHEN WORD GETS OUT THAT THEY HAVE SLAUGHTERED CHILDREN.
THEIR COLONIES START TO WONDER WHO'S NEXT.
THAT'S ONE PERSPECTIVE. ANOTHER IS THAT FEAR IS THE HERALD OF ORDER. REGARDLESS...
AS FAR AS THE REST OF THE GALAXY IS CONCERNED, ELEANIDES...
YOU ARE A BROKEN PEOPLE WHO REFUSED TO LEAVE A PLANET THAT WAS KILLING YOU. IF YOU DIE HERE TODAY...
NO ONE WILL EVER KNOW OR CARE.

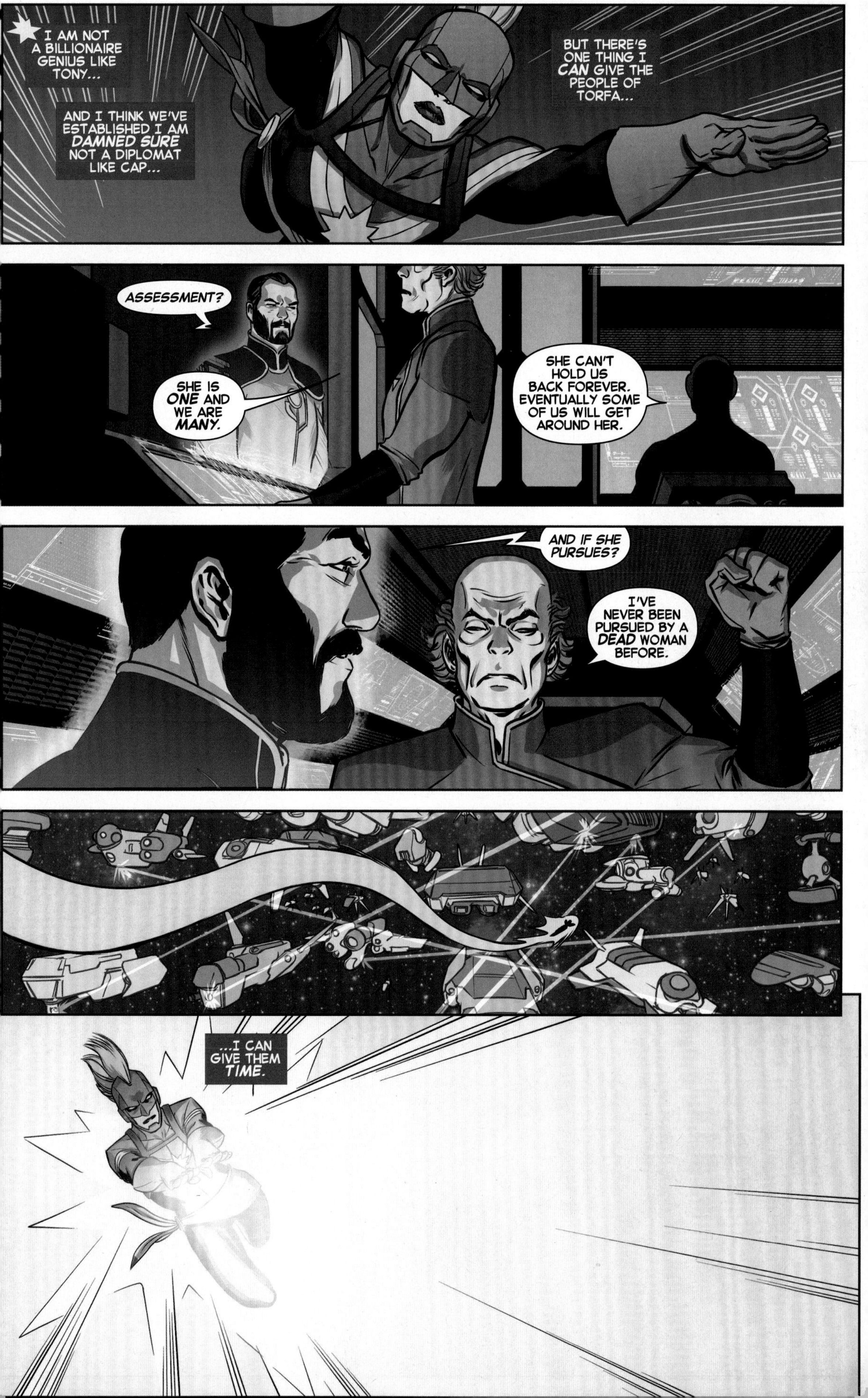
I AM NOT A BILLIONAIRE GENIUS LIKE TONY...
AND I THINK WE'VE ESTABLISHED I AM DAMNED SURE NOT A DIPLOMAT LIKE CAP...
BUT THERE'S ONE THING I CAN GIVE THE PEOPLE OF TORFA...
ASSESSMENT?
SHE IS ONE AND WE ARE MANY.
SHE CAN'T HOLD US BACK FOREVER. EVENTUALLY SOME OF US WILL GET AROUND HER.
AND IF SHE PURSUES?
I'VE NEVER BEEN PURSUED BY A DEAD WOMAN BEFORE.
...I CAN GIVE THEM TIME.

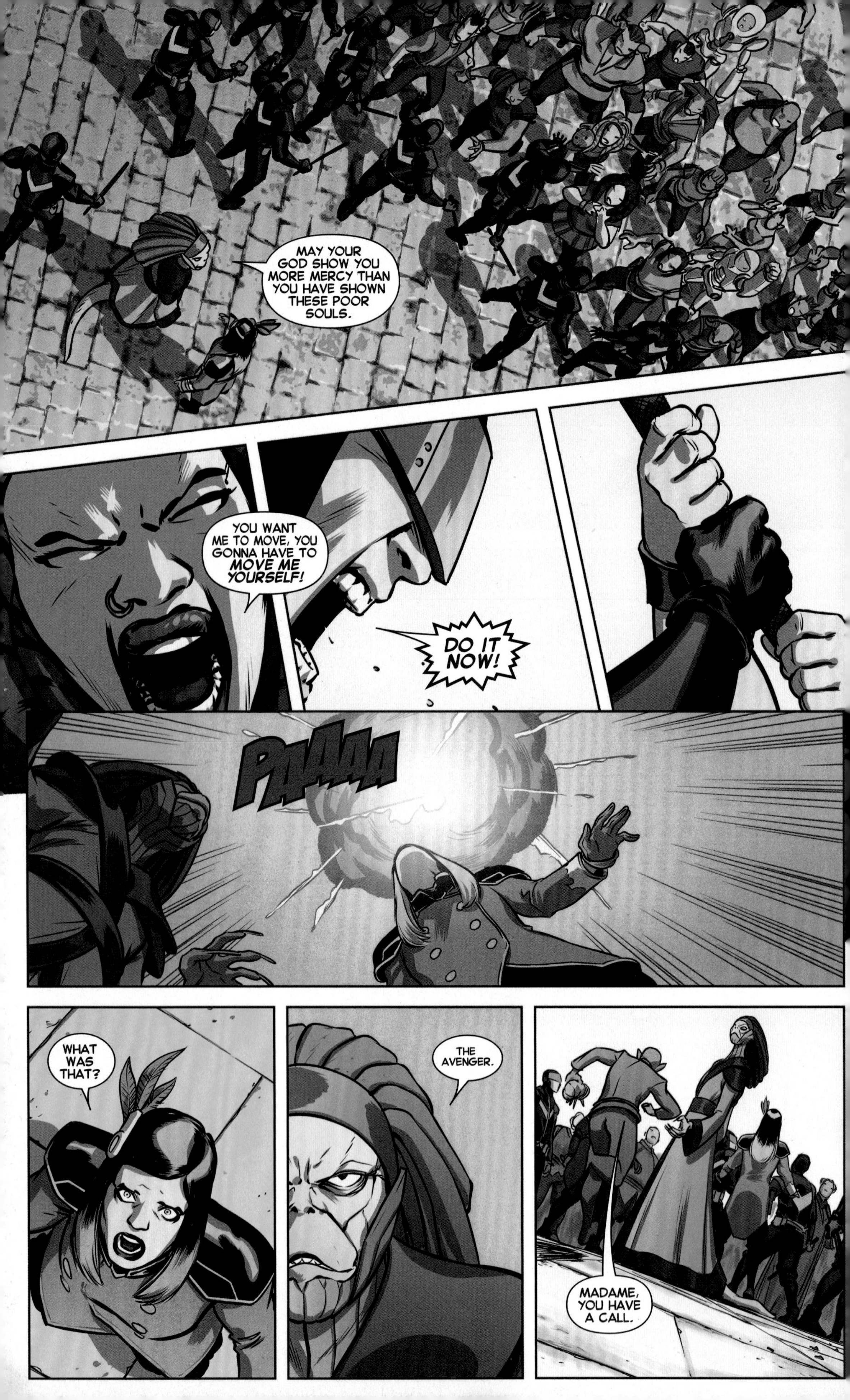
MAY YOUR GOD SHOW YOU MORE MERCY THAN YOU HAVE SHOWN THESE POOR SOULS.
YOU WANT ME TO MOVE, YOU GONNA HAVE TO *MOVE ME YOURSELF!*
DO IT NOW!
PHAAAA
WHAT WAS THAT?
THE AVENGER.
MADAME, YOU HAVE A CALL.

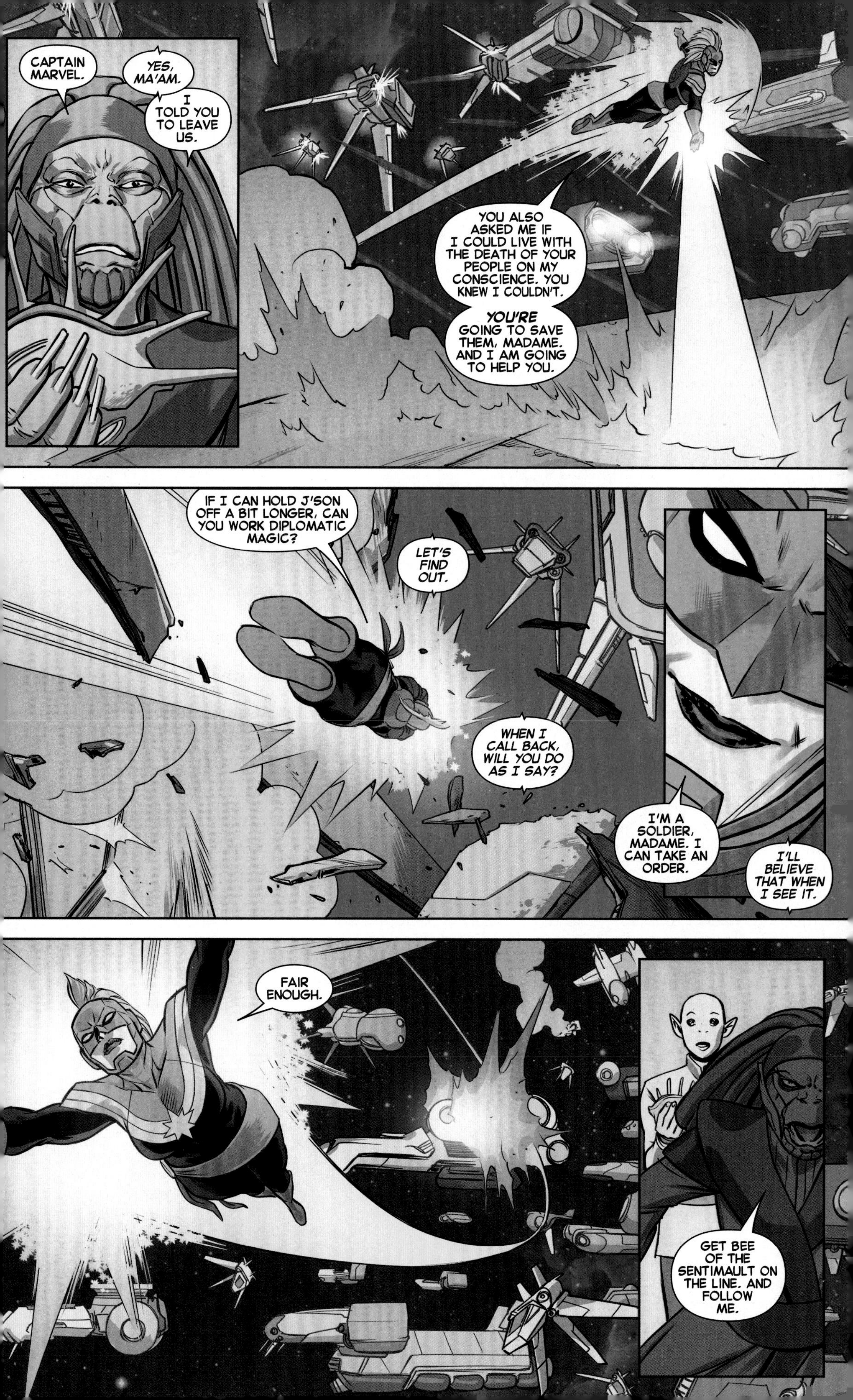
CAPTAIN MARVEL.
YES, MA'AM.
I TOLD YOU TO LEAVE US.
YOU ALSO ASKED ME IF I COULD LIVE WITH THE DEATH OF YOUR PEOPLE ON MY CONSCIENCE. YOU KNEW I COULDN'T.
YOU'RE GOING TO SAVE THEM, MADAME. AND I AM GOING TO HELP YOU.
IF I CAN HOLD J'SON OFF A BIT LONGER, CAN YOU WORK DIPLOMATIC MAGIC?
LET'S FIND OUT.
WHEN I CALL BACK, WILL YOU DO AS I SAY?
I'M A SOLDIER, MADAME. I CAN TAKE AN ORDER.
I'LL BELIEVE THAT WHEN I SEE IT.
FAIR ENOUGH.
GET BEE OF THE SENTIMAULT ON THE LINE. AND FOLLOW ME.

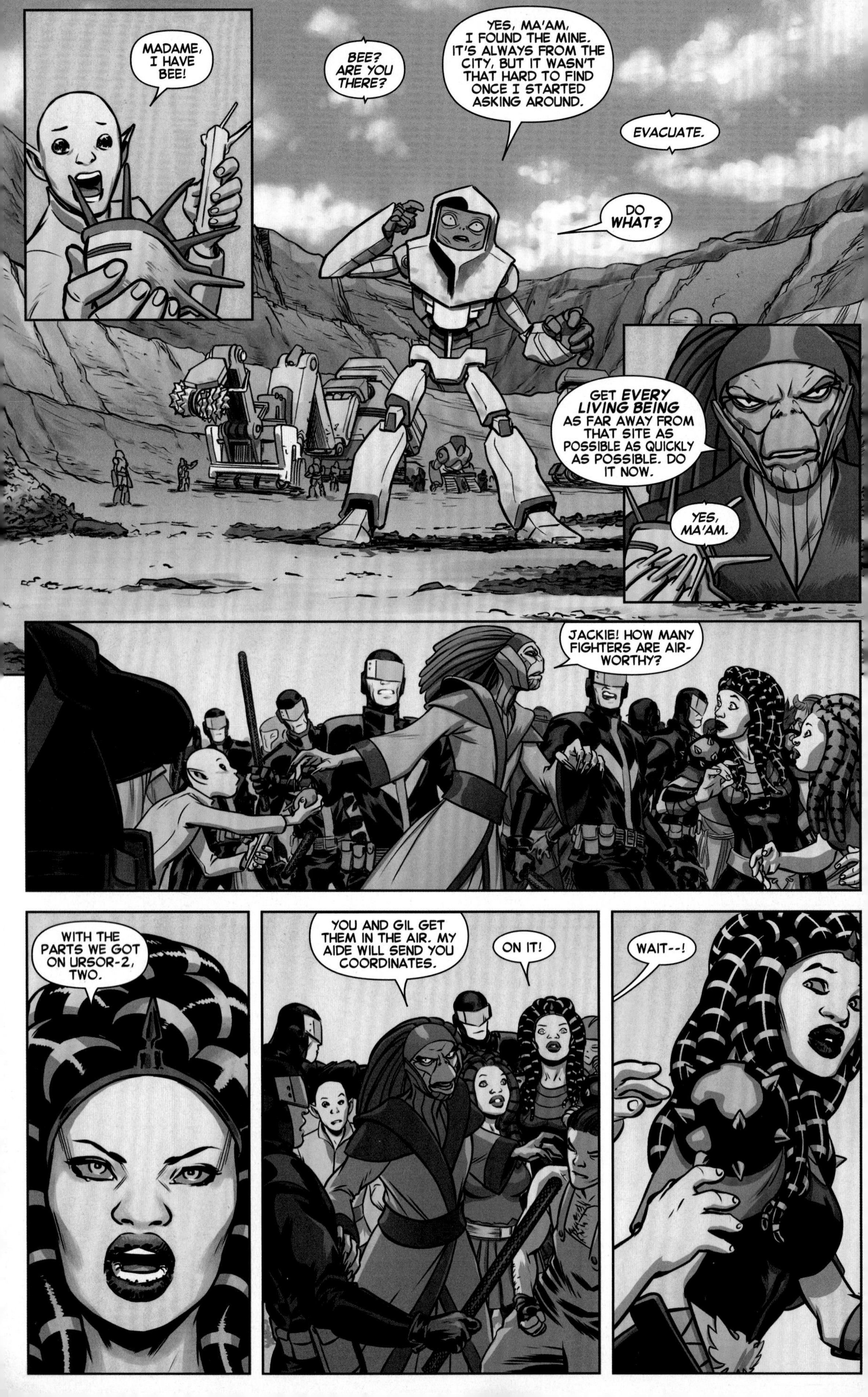
MADAME, I HAVE BEE!
BEE? ARE YOU THERE?
YES, MA'AM, I FOUND THE MINE. IT'S ALWAYS FROM THE CITY, BUT IT WASN'T THAT HARD TO FIND ONCE I STARTED ASKING AROUND.
EVACUATE.
DO WHAT?
GET EVERY LIVING BEING AS FAR AWAY FROM THAT SITE AS POSSIBLE AS QUICKLY AS POSSIBLE. DO IT NOW.
YES, MA'AM.
JACKIE! HOW MANY FIGHTERS ARE AIR-WORTHY?
WITH THE PARTS WE GOT ON URSOR-2, TWO.
YOU AND GIL GET THEM IN THE AIR. MY AIDE WILL SEND YOU COORDINATES.
ON IT!
WAIT--!

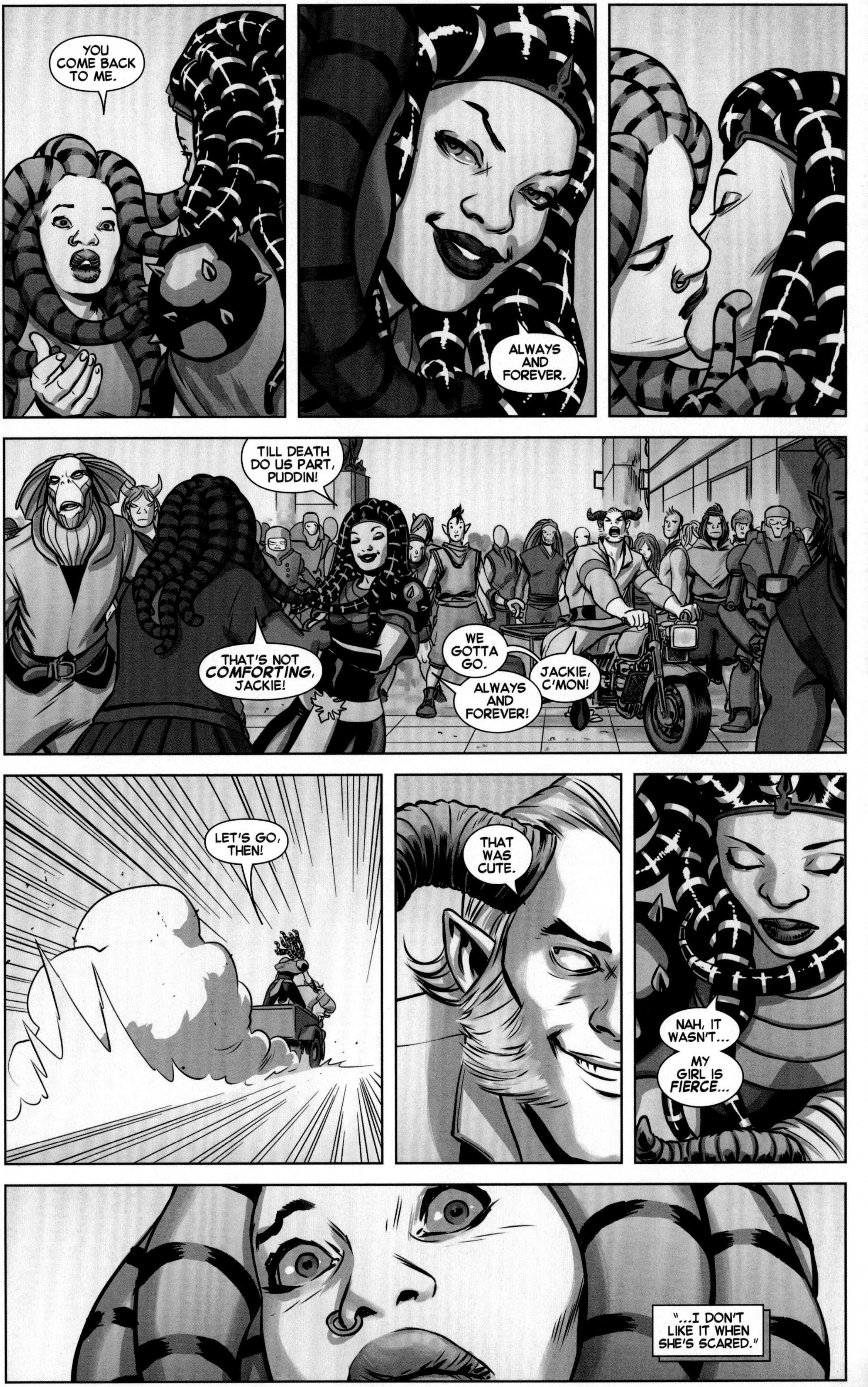

YOU COME BACK TO ME.
ALWAYS AND FOREVER.
TILL DEATH DO US PART, PUDDIN!
THAT'S NOT *COMFORTING*, JACKIE!
WE GOTTA GO.
ALWAYS AND FOREVER!
JACKIE, C'MON!
LET'S GO, THEN!
THAT WAS CUTE.
NAH, IT WASN'T...
MY GIRL IS *FIERCE*...
"...I DON'T LIKE IT WHEN SHE'S SCARED."

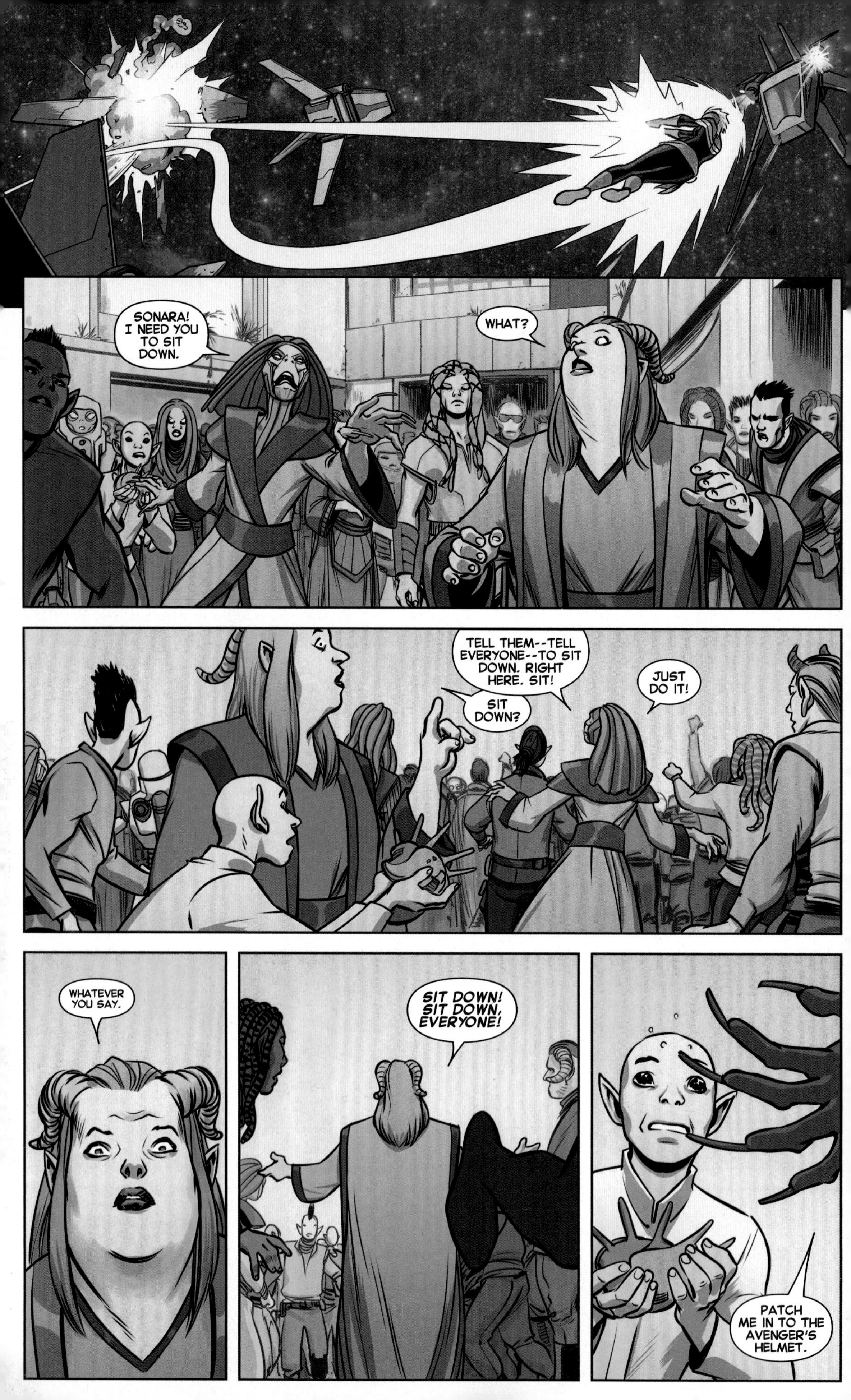
SONARA! I NEED YOU TO SIT DOWN.
WHAT?
TELL THEM--TELL EVERYONE--TO SIT DOWN. RIGHT HERE. SIT!
SIT DOWN?
JUST DO IT!
WHATEVER YOU SAY.
SIT DOWN! SIT DOWN, EVERYONE!
PATCH ME IN TO THE AVENGER'S HELMET.

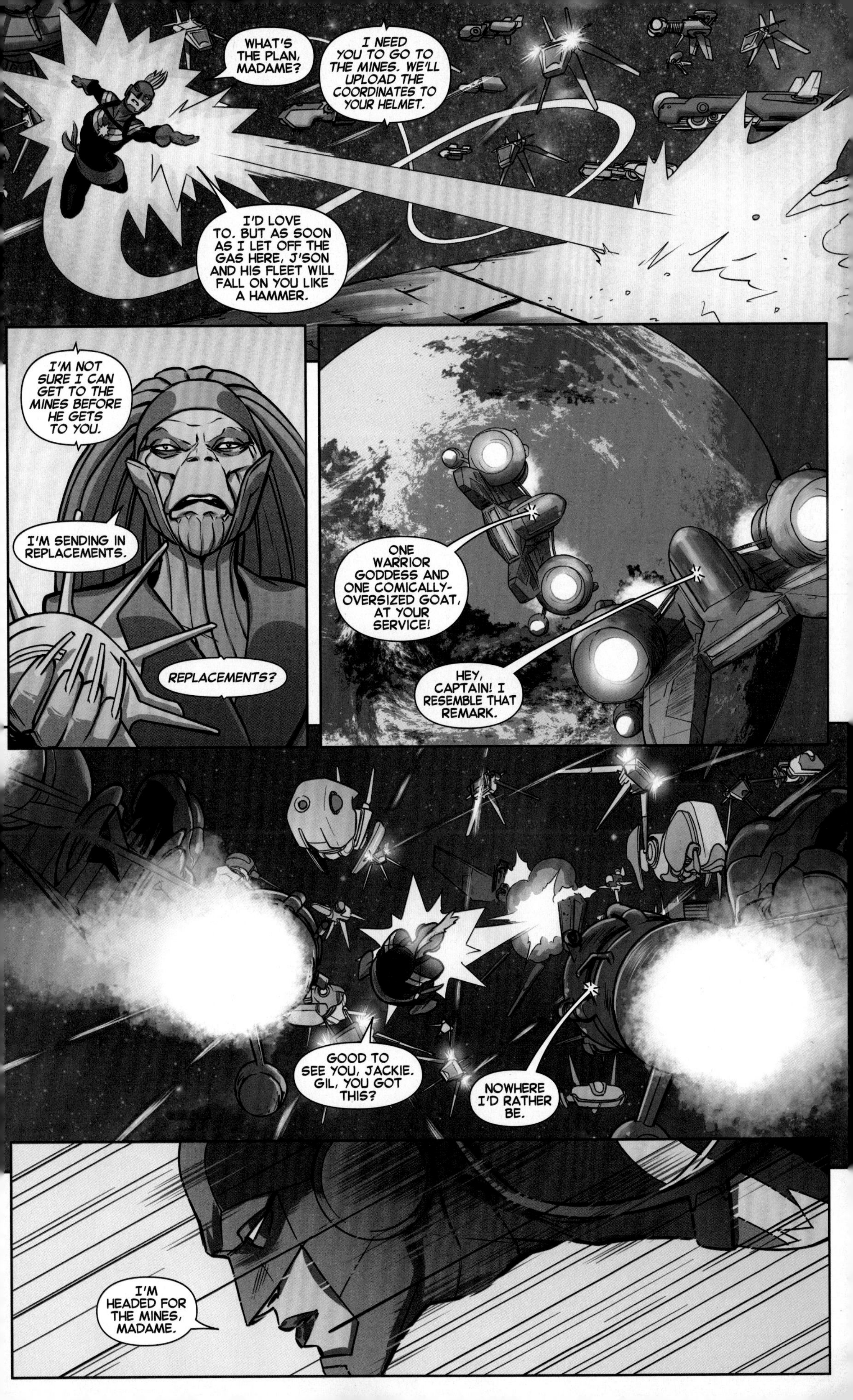
WHAT'S THE PLAN, MADAME?
I NEED YOU TO GO TO THE MINES. WE'LL UPLOAD THE COORDINATES TO YOUR HELMET.
I'D LOVE TO. BUT AS SOON AS I LET OFF THE GAS HERE, J'SON AND HIS FLEET WILL FALL ON YOU LIKE A HAMMER.
I'M NOT SURE I CAN GET TO THE MINES BEFORE HE GETS TO YOU.
I'M SENDING IN REPLACEMENTS.
REPLACEMENTS?
ONE WARRIOR GODDESS AND ONE COMICALLY-OVERSIZED GOAT, AT YOUR SERVICE!
HEY, CAPTAIN! I RESEMBLE THAT REMARK.
GOOD TO SEE YOU, JACKIE. GIL, YOU GOT THIS?
NOWHERE I'D RATHER BE.
I'M HEADED FOR THE MINES, MADAME.

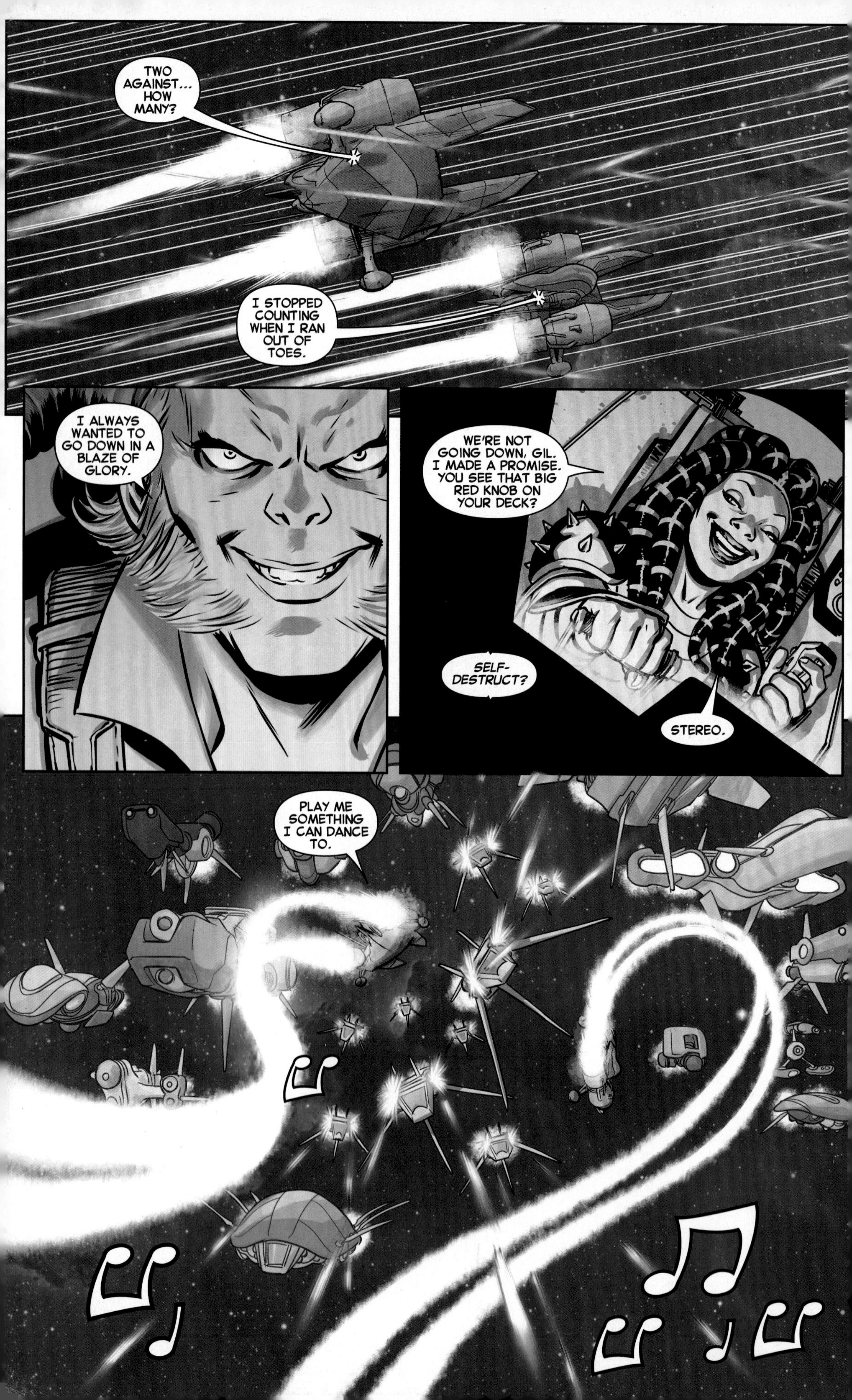
TWO AGAINST... HOW MANY?
I STOPPED COUNTING WHEN I RAN OUT OF TOES.
I ALWAYS WANTED TO GO DOWN IN A BLAZE OF GLORY.
WE'RE NOT GOING DOWN, GIL. I MADE A PROMISE. YOU SEE THAT BIG RED KNOB ON YOUR DECK?
SELF-DESTRUCT?
STEREO.
PLAY ME SOMETHING I CAN DANCE TO.

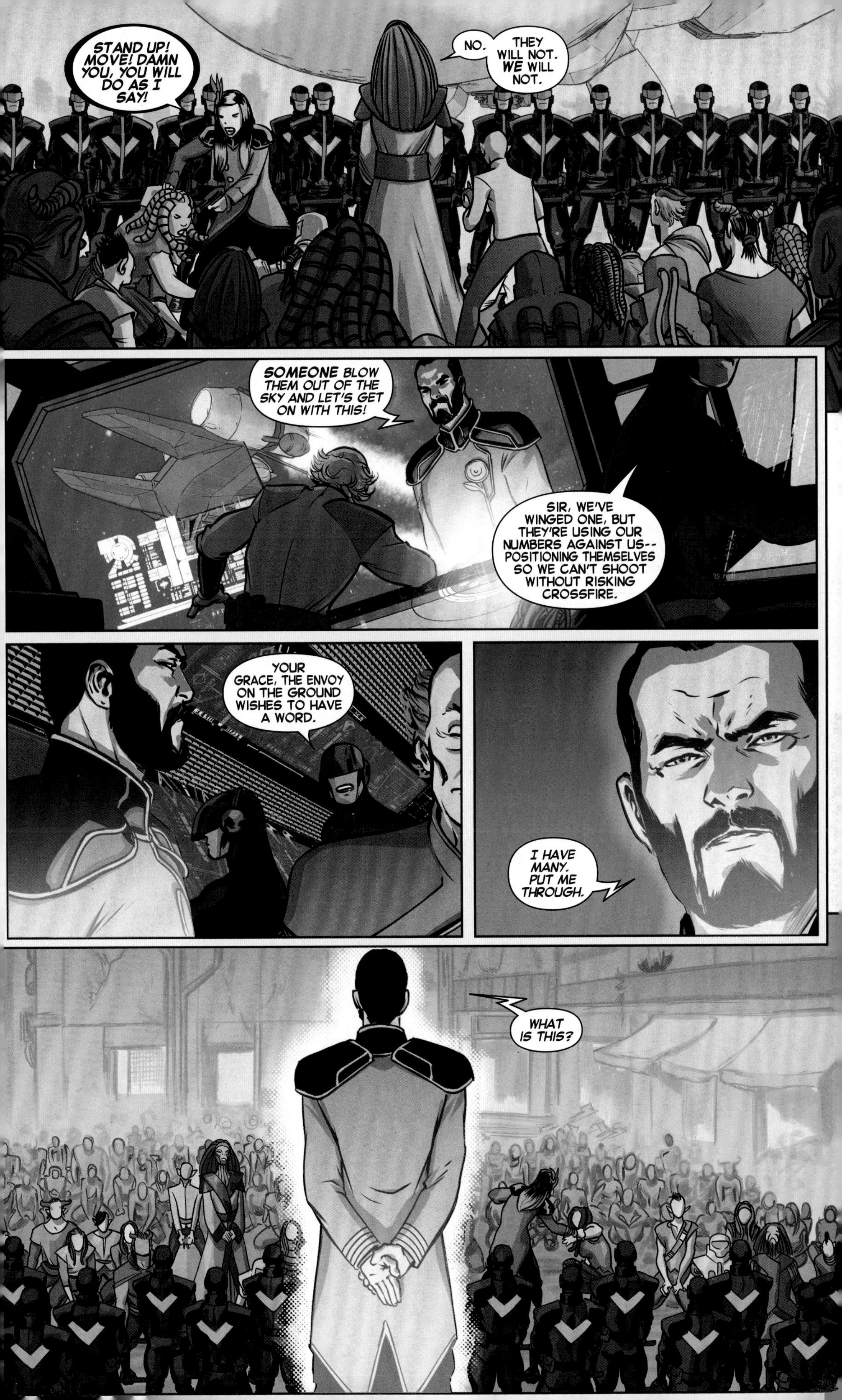
STAND UP! MOVE! DAMN YOU, YOU WILL DO AS I SAY!
NO.
THEY WILL NOT. WE WILL NOT.
SOMEONE BLOW THEM OUT OF THE SKY AND LET'S GET ON WITH THIS!
SIR, WE'VE WINGED ONE, BUT THEY'RE USING OUR NUMBERS AGAINST US-- POSITIONING THEMSELVES SO WE CAN'T SHOOT WITHOUT RISKING CROSSFIRE.
YOUR GRACE, THE ENVOY ON THE GROUND WISHES TO HAVE A WORD.
I HAVE MANY. PUT ME THROUGH.
WHAT IS THIS?

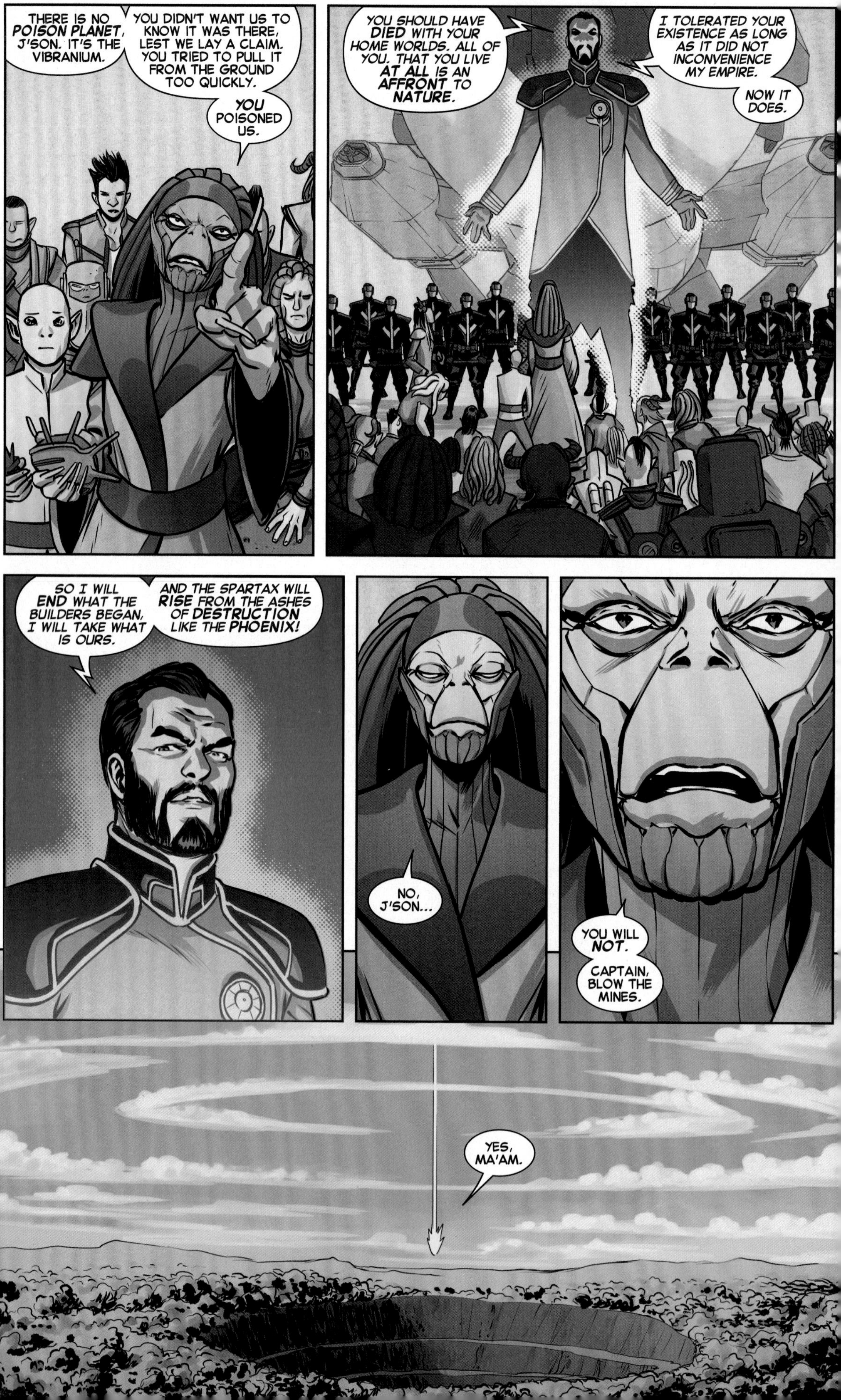
THERE IS NO POISON PLANET, J'SON. IT'S THE VIBRANIUM.
YOU DIDN'T WANT US TO KNOW IT WAS THERE, LEST WE LAY A CLAIM. YOU TRIED TO PULL IT FROM THE GROUND TOO QUICKLY.
YOU POISONED US.
YOU SHOULD HAVE DIED WITH YOUR HOME WORLDS. ALL OF YOU. THAT YOU LIVE AT ALL IS AN AFFRONT TO NATURE.
I TOLERATED YOUR EXISTENCE AS LONG AS IT DID NOT INCONVENIENCE MY EMPIRE.
NOW IT DOES.
SO I WILL END WHAT THE BUILDERS BEGAN, I WILL TAKE WHAT IS OURS.
AND THE SPARTAX WILL RISE FROM THE ASHES OF DESTRUCTION LIKE THE PHOENIX!
NO, J'SON...
YOU WILL NOT.
CAPTAIN, BLOW THE MINES.
YES, MA'AM.

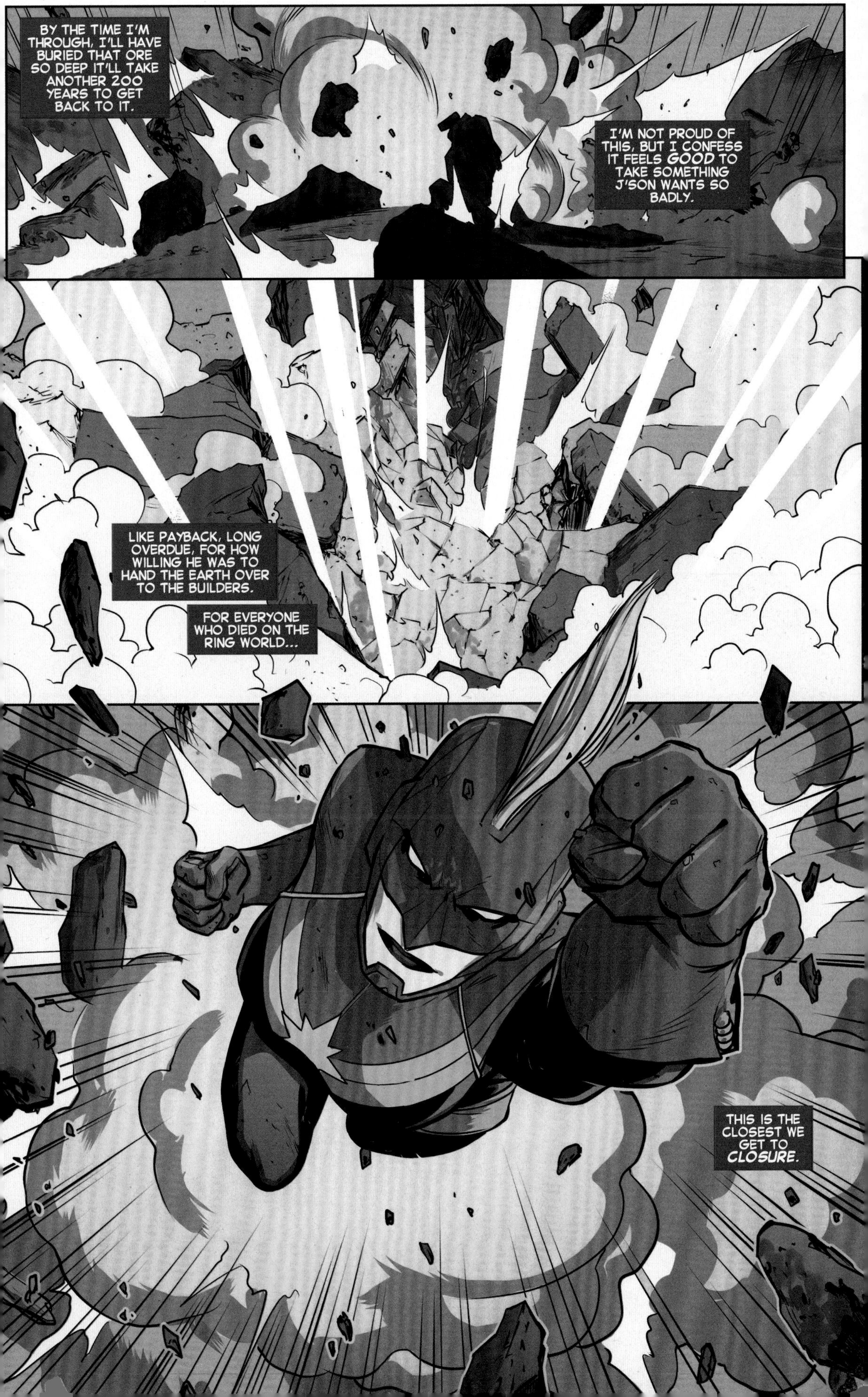
BY THE TIME I'M THROUGH, I'LL HAVE BURIED THAT ORE SO DEEP IT'LL TAKE ANOTHER 200 YEARS TO GET BACK TO IT.
I'M NOT PROUD OF THIS, BUT I CONFESS IT FEELS GOOD TO TAKE SOMETHING J'SON WANTS SO BADLY.
LIKE PAYBACK, LONG OVERDUE, FOR HOW WILLING HE WAS TO HAND THE EARTH OVER TO THE BUILDERS.
FOR EVERYONE WHO DIED ON THE RING WORLD...
THIS IS THE CLOSEST WE GET TO CLOSURE.

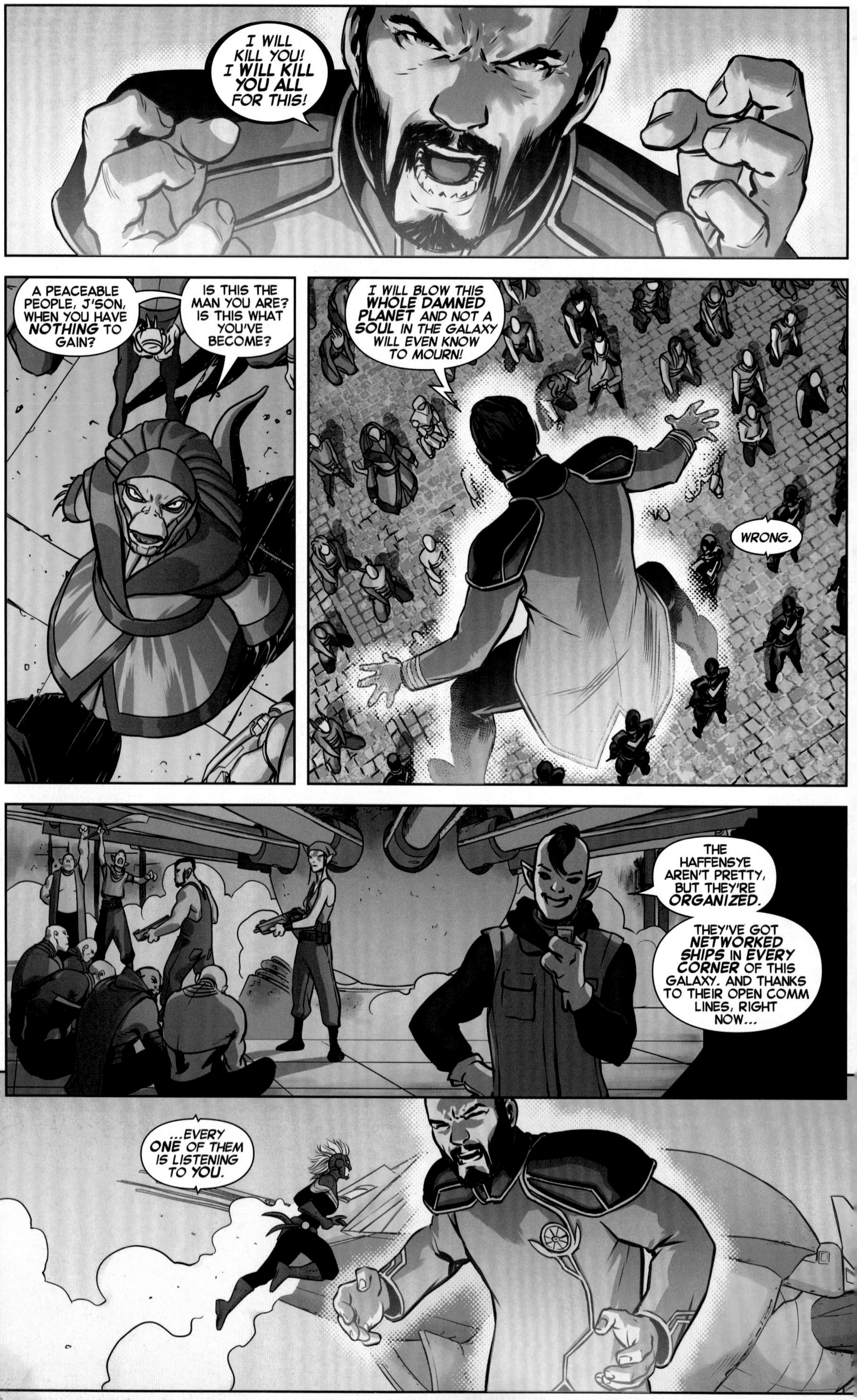

I WILL KILL YOU! I WILL KILL YOU ALL FOR THIS!
A PEACEABLE PEOPLE, J'SON, WHEN YOU HAVE NOTHING TO GAIN?
IS THIS THE MAN YOU ARE? IS THIS WHAT YOU'VE BECOME?
I WILL BLOW THIS WHOLE DAMNED PLANET AND NOT A SOUL IN THE GALAXY WILL EVEN KNOW TO MOURN!
WRONG.
THE HAFFENSYE AREN'T PRETTY, BUT THEY'RE ORGANIZED.
THEY'VE GOT NETWORKED SHIPS IN EVERY CORNER OF THIS GALAXY. AND THANKS TO THEIR OPEN COMM LINES, RIGHT NOW...
...EVERY ONE OF THEM IS LISTENING TO YOU.

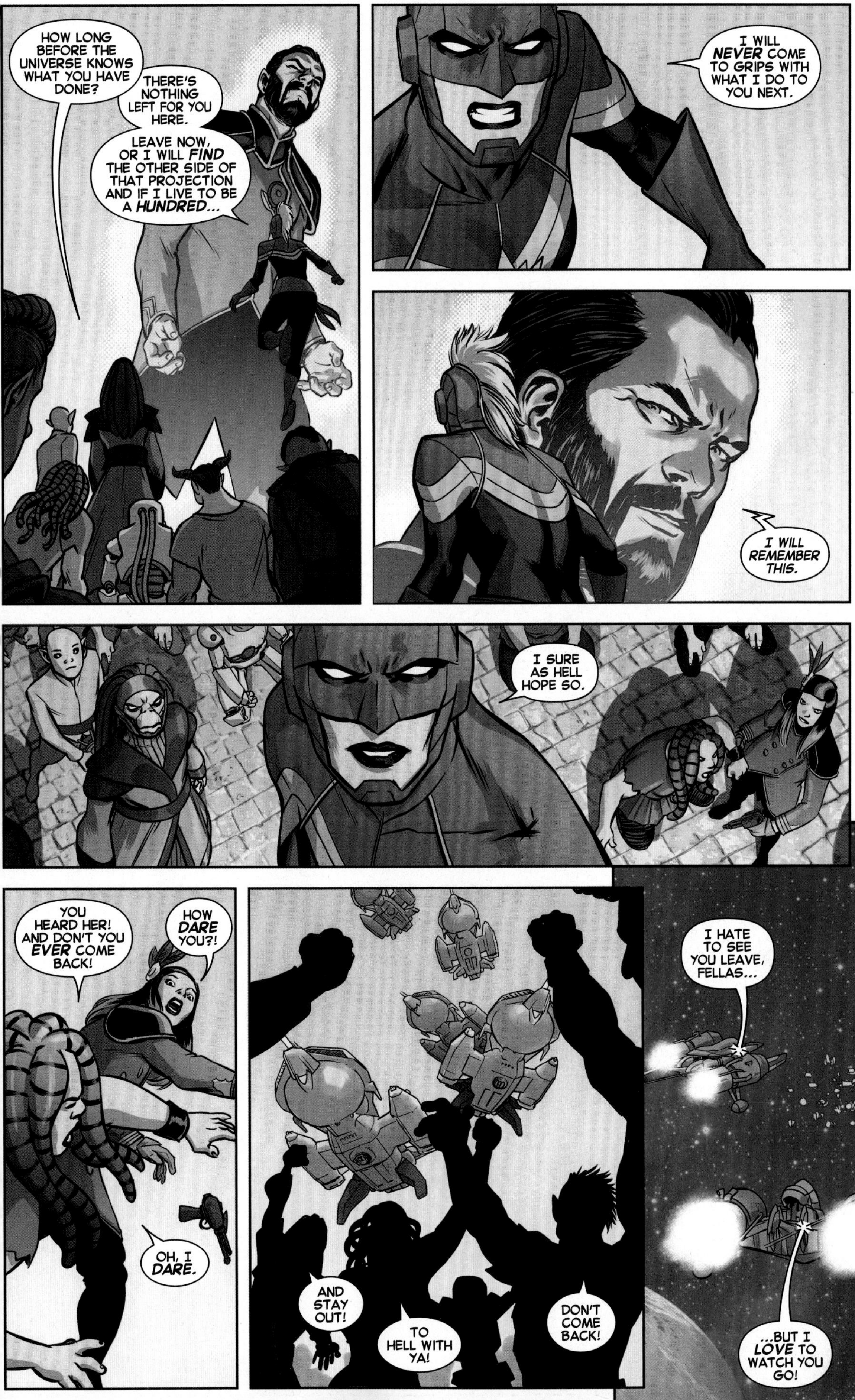
HOW LONG BEFORE THE UNIVERSE KNOWS WHAT YOU HAVE DONE?
THERE'S NOTHING LEFT FOR YOU HERE.
LEAVE NOW, OR I WILL *FIND* THE OTHER SIDE OF THAT PROJECTION AND IF I LIVE TO BE A *HUNDRED*...
I WILL *NEVER* COME TO GRIPS WITH WHAT I DO TO YOU NEXT.
I WILL *REMEMBER* THIS.
I SURE AS HELL HOPE SO.
YOU HEARD HER! AND DON'T YOU *EVER* COME BACK!
HOW *DARE* YOU?!
OH, I *DARE*.
AND STAY OUT!
TO HELL WITH YA!
DON'T COME BACK!
I HATE TO SEE YOU LEAVE, FELLAS...
...BUT I *LOVE* TO WATCH YOU GO!

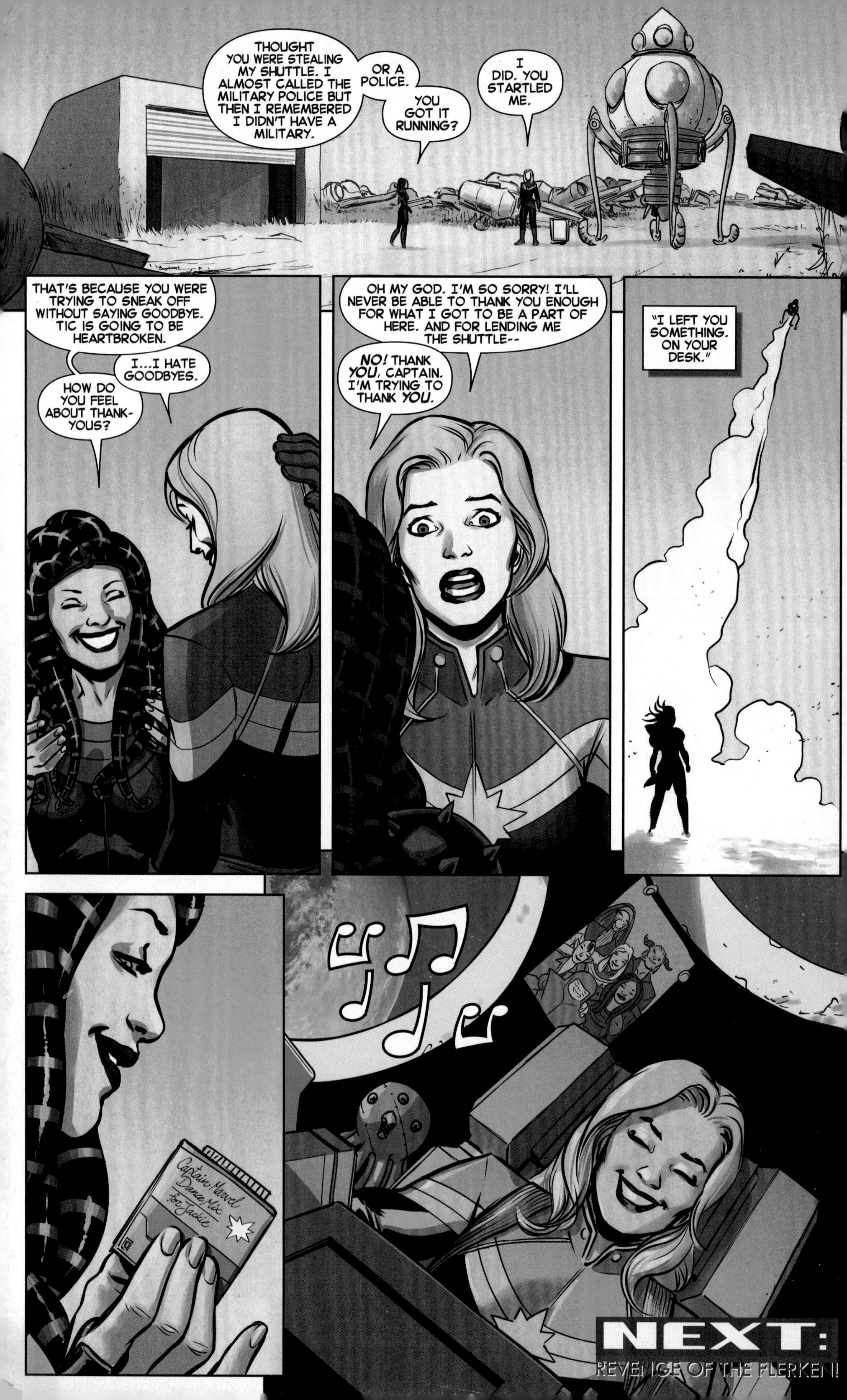
THOUGHT YOU WERE STEALING MY SHUTTLE. I ALMOST CALLED THE MILITARY POLICE BUT THEN I REMEMBERED I DIDN'T HAVE A MILITARY.
OR A POLICE.
YOU GOT IT RUNNING?
I DID. YOU STARTLED ME.
THAT'S BECAUSE YOU WERE TRYING TO SNEAK OFF WITHOUT SAYING GOODBYE. TIC IS GOING TO BE HEARTBROKEN.
I...I HATE GOODBYES.
HOW DO YOU FEEL ABOUT THANK-YOUS?
OH MY GOD. I'M SO SORRY! I'LL NEVER BE ABLE TO THANK YOU ENOUGH FOR WHAT I GOT TO BE A PART OF HERE. AND FOR LENDING ME THE SHUTTLE--
NO! THANK YOU, CAPTAIN. I'M TRYING TO THANK YOU.
"I LEFT YOU SOMETHING. ON YOUR DESK."
Captain Marvel Dance Mix for Jackie
NEXT:
REVENGE OF THE FLERKEN!

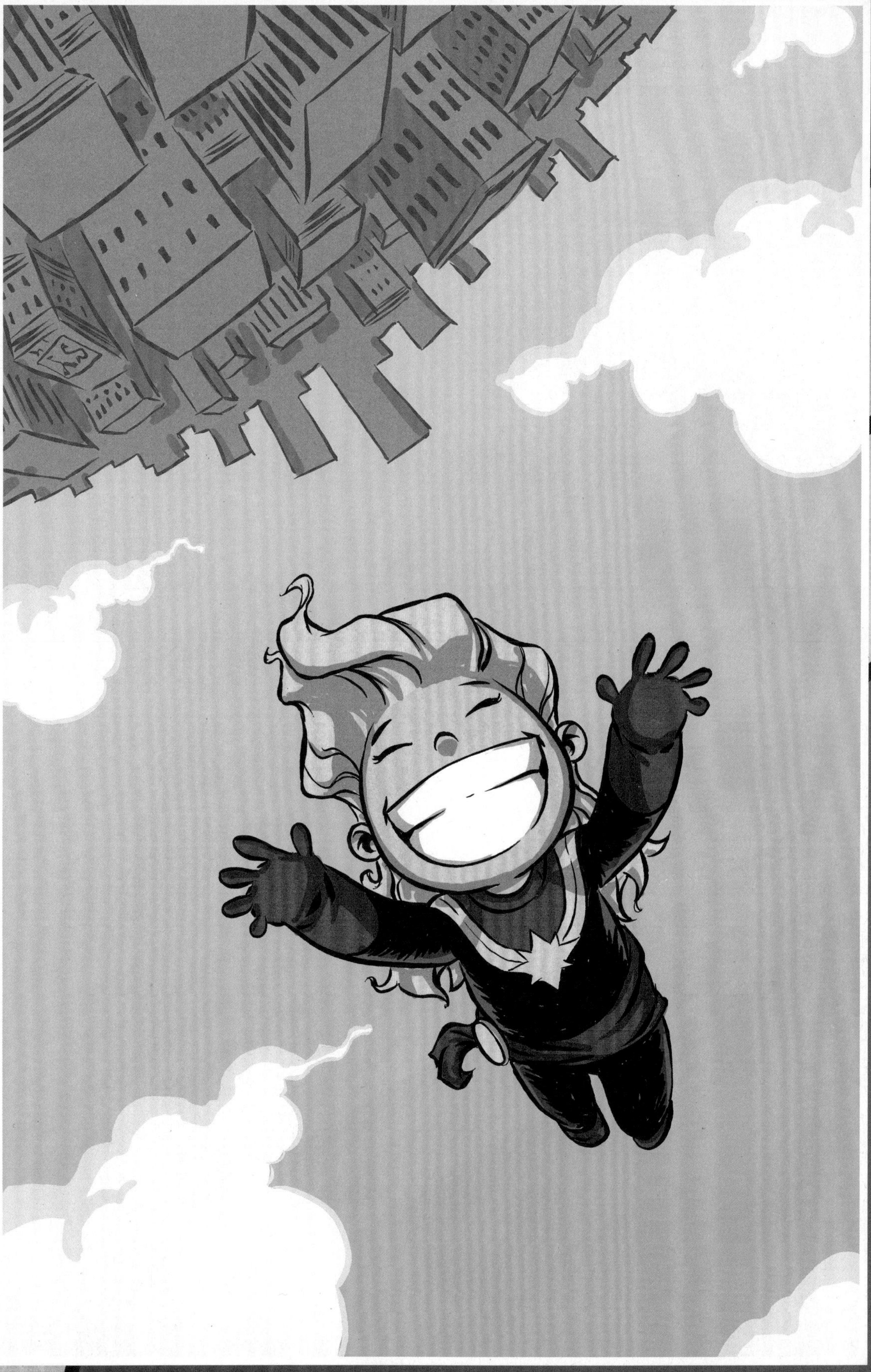

VARIANT BY SKOTTIE YOUNG ONE

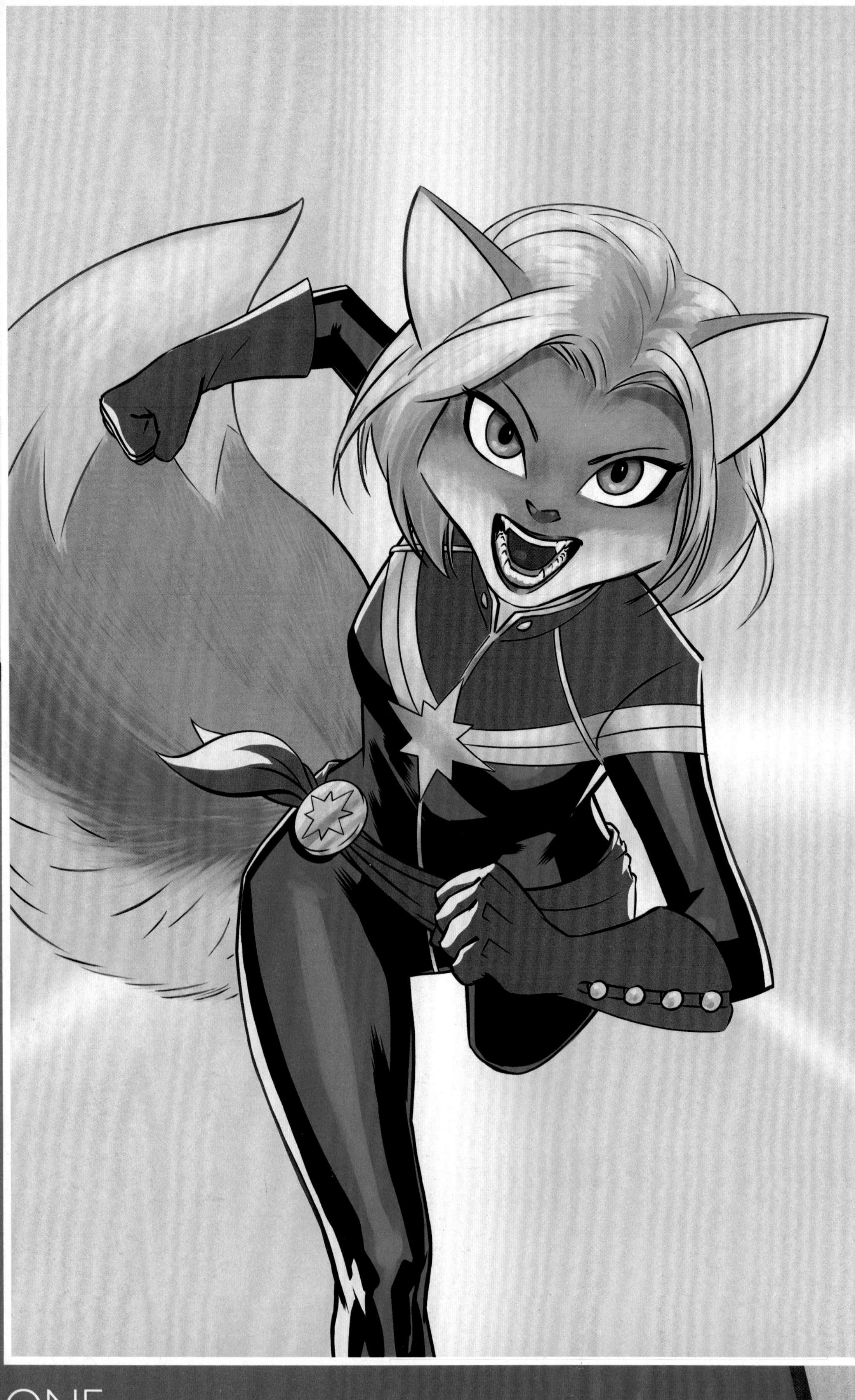

ONE ANIMAL VARIANT BY DAVID LOPEZ

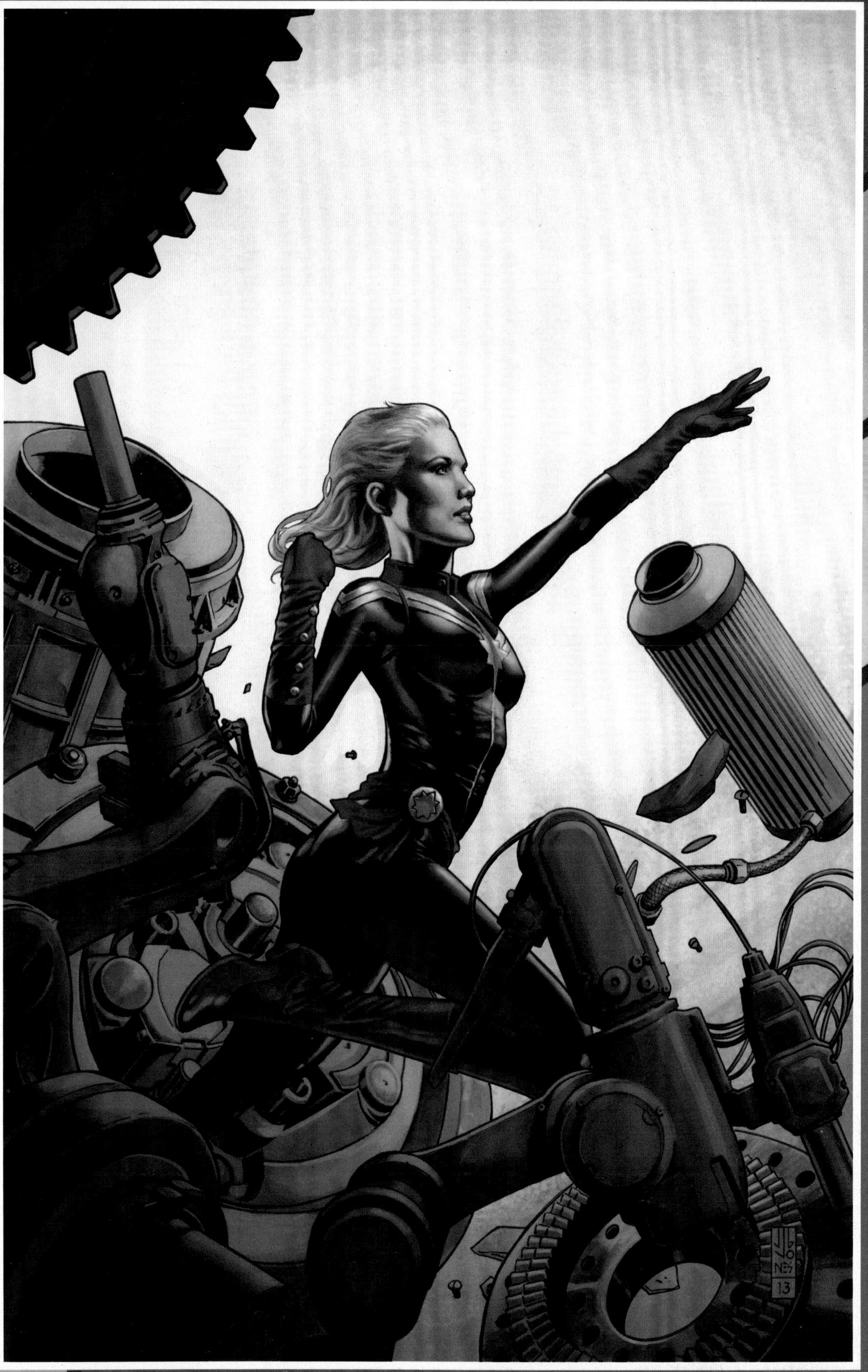

VARIANT BY J. G. JONES & LAURA MARTIN TWO

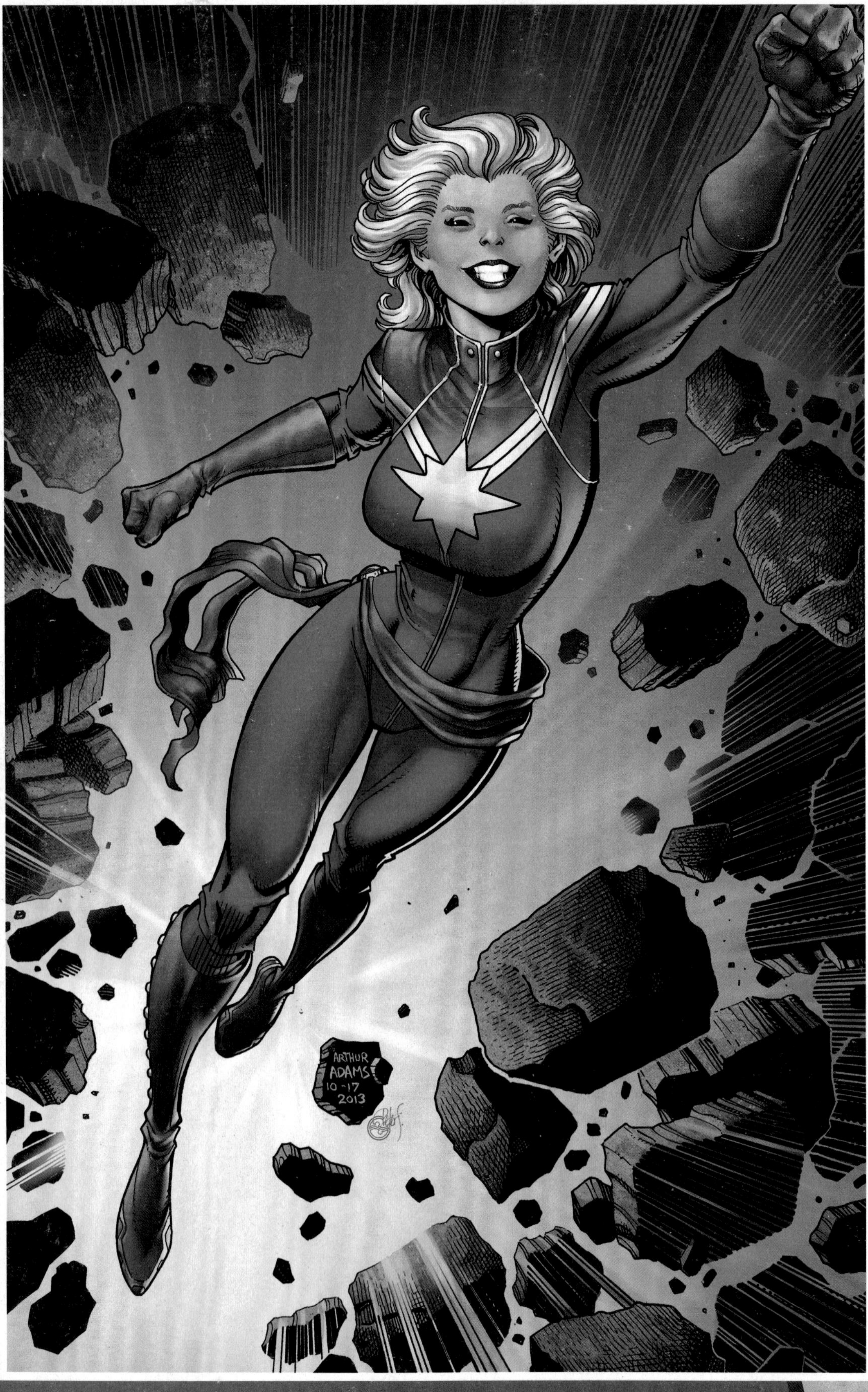
ARTHUR
ADAMS
10-17
2013

THREE VARIANT BY ARTHUR ADAMS & PETER STEIGERWALD